MW00353236

"When my car is not running properly, I try to i
I look for the car repair shop with the best q
Why? Because my car is so very important to me
overall well-being. Likewise, when my body is n
well, I want the best trained, most experienced, and honest medical care I can find. Why?
Because my body is important to me—to my family, for my work, and for my overall
well-being. So it is with church.

"When our beloved congregations are feeling sluggish, filled with anxiety, underper-
forming, and not in alignment with God and community, I want to call the best trained
and most experienced and honest people for consultation and help. For the church, the
visible life of faith, is important to me—to my family, to my work, and for the overall
well-being of our individual lives and our world. So it is here in these pages.

"The experts are speaking, straight from years of courageous church leadership and
directly from the pulpit, the theological classroom, and the offices of denominational
leadership. You can trust them and their words. I certainly have. Blessed reading to you.
May these words begin the path of healing for you and your congregations."

Linda McKinnish Bridges
Founding Faculty Member
President, 2017–2019
Baptist Theological Seminary at Richmond

"At a time when many churches are at a critical juncture, this book is another way for the
Center for Healthy Churches to offer support and encouragement to those who are on
the front lines of ministry. Through personal experience, I have found the CHC to be
very focused on and committed to working alongside churches in helping them to think
through change and move toward greater health and stability.

"This collection of articles shows how leaders within the CHC network have been
able to draw on their extensive experience as consultants and coaches in various parts
of the church to provide gifted insight to church leaders. Their definition of a healthy
church as a community of Jesus followers with shared vision, thriving ministry, and
trusted leadership is right on target and can help provide all of us with a positive way to
move into God's future with a sense of possibility and hope."

David B. Hodges
Dean, Christ Church Cathedral
Episcopal Diocese of Western Kansas

"As a local pastor in a time of cultural change inside and outside the church, I am often left with more questions than answers. The coaches and consultants at the Center for Healthy Churches encourage me with their insight and encouragement in *Just What is a Healthy Church?* This book is filled with biblical and theological insight along with pragmatic approaches for churches in the 21ˢᵗ century as we seek to be defined first and foremost as a community of Jesus followers.»

Jeff Roberts
Pastor, Trinity Baptist Church
Raleigh, North Carolina

"In *Just What Is a Healthy Church?* Bill Wilson and other colleagues affiliated with the Center for Healthy Churches offer reflections on the question posed in the book's title. Their basic contention is that a healthy church is a community of Jesus followers with shared vision, thriving ministry, and trusted leadership.

"While one may or may not wholly concur with the various contributors as how best to answer the presenting question, there is no question that they are raising and responding to a pressing question that is of utmost importance to contemporary Christian congregations. There is much practical wisdom to be gleaned from the vignettes that comprise this volume. This book has caused me to think more deeply and carefully about the ongoing well-being of the bride of Christ. For this—and for the church local and universal—I am thankful."

Todd D. Still
Charles J. and Eleanor McLerran DeLancey Dean and
William M. Hinson Professor of Christian Scriptures
Baylor University, Truett Seminary

Just What Is a Healthy Church?

Bill Owen, editor

© 2020

Published in the United States by Nurturing Faith Inc., Macon GA,
www.nurturingfaith.net.

Nurturing Faith is the book publishing arm of Good Faith Media (goodfaithmedia.org).

Library of Congress Cataloging-in-Publication Data is available.

ISBN: 978-1-63528-110-1

I dedicate this book to the three churches among whom I served as pastor. Each was a mixture of health and unhealth, human as we were, but always straining to move forward, intending to follow the Christ who was always ahead of us. Each one loved him, the church, and my family. For Dry Creek, Immanuel, and Mt. Carmel I am indebted and forever grateful.

Contents

Epilogue: Leadership During Crisis

Foreword

Collective wisdom is a good thing, especially in such an uncertain time for the church in North America. No one who has contributed to the collective wisdom of this anthology would tell you that we are infallible experts. If such ministerial experts ever existed, it was in a different moment in history. What this collection does represent is a community of experienced practitioners who are thinking together about what it means to help churches be the best version of themselves amid all the changes confronting 21st-century congregations.

We think you will find wisdom in these pages that is both timeless (because it points to habits of the heart and mind that the church has always cultivated) and timely (because the ministerial context and thus our strategies for responding to it are always changing). Regardless of the question or challenge that has you thumbing through the pages of this book, our hope is that you will find just what you need to help your church develop a shared vision of thriving ministry.

Matt Cook
Assistant Director
Center for Healthy Churches

Introduction

Every once in a while, one of us who serves as a consultant or coach at the Center for Healthy Churches (CHC) is asked by a church leader, "Exactly what do you mean by a healthy church?"

That's a fair question. Initially, you may be tempted to think, "Well, everyone knows what a healthy church is," but upon further reflection you'd realize that answer is incorrect. There are many ways to define a healthy church, based largely on what metrics you use to think about the word "healthy."

At one of our CHC semiannual gatherings, we decided to come up with a definition of "healthy church" that would help us articulate our understanding of what lies at the heart of the Center's work. We spent several hours crafting a definition. We wanted it to reflect both our own long years of experience in creating healthy churches in congregations we had served as pastors *and* what we have learned from our years of working as consultants with church leaders from around the country.

We quickly came to a shared agreement about what metrics *don't* inform our understanding of "healthy," specifically: the number of members a church has, the size of its budget, and how "successful" it has been. We've seen too many large, "successful" churches that exhibit unhealthy behaviors. We've also worked with too many small churches that exhibit robust health and a vital mission.

After many drafts, we came up with a statement that we feel captures the heart of our work. It also mirrors our understanding of the church's call to be the body of Christ in and for the world. This definition emerged from our discernment:

> A healthy church is a community of Jesus followers with shared vision, thriving ministry, and trusted leadership.

Notice that this is a *qualitative* definition as opposed to a *quantitative* one. We focus on who the community understands itself to be and how it exhibits that understanding in its shared life. Rather than looking at how much a church is doing or what it has accomplished, we look instead at how much that church follows in the way of Jesus.

• A healthy church understands that its most fundamental call is to be *a community of Jesus followers*. This understanding turns us away from institutional concerns and toward discipleship commitments. Such a church is clear that its core purpose is to incarnate Christ's healing and saving ministry in a hurting world, joining God in God's work in that world in the power of the Holy Spirit.

- A healthy church has *a shared vision* that all of its members seek to embody. When a church's vision is fractured, its ministry's impact weakens, both in its members' lives and in the community God has given it to serve. Having a clear and focused vision invites us joyfully to align all our resources—spiritual, mental/emotional, physical, financial, and structural—toward shared Kingdom work.

- A healthy church has *a thriving ministry.* There is a sense of excitement and passion among its members. People experience meaning and purpose as they are given the opportunity to share their gifts. They experience God's deep generosity and grace and are glad to give of themselves and their resources. They understand that their church has all it needs to accomplish the mission God has given it.

- A healthy church has *trusted leadership*—both clergy and lay. A congregation that deeply trusts its leaders can face any adaptive challenge, respond with enthusiasm to any new call, and work faithfully through any conflict that may arise. Clear communication and encouraging words and actions by leaders embolden the congregation to step out in faith.

This way of thinking about a "healthy church" reminds us of Paul's metaphor of the church as a healthy body in Ephesians 4: "(W)e must grow up in every way into him who is the head, into Christ, from whom the whole body, joined and knit together by every ligament with which it is equipped, as each part is working properly, promotes the body's growth in building itself up in love" (v. 15).

Our call at the CHC is to help your congregation "build itself up in love," so that your ministry can become ever more faithful, vital, and full of hope. We would love to talk with you about how we might walk that path together.

PART 1

A Community of Jesus-followers

A healthy church understands that its most fundamental call is to be a community of Jesus-followers. This understanding turns us away from institutional concerns and toward discipleship commitments. Such a church is clear that its core purpose is to incarnate Christ's healing and saving ministry in a hurting world, joining God in God's work *in* that world in the power of the Holy Spirit.

A Healthy Congregation:
A Community of Jesus-followers

Craig A. Sherouse

What is a healthy church? At the Center for Healthy Churches we focus on these major characteristics of church health: a community of Jesus-followers with a shared vision, thriving ministry, and trusted leadership. Vision, ministry, and leadership develop from the foundational characteristic of radical discipleship. A healthy church has a profound commitment to following Jesus and inviting others to follow him.

Jesus' favorite invitation to discipleship was as clear and short as it could be—two words in English and three in Greek (but who is counting): "Follow me!" He said these words to Phillip, Matthew, and Andrew. With these words he invited the rich young ruler and the "wanna-be" disciple who asked to first bury his father. Jesus said his sheep hear his voice and follow him; his disciples take up their crosses and follow him.

Jesus' "school of discipleship" had no home campus. It was a traveling school, with the chief rabbi throwing truth over his shoulder on the journey. Luke uses the journey motif throughout his writings. In the Gospel of Luke, Jesus takes a circuitous final 10-chapter journey to Jerusalem. In the Book of Acts, the disciples and missionaries are always on the move and eight times the church is called "the Way." "Follow me" are the first and last words Simon Peter is recorded as hearing from Jesus. These words enclose Christian discipleship and church health. In John 21, the resurrected Christ asks Simon three times if he loves him, and twice Christ re-invites Simon to follow him. We follow the ones we love.

I started following Beverly (who became my wife) in high school. She followed me to five pastorates in four states. We followed our children to ballgames, concerts, and plays, and now we are trying to follow our six grandchildren in two different states. We follow the ones we love.

We love Christ because he first loved us, and we follow him because we love him. And the more we lovingly follow him, the more we look and act like him. How else could the undependable fisherman, Simon, become rock-solid Peter, a pastor/shepherd who feeds and tends Jesus' sheep? Radical, extravagant, passionate, worshipful love of Jesus leads to faithful following of Jesus. And, faithful following of Jesus shapes us into his likeness and develops congregational health.

My favorite congregation in the New Testament is the church in Syrian Antioch. According to Acts 11, 13, and 15, it was a healthy church. We do not know how big it was, but it was probably small by mega-church standards. Following are a few things we do know about that church:

- We know how big its vision was: The Holy Spirit gave that church a missional vision to share Christ with the Mediterranean world.
- We know how broadly vibrant its ministry was: It was the first church to actively minister to Gentiles.
- We know that it had excellent leadership. That church developed both Barnabas and Saul (only called "Paul" after Antioch) as the leaders they were, and then sent them off because the rest of the world needed them more than Antioch did.

Where in Syrian Antioch did this church find such a healthy vision, ministry, and leadership? How did it become such a healthy church?

You remember that "it was in Antioch that the disciples were first called 'Christians'" (Acts 11:26). "Christian"—we use that descriptive so flippantly that we forget what it really means. "Little Christ" is someone who loves Jesus so radically, so extravagantly, so passionately, so worshipfully that others can see a little of Christ in that person.

The healthy church in Antioch was not known for its "buildings, budgets, and baptisms." It was known for its Christ-likeness, for being a community of Jesus-followers. Healthy churches such as Antioch have changed the world. And healthy churches in the 21st century will also change the world.

Keeping Jesus Right Side Up

Barry Howard

In 2017, an unexpected wave of emotion swept over me as I was preparing to leave the pastor's study of First Baptist Church in Pensacola for the final time as the senior pastor. With an open Bible, an inquiring mind, and a listening ear, I had spent countless hours in that room over the past 12 years.

That room had served well as a place of reflection at times and a place of refuge at others. It was a place where I had offered fervent prayers and a place where I had heard gut-wrenching confessions. It was a place where I had shared generous encouragement and a place where I had uttered occasional rebuke.

It was the same study where I had prepared sermons, offered counsel, planned memorial services, prepared for baby dedications, brainstormed with key leaders, and conferred with trusted colleagues. In that study I had laughed at times and cried at times. Its walls framed treasured memories and had witnessed countless secrets.

With the last of my personal belongings in hand, when I reached the door, I looked back to make sure I had not left anything behind. While scanning the room, I saw it. "JESUS" was upside down. So, my last act upon departing the pastor's study was to turn "JESUS" right side up again.

Among the many plaques, trinkets, and gifts given to me across the years, that sign made of two colors of wood highlighted the name, "JESUS." Rather than being inscribed or engraved, "JESUS" was revealed by the strategic arrangement of the contrast in wood and color.

I'm not really sure how "JESUS" got turned upside down in the first place. A member of the housekeeping staff could have inadvertently flipped the sign while dusting. I could have overturned "JESUS" in my packing frenzy. Or one of the children visiting my study in recent days could have reversed the upright position of "JESUS" while playing with him.

My realignment of "JESUS" became rather parabolic for my final weekend at the Pensacola church. I realized again how easy it is, despite our best intentions, for the church to turn "JESUS" upside down, misrepresenting Jesus to our community. There are several ways to turn Jesus "upside down":

- We turn Jesus upside down when we minimize our faith as mere formulaic transaction.
- We turn Jesus upside down when we buy into consumerist Christianity.
- We turn Jesus upside down when we try to label Jesus as a Democrat or Republican.
- We turn Jesus upside down when we operate the church as a religious institution.
- We turn Jesus upside down when we exclude people who are unlike us.
- We turn Jesus upside down when we veer toward the extremes of legalism on the right or liberalism on the left.

- We turn Jesus upside down when we contentiously frame worship as contemporary or traditional.
- We turn Jesus upside down when we take his words and teachings out of context to affirm our own presuppositions.
- We turn Jesus upside down when we preach partisan politics from the pulpit.
- We turn Jesus upside down when there is a huge disparity between our words and actions.
- We turn Jesus upside down when we confess his Lordship but we neglect worship.
- We turn Jesus upside down when we avoid addressing tough topics and tough issues and allow injustice and untruth to go unchallenged.

To maximize our impact and influence in the community, the church must keep "JESUS" right side up, from the pastor's study to the pew. Consider these ways we can keep Jesus "right side up":

- We turn Jesus right side up when we faithfully share the love of God in word and deed.
- We illustrate Jesus right side up when we invest time and resources in "the least of these," the disadvantaged and underserved in our city and around the world.
- We proclaim Jesus right side up when we "make more space for grace."
- We exemplify Jesus right side up when we leverage our diversity within the body of Christ.
- We present Jesus right side up when we perceive other churches to be our colleagues, not our competitors.
- We portray Jesus right side up when we open the doors of our church more widely than ever before, recognizing that many disconnected individuals need to walk alongside us before determining to join us on this journey of faith.
- We embody Jesus right side up when we confront racism and courageously contend for equality.
- We preach Jesus right side up when we refuse to give up on anyone, even those we perceive to be the most hopeless and hardcore of sinners.

And so, as I prepared to transition into a new season of ministry, my final action upon departing the pastor's study was to turn "JESUS" right side up. And our challenge is to keep turning Jesus right side up in a world where far too often the message of Jesus is turned upside down.

Jason's Upside-down World

Bill Wilson

If asked to identify a favorite New Testament character, most of us go with the predictable and obvious: Barnabbas, Mary, Nathaniel, Peter, Lydia, Timothy, Phoebe. You know the list.

Let me remind you of an obscure character who can remind us of an important truth about church health. His name is Jason, who lived in northern Greece in Thessalonica. In Acts 17:1-9, Paul and Silas are coming through town on one of their missionary journeys, making great headway at the local synagogue and persuading many Jews and devout Greeks "and not a few of the leading women." Their success is not well received by the synagogue leaders, however, and so a band of ruffians is hired to find Paul and Silas and run them out of town.

In the midst of the search, the posse shows up at Jason's house and drags Jason and some other believers before the city authorities. The accusers make a telling comment: "These people who have been turning the world upside down have come here also, and Jason has entertained them as guests" (v. 6). Jason bonds out of jail, and Paul and Silas escape the vigilantes. While Jason disappears from the pages of the New Testament, his spirit lingers on. His risky "bed and breakfast" serves as a key link in the spread of a gospel message that reverses the established order of the day and heralds a new way of thinking and believing about God.

Hosting those who bring a new, upside-down day is always risky business. In the 21st century, hosting can take the form of considering an idea, proposing a new method, suggesting an alternative, or raising a question. Sometimes hosting takes the form of saying what everyone is thinking but no one is willing to say. Upside-down ideas are those that challenge the established order or way of thinking or of being a church. Healthy churches need to have a steady diet of hard conversations about such ideas. If not, we will grow rigid and inflexible and run the risk of missing the movement of the Spirit.

Of course, that is easier said than done. The established order may give lip service to wanting change and innovation, but the truth is that most of us find change offensive and obtrusive. The way we do things brings some order to the chaos of our life and enables us to avoid the surprises that fill most of our days at work and at home. Those who bring or suggest change are often labeled as troublemakers or misfits and their ideas dismissed as unreasonable. Some days our church is the one place we can go that reminds us of how life used to be, and we cling to that fading dream with a vengeance.

The spirit of Jason is the spirit of adventure and a willingness to embrace the possibility of the new. Jason's world was turned upside down by these gospel messengers and by the revolutionary person they gave witness to. Jesus spent much of his teaching time upending the commonly held perceptions of his day, for example:

- Instead of leadership being determined by position and power, Jesus suggested that a true leader is a servant first.
- Instead of power being the avenue through which God works, Jesus suggested it is weakness.
- Instead of finding our life by holding onto it, Jesus suggested we find life when we lose our life.
- Instead of the rich receiving God's blessing, Jesus called the poor blessed.
- Instead of loving self and looking to our needs first, Jesus suggested loving our neighbor and seeking his kingdom first.

At every point, Jesus turned the world upside down. He continues to inspire his followers and churches with upside-down thinking and acting. Our world will surely resist now as his world did then. Our goal must be to work among those who are accused of harboring such radical ideas and hosting such dangerous possibilities. Turning the world upside down was hard work in Jesus' day, and it is hard work today. In the end, upside down brought abundant life and unconditional love to a world desperately in need of both.

The next time you are asked to name your New Testament heroes, consider Jason and his upside-down world. Even more, consider adopting his spirit and helping to create a readiness at your church to be turned upside down!

Everyone Needs to Go to Arabia

Bill Wilson

One of the pressing concerns of 21st-century individual and congregational spiritual life is the question of depth. To be blunt, there isn't much. Study after study has revealed the sad truth that much of what we call faith and commitment is actually a thin veneer of religious ritualism that wilts at the first hint of stress. It is stunning to watch long-term, regular participants in a congregation's life resort to all manner of psycho-babble or afternoon talk show wisdom when confronted with a crisis. Every pastor has watched in dismay as lifelong believers revert to their worst and darkest selves when things don't go their way.

The self-absorption of our culture has come to define our churches. Affluenza is not just a cute way to describe the American way of materialism; it is what robs would-be disciples of the joy of authentic stewardship of all our life and possessions. The list goes on and on.

I propose a cure for this "mile wide, inch deep" variety of faith that plagues the Kingdom: Everyone needs to go to Arabia.

Now, I am not a travel agent, and I get no kickback from the airlines. To fully appreciate this invitation, you must know your Bible trivia. Specifically, what did Paul do after his conversion on the Damascus road? You'll find that story in Acts 9. Christianity's most ardent opponent, a genuine first-century terrorist, is dramatically converted and transformed. Think of a leading ISIS terrorist confessing Christ and leading the Christian church in the Middle East. Not surprisingly, other disciples are incredulous at this turn of events, and eventually, the church leaders send the newly converted Paul away. Where does he go? For the answer, one must turn to Galatians 1:17. He goes to Arabia.

We are given no details of Paul's time there. Much like the 18 years between the story of Jesus and his parents in the temple and his baptism, we have a gap in the narrative. Paul is gone approximately three years. Many legends exist about his time in Arabia, but the biblical text is silent about what takes place during those days. We can only deduce what happens by the transformation that is obvious when he returns: Paul is a different man. He left a zealot and returns a theologian. He left filled with raw enthusiasm and returns with passion for the Kingdom. He left shrouded by doubt and returns grounded in conviction. It seems clear that while in Arabia, Paul went deep.

What will it mean for you or your church to go to Arabia? To go to Arabia means we must learn to listen to God's voice rather than his competition. Henri Nouwen wrote about how difficult it is for us to hear the voice of God; of how we have become deaf, unable to know when God is calling us, and when we hear God, unable to know in what direction he is calling us. Nouwen described modern life as absurd. Interestingly, the root word for absurd is the Latin word *surdus*, which means deaf. Arabia is a place to listen for that voice you have been ignoring.

What would it look like for your congregation to go to Arabia? What would it look like for our clergy to go there? Far too often, deep is the part of life we studiously avoid. It's so tempting to let others think for us, to settle for what comes easy, to walk away when things get a little complicated. To go to Arabia would mean we would have to think deeply, wrestle with God, and lean into our pain and shortcomings. Sadly, that seems to be far down the list of priorities for most of us. Our congregational life is filled with pressure to produce, with incessant programs, with demanding consumers (parishioners), and with more noise than quiet.

For the sake of our congregational and individual health, we need a trip to Arabia. Would you be willing to follow the example of Paul and Jesus and take some time away from the noise, pressure, and the whirlwind to listen for the voice of the Spirit calling you to a deeper life? With a little more work on our foundations, perhaps we would not crumble so quickly under pressure. With a deeper reservoir of faith, perhaps we could exhibit an extra measure of grace to those around us. With a stockpile of thoughtful prayers, perhaps the crises we face would not overwhelm us so easily.

Everyone needs to go to Arabia. This means you.

The Practice of Warming

Bill Owen

Even though the days are shorter in the fall, I love the cool, crisp air and the changing colors. It's nice cutting the AC down at home. Pleasant evenings find Cindy and me sitting in the backyard around a crackling fire and reminiscing. I've even noticed that Cindy and I are sleeping a bit closer together! I'm reminded of a verse in Ecclesiastes: "Also, if two lie down together, they will keep warm. But how can one keep warm alone?"

Over the years in pastoral ministry, it has been a privilege to counsel couples in preparation for marriage. Often, I asked them to tell me exactly what they cherish about each other. They would tell stories of how they first met, where they were for their first kiss, and other fond remembrances. I would be careful to write their answers down. I would then weave their words into the homily for their wedding day. Afterwards I would give them a copy, urging them to read those words again when times get tough.

And, you know as I do, times always get tough. There comes a day in almost every relationship when we are so far from one another that the relationship gets cold. And it is then that we need to *warm* one another. It's not just true in marriages; it's true in most any relationship—with friends, neighbors, co-workers. It's true also in churches.

Marital therapist John Gottman writes: "Fondness and admiration are two of the most crucial elements in a rewarding and long-lasting romance. Although happily married couples may feel driven to distraction at times by their partner's personality, they still feel that the person they married is worthy of honor and respect."

That's why Gottman's number-one strategy for helping couples in marital trouble is *not* to plumb their problems with each other. It is to get them, figuratively, to "lie down together." Gottman asks them to get close to one another and do one of the following exercises each day to heat up the fondness and admiration they've simply become too cold to feel as they once did. Feel free to try these at home, at church, or wherever relationships seem hard:

- Describe a character trait or physical attribute you find endearing or lovable about the other.
- Think of a good time in your relationship and talk about what was so good about it.
- Name one thing about the other that makes you proud.
- Describe one strong value, belief, or interest you have in common and why it is important to you.
- Talk about a common goal you once had or could still forge together.
- Describe a time when you felt very supported by the other.
- Tell the story of your meeting and why you decided to bind your lives to one another in the first place.

• Discuss a vacation or play time you remember sharing together and what was so special about it.

• Describe a tough time that you managed to weather together.

Gottman wasn't the first to offer this type of counsel. The Apostle Paul spoke these words: "Whatever is true, whatever is noble, whatever is right, whatever is pure... lovely... admirable—if anything is excellent or praiseworthy—think about such things... And the God of peace will be with you" (Phil. 4:8-9).

Church relationships are not unlike marriages. If you want a church that is filled more with a sense of peace and promise than of problems and pain, think on these things and see if it doesn't warm up that old fondness and admiration.

At the Center for Healthy Churches we can lead your church in such an appreciative, healthy, and collaborative process.

Do You Ever Change Your Mind?

Bill Wilson

I once listened to a friend as he described the challenge his church had faced as they navigated a difficult congregational decision. It was no surprise to hear him talk about people taking sides, expressing opinions, twisting facts, assigning motives to the opposition, and generally imitating our culture's standards of behavior. Sadly, that is the norm for most leaders in congregations that attempt to engage in thoughtful conversations about difficult topics.

This congregation emerged from the painful path of making their decision bloodied and battered, smaller, but intact. Since that time, healing has begun and they are now moving forward and giving their attention to the future God has in store for them. That pastor's comment about the process caught my attention: "No one really seems to change his or her mind anymore, you know."

As a pastor, I quickly learned that most of the people in my congregations had concretized their opinions and attitudes early in their adult life. One of the hardest shifts in moving from being a youth minister to serving as a pastor was that I no longer spent the majority of my time with adolescents who were still young enough to be open to teaching, new ideas and contrarian thinking and who had a genuine interest in growth as a disciple. When I became a pastor, I had to put away such childish things. Most of the adults I worked with had their minds made up about a multitude of things and were not really interested in changing them.

Once someone abandons their openness to learning, it usually takes a "Damascus road experience" to break through their dogmatism. It was certainly true for many of the adults Jesus met and invited into an experience of life transformation. It was often at a time of crisis when people changed their mind and embraced the narrow way that Jesus was offering: being struck blind, losing a child, being shunned by a community, suffering from an incurable illness, threatened with torture and death, etc.

As a minister, I've watched for 40 years as the same phenomena plays out. Most of us only change our mind in the face of intense pain, loss, or some type of crisis. Our rigid opinions and convictions crumple in the face of an experience that shocks us into a new way of thinking. Chest pains, marital discord, prodigal children, getting fired or laid off, a bad biopsy result, a near-fatal accident all have the effect of breaking through our illusion of immortality or always being right, and we open ourselves to the richness of changing our mind about ourselves, someone else, or something.

How about congregations and faith communities? Can we change our mind? Does it always take a crisis for this to happen? Is there a healthier, less painful path toward an open mind? I certainly hope so. Crisis is a cruel teacher. Some of us don't survive the illness or the accident or the marital discord or the depression that failures bring. Our opportunity to learn new things is lost. There must be a better way.

I remain hope-filled for churches that are willing to learn and change their minds. I pray we can do so without a paralyzing or devastating crisis. Here's what I have seen that must happen for us to come to that point:

- *We must cultivate humility.* Much of our resistance to changing our mind about people, topics, or issues is rooted in an unhealthy pride virus that infects us. Reinhold Niebuhr had it right: our pride is at the heart of our resistance and rebellion against God's desires and dreams for us. Congregations comprised of individuals who learn to confess their own sins, rather than the sins of others, are most likely to be those who are open to God's unfolding revelation of truth.

- *We must more fully experience church as mission, rather than temple.* One part of the genius of Jesus' leadership of his early followers was to replace their fixation upon a place with their devotion to a movement. While he certainly spent his fair share of time in and around the temple, Jesus was much more engaged with, and animated by, the individuals and the needs in the communities he encountered. It dumbfounded the religious authorities of his day, as it does ours. Our American insistence of church as a location rather than a way of life is perhaps the saddest misstep we have made. Thriving churches reverse this travesty and reprioritize appropriately.

- *We must adopt the posture of a disciple, rather than a master.* Disciples are open to the teachings and insights of others because they have recognized their own limitations and blind spots. When we begin to think that we know all there is to know about a type of person, an issue, a theological point, a matter of church practice, or any point of contention, we have moved from the humble posture of a disciple to the proud posture of a master. Beware.

What would it look like if we were to become people who are genuinely open to the idea of changing our mind to more nearly align with Christ? I believe we might become more of the church Jesus intended us to be when he sent us out on our mission. We might actually turn this world upside down.

Reclaiming Enthusiasm

Bill Wilson

Stagnant, boring, aimless, tired, tepid … What do these words describe? You? Your minister? Your church? Your Sunday school class? Your career?

All too often I hear ministers and parishioners alike using such words to describe all of the above. Far too many of God's people and God's churches find themselves with a shortage of passion and energy for the journey before them.

Many churches seem to be going in circles, without energy and lacking a sense of missional direction. Ministers talk about burnout and seem to have lost their focus. A sense of calling and passion has slipped away. Lay persons show up without preparing to worship. Life at the church becomes predictable. New ideas and suggestions meet with practiced indifference. Is it any wonder that eventually parishioners talk about their pastor and ministers describe their congregation using such words?

Do you know how we got the word "enthusiasm"? It comes from the Greek and is a blend of two words: *en* (in) and *theos* (God). Enthusiasm, as originally defined, means having God within us. Over time, enthusiasm came to mean "any rapturous inspiration like that caused by a god." Today we are more likely to use this word to describe our feelings about a favorite athletic team or hobby rather than to describe what God is doing in and through us.

Perhaps we need to revisit this word and reflect on its origins. The truth that God within us sparks enthusiasm and ardor is both biblical and healthy. When faith is healthy it begins within and is passionate, heartfelt, spontaneous, and authentic. It is less concerned with meeting the expectations of others and more concerned with giving witness to the One who gives us purpose and direction. It is when our religious practice flows out of guilt or meaningless repetition or thoughtless habit that it is thin, shallow, and unable to hold up to the demands of life in the 21st century.

When our life in Christ flows out of a personal relationship that defines everything about us and gives us a center to build the rest of life around, enthusiasm is inevitable. Christ as the organizing center of all of life not only holds life together, but also gives life meaning beyond the ups and downs of circumstances. Without that deep indwelling of the Holy Spirit in our congregation and the individuals who make up the congregation, we are prone to become like the shallow soil of the parable of the sower—unable to root deeply and endure the inevitable dry season.

Individuals can be enthusiastic, but so can congregations. When the body of Christ is *en theos*, that is, when local church life is grounded in God's presence rather than ritual or personality or practice, then healthy enthusiasm becomes a defining trait of God's people. The healthiest churches I know are not clergy-focused or program-focused or doctrine-focused. They are Christ-focused. Whether it be acts of worship or mission endeavors or teaching opportunities or fellowship events or outreach efforts, the persistent emotion underneath them all is a deep and authentic enthusiasm.

Ralph Waldo Emerson had it right: "Nothing great was ever achieved without enthusiasm."

When God's people are filled with the character and spirit of Christ, then great things are possible. Check your vocabulary, and let's see if we can inject some new words into our conversations: passion, energy, enthusiasm, meaning, purpose. These words describe the kind of church and church leader our world needs today.

When Church Gets It Right

Bill Owen

As soon as I walked into the church building, I felt it. The day was significant. In fact, it's what brought me there. The preparation was obvious. The choir was poised, the orchestra full, and the worship brochure four-color. But it was more than that.

There was a flow that was undeniable. The pews were teeming with expectancy. "Installation Sunday" marks a new chapter in a church's history, and today was special.

As I sat there, I thought about how good church is when it's at its best. If worship on an "ordinary" Sunday could be like this, I mused. Beyond the single purpose and obvious preparation, what was it that gave this day such flow? The early church tried to communicate this notion as a mutual participation in the Divine.

If you have been to a Greek wedding, you may have seen it played out in a dance. It's called *perichoresis*. There are not two dancers, but at least three. They move in circles, weaving in and out in this very beautiful pattern of motion. They go so quickly and effortlessly that they become a blur, their individual identities part of a larger dance.

The early Cappadocian church fathers looked at that kind of dance and said, in so many words, that's what God is like—not one but three, not three but one.

Whatever is going on in God is a flow that's like a dance; and God is not just the dancer, but God is the dance itself! Richard Rohr says it this way:

> Trinity is the very nature of God, and this God is a circle dance, a centrifugal force flowing outward, and then drawing all things into the dance centripetally . . . Scientists are discovering this reality as they look through microscopes and telescopes. They are finding that the energy is in the space *between* the particles of the atom and *between* the planets and the stars. They are discovering that reality is absolutely relational at all levels. When you really understand Trinity, however slightly, it's like you live in a different universe.

And, I might add, it's like being part of a different kind of church—the flesh-and-blood participation in the divine "flow." That's when the church is at its best. What might that look like? Perhaps . . .

- When the church moves from the center to meet with others on the edges, you join the flow.
- When the church is honest and humble about the darkness within its own walls and lets the light shine in and does needed interior work, you join the flow.
- When the church gives itself to that which is larger than itself, you join the flow.

If the Divine is a community of love in which the members of the Trinity move and encircle one another in loving community and service, then God is not someone on a cloud somewhere, but right here among us—like a dance or a "flow" that we enter into.

This "flow" is the essence of church when it is at its best. It's when God and the church are in sync with one another. It's like entering a sacred dance. You can feel it—the energy. You can hear it—a holy hum.

I want to join this kind of flow. I believe others will as well.

At the Center for Healthy Churches we lead churches through healthy processes that enable churches to get in sync with God, one another, and their local community. Such transition results in renewed purpose and vision, conflict transformation, energized ministries, and staff.

Learning to Navigate Diversity

Barry Howard

One of the most enriching and fatiguing things about church life these days is the vast diversity within most local congregations.

During a recent time of self-reflection and ministry evaluation, I spent some time thinking about why I feel more fatigued these days than I did a few years ago. There are likely many contributing factors including my age, my length of tenure, and what Paul called "the daily pressure of my concern for the churches" (2 Cor. 11:28). But it dawned on me that a part of this new mental fatigue is caused by the continual task of navigating diversity within the church, a phenomenon for which I was neither trained nor prepared.

To further process my notion, I started listing the ways the church is more diverse today than it was when I began my first tenure as a pastor. I quickly identified 10 areas of church ministry that illustrate this proliferation of diversity:

1. *Generational diversity:* There are now 4-6 generations present on any given Sunday in many multi-generational churches.
2. *Translation diversity:* Rather than one standard Bible translation, members of my congregation read a variety of different Bible translations, and I am sure there are a dozen or more different translations present each time I preach.
3. *Racial and ethnic diversity:* There are multiple races, ethnicities, and cultural backgrounds present within most congregations.
4. *Worship time diversity:* Many churches have multiple worship services.
5. *Worship style diversity:* Our church has two Sunday morning worship services, each involving a different style of worship.
6. *Curriculum diversity:* Rather than a standard denominational literature, there are multiple curricula used by Sunday school and Bible study groups in our church.
7. *Missional partnership diversity:* Rather than having a singular missional partnership, many of our churches contribute to and network with multiple mission partners.
8. *Denominational background diversity:* Years ago, it was a rare occurrence for a person to join our church from a different denomination, but today there are persons from various denominational traditions represented in our congregation.
9. *Political diversity:* In my first church, I would venture to say that the congregation was pretty evenly divided between the two primary political parties. Congregants today may be affiliated with political parties, subsidiary groups within each party, PACs (Political Action Committees), and lobbying groups.
10. *Theological diversity:* Multiple strands of theological influence, from both academic and folk theology, are represented in the DNA of most local congregations.

Unfortunately, there was no course offered in seminary titled "Navigating Diversity." Churches basically are going to do one of two things in regards to diversity. They will either limit diversity, by becoming a highly specialized and homogenized church. For example, they will focus on ministry to one or two generations, or "only" allow one Bible translation, or only promote one theological perspective. Or, they will embrace their diversity and leverage it for Kingdom purposes.

Does this expanded diversity have a positive or negative effect on a congregation? I think it depends on how ministers and ministry leaders circumnavigate the diversity.

From a potentially negative perspective, there are many ways diversity makes ministry more challenging:

- It becomes more challenging to communicate across diverse platforms.
- Planning a program of discipleship, ministry initiatives, or activities can become cumbersome.
- Navigating the tension created by extraordinary diversity can weary the staff.
- The greater the diversity, the greater the potential for conflict.

But from a positive perspective, a high level of diversity provides many Kingdom opportunities and benefits:

- Those in a diverse congregation learn to respect varying points of view.
- Multiple generations, ethnicities, and spiritual backgrounds tend to provide multiple perspectives that enrich the overall ministry of the church.
- If a diverse congregation is diligent "to preserve the unity of the Spirit in the bonds of peace" (Eph. 4:3), that congregation can be a powerful witness to the transformative power of the gospel.
- A diverse congregation usually is comprised of diverse spiritual gifts, talents, and skills.
- A highly diverse congregation is a vivid picture of God's universal family.

Local churches are more diverse today than at any point in their history. And indications are that diversity will increase exponentially. To effectively navigate diversity, churches in the future—especially highly diverse congregations—must share a common commitment to following Jesus, to look to the Bible as their spiritual compass, and to covenant to engage in worship and ministry in a sphere of mutual respect.

Ministers and church leaders are discovering that negotiating and arbitrating diversity in a "big tent church" is highly demanding, a task requiring non-partisan pastoral guidance. However, a church that embraces its diversity and learns to navigate it wisely may discover the diversity to be a wellspring of Kingdom potential.

Unity of the Spirit

David Hull

I like the story of the man from the Northeast who was in the South for a conference. He went to a diner for breakfast and asked for eggs, sausage, and toast. When the server brought the order, he noticed a little white puddle on his plate. "What's that?" he asked. "Grits," she replied. "What is a grit?" he continued. She rolled her eyes and said, "Honey, they don't come by themselves."

Neither do Christians who are trying to be devoted followers of Jesus. Instead, we connect in a community. This has been the commission of Jesus from the very first days of his ministry. He drew his followers together into a community and said to them, "By this everyone will know that you are my disciples, if you have love for one another" (John 13:35, NRSV). Christians . . . honey, they don't come by themselves!

From the earliest days of the church, our challenge has been living together in a community of love. After two thousand years, this challenge has not grown any easier. The culture today is divided by politics, ideologies, generational differences, economics, race, and the list goes on. The church cannot avoid these cultural differences.

In his *Letters*, C.S. Lewis wrote: "The Church is not a human society of people united by their natural affinities, but the Body of Christ, in which all members, however different, (and He rejoices in their differences and by no means wishes to iron them out) must share the common life, complementing and helping one another precisely by their differences." How can we live together as a community of love in these very divisive days?

I love how Ephesians 4:2-3 (NRSV) says it. In this great epistle about the church, we are instructed to relate to each other in the church "with all humility and gentleness, with patience, bearing with one another in love, making every effort to maintain the unity of the Spirit in the bond of peace."

Notice the words. We are not called to have a "spirit of unity." Instead, we are called to have a "unity of the Spirit." That is what verse 3 says. The difference between those two phrases is not just semantics; it is a matter of focus. A "spirit of unity" focuses on unity. The goal is unity. When this occurs, several possibilities exist:

- We get discouraged before we even begin. We look around and see diversity and animosity and declare that we will never all come together on anything.
- We force uniformity. Not the same thing as unity, uniformity is sometimes seen as the next best thing. The way to achieve uniformity is for someone to declare, "It's my way or the highway." Those who agree will stay; those who disagree will leave. Uniformity is the result.
- We fear conflict. If unity is our absolute goal, then we will go to great lengths to avoid any conflict that might disrupt the unity we desire so much. In the long run this is not healthy for a church: it leads to a lack of courage and conviction.

As Christians, we are called to have a "unity of the Spirit." Do you see the difference? It is a matter of focus, or priority. The focus is on obedience to the Holy Spirit, and unity is simply a byproduct. The number-one priority of this approach is to focus on the power of the Holy Spirit in our lives. We seek the presence of God with us in a daily commitment to live "by the Spirit," not by the ways of "the flesh." The focus is not on unity, but on the Spirit. When the focus is on the Spirit, unity comes to us even in our differences.

The same lesson can be learned from another area of life. The November 1994 issue of the *Atlantic Monthly* included an article about the superstar tenors Jose Carreras, Placido Domingo, and Luciano Pavarotti performing together in Los Angeles. When a reporter tried to press the issue of competition between the three men, Domingo said: "You have to put all of your concentration into opening your heart to the music. You can't be rivals when you're together making music." The same is true of Christians who "put all of our concentration into opening our hearts" to the Spirit.

The great missionary E. Stanley Jones said it so well: "Talk about what you believe, and you have disunity. Talk about Who you believe in, and you have unity." That is what "unity of the Spirit" means.

What will be the focus of your church?

Preaching from a Purple Pulpit

Jim Kitchens

Except in rare cases, there is always a bit of tension between a pastor and his/her congregation when it comes to preaching, especially prophetic preaching.

We all know a few congregations where a liberal pastor and a liberal congregation seem to be perfectly matched. We also know a few conservative churches where the same is true. But we also know how few and far between such perfect matches are, and we suspect that even those pastors hear from an angry parishioner at the back door of the church every once in a while.

For most of us who preach, however, the context is quite different. We preach in congregations that some are calling "purple" churches: neither all "red" (conservative) *nor* all "blue" (liberal). We preach to pews filled with Republicans *and* Democrats, with a sprinkling of Independents and Libertarians added in.

This inherent tension between pulpit and pew has escalated dramatically in some churches during the Trump administration. Some congregations—and pastors—are showing signs of being stretched to the breaking point.

Many of us who are pastors find ourselves asking, "How do I do this? How do I engage the issues the Spirit has laid on my heart *and* maintain my relationship with these people I love—even if I disagree with them sometimes?"

There is, of course, no "one size fits all" answer to these questions. Every pastor finds him/herself in a unique context and will have to balance many factors in play in that particular congregation.

There are, however, some things I can suggest that may help you sustain yourself during this particular season *and* maintain your relationship with your congregation over time.

• *Most importantly, attend to your prayer life.* Make sure you are spiritually grounded as you take on the taxing work of speaking the truth in love. Remember, in the heat of the Reformation, Martin Luther said, "I have so much to do, that I shall have to spend the first three hours in prayer." Part of my current spiritual discipline is to start my morning with the daily meditation sent out by the Franciscan mystic Fr. Richard Rohr. His insights always help me frame my day faithfully.

• *Find colleagues with whom you can wrestle honestly about how you all are going to minister with your congregation in these days.* I belong to a weekly *lectio divina* group who meditates together on an upcoming gospel passage in the lectionary. Having a group where I can listen deeply to scripture, sit in silence with God, and share insights into the passage with others gives me a solid grounding for the work ahead.

- *Focus on issues, not on people.* Rather than calling out the president by name or castigating his administration's actions, focus on the deep traditions in our faith that speak to the issues at hand. For example, remind people of the repeated admonition in both Jewish and Christian traditions to care for the alien and the sojourner rather than attacking the president's proposal to build a wall. As one colleague recently suggested to me, "Let Jesus do your dirty work."

- *Remember that the work of developing prophetic faith in people is a long-term process—a marathon, not a 100-yard dash.* Speak your prophetic word into a deeper frame in which you hope to mold your congregation into a more faithful community of Jesus-followers over the long haul. As David Frum, a senior editor at *The Atlantic,* pointed out in an article, "The outrage may get you started, but only hope keeps you going."

I often use the metaphor of stretching a rubber band to describe how best to move a congregation to new understanding. Whatever the issue, I always stretch that band in the direction I understand God is drawing us. But I am always aware that I can stretch that band so tautly that it will break, severing the relationship between the congregation and my leadership. Consider how much tension you want that band to be under so that your congregation will keep moving forward.

- *Finally, remember that we are a people of hope and belong to a God who is always leading us toward greater justice and truth, toward true shalom.* Meditate on Martin Luther King's assurance that "The arc of the moral universe is long, but it bends toward justice." Know that God will bring us all into the Beloved Community over time.

Some of my suggestions may speak to you; others may not. Feel free to incorporate the ones you find helpful for your own context. Develop additional practices that will feed you over the long term. And know that there is a whole community of preachers out there who are praying for one another … including you.

How to Be a Family of Faith

Joel Snider

About 20 years ago, the congregation I was serving adopted five core values. The one that spoke to our internal relationships said, "In relationships . . . Family." Our church covenant expanded this core value to read: "As a group of gathered believers, we understand ourselves to be a part of a family of faith. Therefore, we shall love, forgive, admonish, encourage, serve, and pray for one another—always in the spirit of being sisters and brothers in Christ."

We sought to model healthy family dynamics on a larger scale. We took what we knew about strong family systems and applied them to the congregation. In two decades of experience, we learned these lessons:

- *Communication is essential.* Families in crisis often complain of communication problems. Church families are no different. No one likes to be left out of the loop; those who missed information may feel estranged. For instance, it is embarrassing to be the only person who did not receive notice of a meeting's time change. We learned we must tell something 16 times to communicate it broadly within the church family.

  If we had an event that people didn't know about, we would look at each other and say, "16 times," as an admission that we failed to disseminate fully what people needed to know. We tend to overestimate how much attention people give to communication from the church, and we underestimate how often we need to give it; 16 times may seem like too much, but experience bears out the number.

- *Listen, too.* Listening is an important part of communication. People want to be heard. For our most critical decisions, we built in discussion times and listening sessions. These types of sessions must be genuine and not a pretense. Nothing is more insulting than to say feedback is important, and then to discount it in a public meeting.

  Discussion leaders have to communicate clear acceptance of input by controlling what they say and by eliminating nonverbal signs of impatience. Members of the church family know whether or not you are serious if you ask, "Are there any more questions?" The wrong inflection at the end of the question implies, "Of course not," cutting off conversation before people are ready to stop. It takes time to create a culture of open discussion and honest feedback, but it is what healthy families do.

- *Go toward the problem.* Dysfunctional families let resentments and anger build until they reach an explosive point. Members of these families would rather pretend everything is in order to avoid responsibility for their part of a problem or possible conflict. Healthy families, however, deal with differences and misunderstandings as they arise.

In a church setting, it is a rare mistake or misunderstanding that becomes easier to address as time goes by. The best time to confront an issue is immediately. Consequently, in my congregation when discussing a church member who was disappointed or disengaged, our ministry staff often challenged each other with "Go toward the problem." As uncomfortable as this approach may be, it will be easier in the present than in the future.

- *Talk to each other, not about each other.* Families with poor dynamics may find a family member attempting to gather the support of others against a single member. Psychologists speak of "triangling" when one person manipulates a second individual against a third. The instigators of triangles try to exert their will by using the pressure of numbers. They also avoid responsibility for their own opinions by getting someone else to express it for them. In healthy families, members take responsibility for their own feelings and desires. They are not afraid to say "I" and do not need to manipulate others in order to say "we" for added pressure.

  My church's staff had a covenant that if a church member complained about one of us to another member of the staff, the minister receiving the complaint would tell the church member to speak directly to the other minister. The same principle held true when a member of the congregation wanted a minister to confront another church member about a problem. Rarely did we need to solve a problem between two other people.

Thus, what makes for healthy family relationships makes for healthy church relationships.

Dysfunctional patterns at home are equally as dysfunctional at church. Build a culture of health by modeling positive behaviors yourself. If you serve in a multi-staff congregation, agree with other ministers how you expect each other to act and then hold each other accountable. Do the same for the entire church. Health will breed more health. The culture of the church will begin to work in favor of strong relationships and stand against dysfunctional attempts to hijack the congregation for purposes other than serving Christ.

Things We Never Needed

Mike Queen

O soul, are you weary and troubled?
No light in the darkness you see?
There's a light for a look at the Savior,
And life more abundant and free!

Turn your eyes upon Jesus,
Look full in his wonderful face,
And the things of earth will grow strangely dim
In the light of his glory and grace.

My friend, Bill Wilson, sometimes recites these words from an old hymn when working with a church that is experiencing anxiety over some pastoral change or facing a significant congregational decision or simply when the members find themselves in a crisis of budget reductions and/or declining attendance.

"Turn Your Eyes Upon Jesus" paints a clear picture of this anxiety: a weary and troubled soul, no light in the darkness. Somewhere along the way most congregations, and people, have felt the destabilizing grip of anxiety and lostness because they do not have a clear sense of who they are and in what direction they are headed.

Of course, the refrain of the hymn offers the only real antidote for this anxiety and lack of direction: the wonderful face of Jesus. It goes a step further to tell us what happens when we turn our eyes upon Jesus. It reminds us that "the things of earth will grow strangely dim in the light of his glory and grace." What, exactly, do these words mean?

In the midst of such anxiety, we often hear church leaders say things such as these: "If we just had a better preacher or more parking... If we just did contemporary music or renovated the sanctuary... If we had more for the youth to do... If we just gave more to missions... If we..." Most everyone, it seems, has a suggestion as to what needs to be done—usually by someone else—to "fix" whatever it is they see as wrong with the church. Rarely do leaders begin with the question, "What does Jesus want us to do right now?"

All too often we are preoccupied with "the things of earth"—temporal things—remodeling the church, setting budgets, paving parking lots, replacing a pastor or staff member. Those things are easy when compared to living out the gospel. We have substituted the things we can control in the place of Jesus' call to the hard work of disciplined discipleship. No wonder we have feelings of anxiety and a lack of direction in many of our congregations and for many of our clergy. The good news is that Jesus loves us so much that he never stops calling us back to him when we lose our way or chase after "the things of earth."

One of my favorite modern-day poets is singer/songwriter, Grace Potter. When I first heard her sing "Things I Never Needed," I assumed it was a song about love gone bad. But upon further reflection, her words could easily be taken as a haunting prayer to God from someone who is anxious about her future or who has lost her way in the past. I invite you to read Grace's words slowly, and you be the judge.

Take away this sense of regret
Take the things I need to forget
Take the mistakes I haven't made yet
They're all I have left

I don't want to be the one who lets you down
All I did was run myself around
I wish I could have seen through your eyes
Maybe then I would have realized
I'm the only one who is bleeding
For the things I never needed.

As one who has been privileged to be in ministry with some incredibly wonderful congregations, I am keenly aware that there were still too many times when we—both the church and I—were driven by the "the things of earth." Sometimes we chased after things we never needed. Sometimes those things seemed to salve our anxiety or make us feel better about what we were doing. None of them were bad, but always...they were temporary.

As important as they were, new buildings and new programs did not change us. It was only when we humbled ourselves before God and literally turned our eyes upon Jesus that the truly transformational things in the life of our congregation occurred—for example, feeding the hungry each day in our fellowship hall or taking the gospel into the county jail four days a week. Those were things we might have missed because we were focused on the things of the earth, focused on things we never really needed. It took a while. There was some pain on the journey. But once we learned that lesson, we were never again the same.

So, when you feel deeply in your bones that something is of God—"a Jesus thing"— and you humbly pursue it; know this: It will change your life. It will change your church. And it just might change someone else's world.

Singing Is Praying Twice

Doug Haney

On the bookshelf in my office is a gift from a church member and former adult choir member, Frances. The ceramic plaque reads, "Singing is praying twice." It's an adaptation of a quotation usually attributed to St. Augustine, "One who sings prays twice."

What does this mean? At its best, singing together in worship helps us express our praise of God, creates a space for us to offer ourselves to God, and binds us to one another in community. Pastors and ministers of music and worship leaders dream that worshipers would experience the presence of God weekly. Singing well helps us pray more deeply and puts us in a place to hear the voice of God.

Churches vary widely in the assets they have to support singing. "Sustained excellence" is the way a colleague in another state recently described music ministries with strong legacies and abundant resources. But what about the many churches that continue to be faithful Sunday after Sunday but are in a musical recession or simply lack leadership or resources?

Sing anyway. There is an expectation that when we worship together, we are going to sing. So, let the people sing. Take some time to figure out what your people sing and sing well.

At Wilshire Baptist Church, to celebrate the 500th anniversary of the Reformation, we planned a hymn festival for morning worship. Our theme was "Hymns We Love." I did an informal poll of some key leaders in our church—staff, deacons, Worship and Music Committee, and a few other members—and asked them the question, "What hymns do you think our congregation loves and sings well?"

Based on this information, we selected about a dozen hymns in a variety of styles: classic traditional hymns, gospel hymns, new hymns. Some hymns were accompanied by organ and brass, others by piano, mandolin, and violin. There were a few moments the people sang without accompaniment, the voices filling the sanctuary. Simply put, it was wonderful.

What is the soundtrack of your congregation? What are your congregation's heart songs? What are the hymns that speak to the identity of your community of faith? Can you list 10 hymns or songs that make up a core playlist? This is an opportunity to get to know your people and for them get to know one another. The conversation is just as important as the information.

Another way to engage your people in singing and praying twice is to invite church members to write new texts. A few years ago, a Wilshire member who is a writer and I led a three-session hymn-writing seminar. About a dozen church members met weekly to learn how to create texts for worship. Several people composed original hymns.

LeAnn Hampton composed the following pair of stanzas, using the traditional melody of the Doxology (OLD 100th), which we sang in worship that summer as the offering was presented.

Our God is making all things new,
A promise that we know is true.
Through eyes of faith we long to see
A love-transformed community.

A place where truth and justice reign
And healing triumphs over pain,
Where all have dignity and worth
And peace is passed throughout the earth.

James Steel, a member of the sanctuary choir, composed "We Adore You, God, Creator," sung to the hymn tune NETTLETON, a melody most often sung to the familiar text "Come, Thou Fount of Every Blessing."

It is such a beautiful gift to the church when poets and writers create something new for the church. Such gifts are received with gratitude. "Sing to the Lord a new song" must surely be an imperative for every generation. Even "Amazing Grace" was a new song once upon a time.

Years ago, I served a small church in Mobile, Alabama. One Sunday evening we built the service around singing familiar gospel hymns. Following the singing, the pastor asked people why they loved these particular hymns. With just a little encouragement, the people began to tell their stories and how these hymns were woven into the fabric of their lives. The songs were part of the journey of faith, and I began to realize there was much more going on in the hearts of people than simply the notes on the page.

Those who sing pray twice.

Are You Ill?

Bill Wilson

My grandmother often used a word to describe herself or other people. It was the word "ill." She did not use it to describe someone who was sick with a cold or the flu. She used it to describe an attitude, a demeanor, or a spirit. For example, if someone were rude or stern with her, she would describe them as being "ill." If someone were sour or negative and brought a wet blanket to every gathering, she described them as "always being ill."

While not meaning that they were physically sick, she was accurately describing another kind of sickness. This sickness is spiritual and emotional. It is the dreaded disease characterized by grouchiness, sullenness, and negativity. Unfortunately, it is a disease that is present in pandemic proportions in local congregations today.

The "ill spirit" that pervades many local churches is born of personal frustration, anxiety, unmet expectations, and general unhappiness. It is often brought into the life of the church from the workplace, the media, the economic realities we live in, our dysfunctional families, or our own personal emotional struggles. We show up at church "ill," and at the first opportunity we share our "illness" with all those within reach.

I recently was in a congregational meeting that was punctuated with mean-spirited comments and actions. The entire evening had an unpleasant feel to it. The trust level among those present was so low that nothing was taken at face value. Everything was subject to skepticism. In the end, the gathering was embarrassing. I walked away feeling sad that a people who call themselves Christian could treat one another in such brutal and unhealthy ways. I wondered:

- How is it that some people are able to attend church for a lifetime, call themselves Christians, and yet so easily revert to being un-Christlike in the way they treat others?
- How are we able to produce so many righteously mean Christians?
- How have we managed to create a theology that allows such a disconnect between the One we claim to follow and the way we live?

Dallas Willard, theologian par excellence, suggests that we have made secondary the inner transformation that Jesus made primary. When we neglect the spiritual disciplines, our surface spirituality melts away quickly when emotions get heated or issues become intense. Far too often, our inner self has been shaped and formed by the culture we live in rather than the Christ we follow. Willard suggests: "The greatest need you and I have is the renovation of our heart. That spiritual place within us from which outlook, choices, and actions come has often been formed by a world away from God. Now it must be transformed."

I once spent a very pleasant weekend with a group of Baptist deacons who wanted to talk about transformation. We began by admitting that most of us are a bit frightened by the idea of transformation. We are more interested in slight modifications or subtle adjustments than genuine transformation. After all, we are bright, intelligent, self-made men and women who tend to become self-absorbed and somewhat proud of our lives. The last thing most of us want to be accused of is being a zealot or a religious fanatic. Transformation sounds like more than we signed on for.

I am convinced that the tidal wave of "ill" people surging through our churches is a direct result of our failure to take seriously spiritual transformation into Christlikeness as the exclusive primary goal of a healthy local church. Such a priority would permeate our efforts at worship, evangelism, education, age-group ministries, small groups, etc. Such a focus would fundamentally change many of us.

Transformation is not optional for Christ-followers. It is why we are here and what we are to be about. Reforming our lives from the inside out will surely change us and reshape us in profound ways. It might even make a difference in the way we conduct ourselves in a church business meeting when emotions are high and tensions are up. If not, then we may need to admit that we have managed to hear dozens, even hundreds, of sermons, Bible studies, Sunday school lessons, and the like but have managed not to take internally those teachings.

Rather, what if we sought diligently to personally cultivate a loving spirit that became a defining characteristic of our congregation (John 13:35)? What if we took seriously the idea that our transformation is why Jesus came and lived among us (John 10:10)? What if the fruit of the Spirit, rather than being called "ill," became the defining trait of each one of us (Gal. 5:22)? Such would be a church that would honor and not embarrass our Savior.

It Goes Without Saying

Bill Wilson

Have you learned that nothing "goes without saying" anymore? That sobering truth runs counter to our tendency to think there are some universally shared assumptions on which we all agree. We may think that everyone agrees with us about what a family looks like, or what the Bible teaches regarding some pressing social issue, or which is a more effective worship style. We stand before a congregation or a denominational group or even our own family and make huge assumptions that have no basis in reality.

I once heard a high-profile preacher state with conviction: "It goes without saying that the pastor is the leader of the church." You could feel the tension in the room rise several notches. Then one insightful soul behind me whispered, "You'd better let Jesus know about that."

A few years ago I heard Robert Jones from Beeson Divinity School at Samford University deliver some lectures about preaching. He suggested that churches and clergy are especially prone to making these assumptions with regard to scripture. Lamenting the biblical illiteracy that plagues most congregations today, Dr. Jones urged his audience to go back to the fundamentals and reestablish the things we hold in common. Don't take for granted, he said, that the building blocks of the faith are firmly implanted in the hearts and minds of your parishioners. In fact, he suggested, assume that they are not. Our biblical illiteracy means that seemingly clear-cut truths must be regularly revisited and reaffirmed, for example:

• Does it go without saying that prayer is a daily priority in the life of a believer?
• Does it go without saying that sacrificial giving is the norm for God's people?
• Does it go without saying that judging others has no place in Christ's church?
• Does it go without saying that humility is more important in godly leaders than charisma?

You get the idea. There are many things we may assume are shared values that are actually called into question every day.

One of the signs of a healthy church and a healthy leader is giving focused attention to the fundamentals. Making Jesus the filter through which all such questions pass keeps us true to our calling. If a church can get clear about whose church it is, for example, much of the strife that characterizes congregational power grabs is negated. If the pastor thinks it is his or her church, or if the members think it is their church, or if the deacons think they own the place, or if the super-pious Sunday school class thinks they call the shots, or if the contemporary worship group or the traditional worship group or the experimental worship group think they are in charge, the result is always the same: a fractured fellowship plagued by chaos and confusion.

When we not only say but also believe and practice that the church belongs wholly to Jesus Christ, and that all decisions and power and vision must pass through him and his example, then much of the chaos and confusion fade away.

Let's spend some time in our churches articulating the things that we believe should go without saying. Here's a short list of ideas to get you started. They will need constant attention and high visibility if your church is to move toward health. Do the following ideas go without saying in your community of faith?

- We will address each other using the biblical injunctive, "speak the truth in love."
- We will regard our differences as a gift rather than a problem.
- We believe God loves the whole world, so we will love others as God has loved us.
- We will find our life by losing it.
- We will regard worship as an offering to God, not entertainment for ourselves.
- We will put our trust in God, not conventional wisdom.
- We expect to suffer and sacrifice and will not complain when we do.
- We will make time in our schedules for God.
- We will direct attention to God, not ourselves.
- We want to live in a constant state of gratitude.

Some things really should go without saying. Of course, the only way something becomes a shared belief that goes without saying is when we say it over and over again and make it a core value that permeates all we say and do. Perhaps this is a good time to be crystal clear about such things.

The 8 Deadly Sins of the Church

Bill Wilson

All organizations, including churches, have a reason for being. Only a few actually know that reason and articulate it and live into it. Sometimes the reason is clear and crisp; other times it is fuzzy and nebulous. Some choose their "why" intentionally, while others do so accidentally or allow others to choose it for them.

To have a vibrant future, a congregation must have clarity about its purpose. Those churches that define and differentiate themselves in a healthy way will be the ones that have a chance to manage the challenges of the 21st century successfully. Those that do not will probably not survive past mid-century.

When it comes to our primary purpose for being, it has been helpful for me to observe churches and try to understand what resides at the center of their attention, focus, funding, and shared vision. I'm into my fifth decade of local church ministry and have had the privilege of walking alongside many congregations and faith communities from a wide array of traditions as they seek to be faithful to their calling. This pivotal question, "What is your primary reason for being?" has emerged as my first question for assessing the health of a congregation.

In alphabetical order, here are eight common scenarios I've observed, followed by one that I can only hope will continue to emerge as a healthy alternative. Please know that this is simply an exercise in hyperbole: no church fits neatly into any one category, and there are many more categories than are listed here!

1. *Building-centric:* Congregants in this church have come to see their facilities as their primary identity and reason for being. Every decision is run through a filter that assumes the primacy of the facilities. Nothing can be considered without examining how it will impact the facilities or the campus. The church eventually exists to care for its facilities, and its mission is dictated by the building(s).

2. *Denomination-centric:* This church is waning and rapidly disappearing, due to the implosion of denominational organizations of every type. Its primary task is to play out the role and programs dictated by its denomination. Very little original thought or local initiative is required. Like a chain restaurant, the church simply serves up whatever the denomination sends.

3. *Doctrine-centric:* At the heart of this church is a rigid adherence to some faith confession or doctrinal stance. This can be a very conservative and strict church that tolerates little deviance from a shared doctrine, or it can be a very liberal and permissive church that tolerates little deviance from a shared doctrine. Both types of churches are marked by smug intolerance; demeaning of those who differ; and a lack of humility, compassion, and basic love for the people God places around them.

4. *Laity-centric:* This church places its primary authority in its lay leaders and guards that authority aggressively. Clergy and staff are seen as hired hands who are simply passing through and are tolerated and often relegated to observer status. The laity defines the church's mission and vision, and it often ends up looking like a self-designed organization that mirrors its creators' biases, prejudices, and preferences.

5. *Money-centric:* This congregation is concerned primarily with money. With a scarcity mindset, members make the money question the first and most important consideration when seeking to make their way into the future. These folks often blame others for their debt or shortfalls, and fail to practice biblical stewardship themselves. Their frugality chokes off creativity and innovation, and they descend into a death-spiral of hoarding and active resistance to a theology of abundance.

6. *Pastor-centric:* Persons in this church believe their pastor is the answer to every question or challenge the church faces. Nothing is decided or done without pastoral approval. Members often adore their pastor and believe he/she is the reason for their success. Conversely, when the church begins to wane, they are quick to turn on their pastor and place the blame for every difficulty at his/her feet. This love-hate relationship can turn quickly. Pastors who willingly step up on this pedestal often learn the hard way how painful the fall from a pedestal can be. Churches that succumb to this temptation often fall the fastest and the hardest when the beloved pastor is no longer on the job.

7. *Program-centric:* This church believes the answer to every challenge is a new program. Its people tend to be exhausted and jaded from being sold multiple bills of goods by pastors, consultants, denominational bodies, etc. Members believe they just "try harder," and that the secret to their future is a program that can be bought or a book that can be read.

8. *Staff-centric:* Persons in this church believe they exist primarily to pay the salaries and benefits of their staff, and they expect staff members to do the vast majority of ministry. The congregation sees its role is as judge and jury regarding the staff's abilities. Staff members who accept this deal come to believe they are indispensable and unreplaceable. This model seldom ends well.

A healthy alternative is the *mission-centric* church that seeks to align every part of its congregational life with the mission of God. Jesus was clear when asked what our reason for being is: to love God, to love our neighbor, and to make disciples. When the Holy Spirit raised up the church in Acts 2, worship, evangelism, missions, community, and discipleship were the ways those first Christ-followers chose to live out their common life together. These remain our missional marching orders. When we distort or confuse them, we do so at our own peril. When we refocus our congregation around them, amazing things happen. Mission-centric churches—of every size, shape, and theological persuasion—are the key to our future. May their tribe increase, and quickly.

King David and Church Culture

Joel Snider

In 1 Samuel 24–28, we read about a major set of events in David's relationship with King Saul. It was a rocky relationship at best. Saul's roller-coaster personality did not lend itself to stable interactions, particularly with someone he found as threatening as David. The accolades of the people, "Saul has slain his thousands and David his ten thousand," only increased the king's insecurities. Saul tried to kill David often enough that David had to flee from his homeland, finding it safer to live among the Philistines rather than in Saul's Israel.

Twice during this period, David had the chance to kill Saul. Although Saul failed in all his attempts to kill David, David simply refused to kill Saul even though occasions presented themselves. One of the scenes is genuinely comical, with Saul's vulnerability shown while he used the bathroom. His defenses and his pants were down. David could have stabbed him while in the cave but did not.

After refusing to take the opportunity to kill Saul, David's words are often described as noble: "I will not stretch out my hand against my lord, for he *is* the Lord's anointed." Was David simply righteous? Subsequent history would say "no."

David was a political creature. He understood better than most of his contemporaries the dynamics involved in the transition of Israel from a tribal confederacy to a kingdom ruled by a monarch. David saw that his actions set precedents that would become part of Israel's culture.

If David slayed the monarch, then others could justify slaying him when he took the throne. It was much wiser for David to weave respect for the "Lord's anointed" into the fabric of Israel's culture than for him to institute regicide as a practice sanctioned by the king himself.

What does this story have to do with church culture? Our combined actions shape the culture of our community of faith, or more directly put: Unless challenged, the way we treat others becomes an accepted way we can expect to be treated in the future. The way we function in a crisis today becomes the accepted way to function in future crises.

This dynamic is particularly important in disagreements. Many congregations have at least one chapter in their history when someone resorted to anonymous mail during a controversy. Is that the way you want your church to decide issues? Remember, the tactics you sanction today can be used against you.

If a controversial congregational vote is pending, how do you attempt to achieve your desired outcome? If you try to stack the meeting with people who will vote with you, that tactic may become an accepted part of your church's culture. Someone may stack the meeting against you the next time. Do you want a culture of discussion and consensus-building, or a culture of "who can get out the vote"?

David's story shows us that the actions we utilize, accept, or tolerate become part of our individual congregational cultures. David shows us that *how* we do things in our churches is as important as the decisions we make, the policies we implement, or the actions we take. He would not take the throne by force because he did not want to legitimize force as a way for an adversary to dethrone him in the future. Yes, Absalom tried that route, but the nation resisted it because force was not an accepted way for a king to take the throne in Israel.

If you think the outcome of a church action is more important than the way the outcome is achieved, you need to read the Gospels again. Jesus would not turn stones to bread or worship Satan to become the prince of this world. He would not forsake the cross to try to save us another way. How he became the Savior is as important as being the Savior. How the followers of Christ function is as important as claiming Christ.

The Center for Healthy Churches assists churches in developing processes that honor Christ and strategies for ministry that accomplish Christ's purpose in the world. We believe that how churches do things is as important as what they do.

Pebbles in Your Pocket

Steve Scoggin

Times of transition in a church are anxiety-filled during which we see parishioners exhibiting both hope and fear. William Bridges defines a time of transition as an ending followed by a period of "lostness and emptiness" before life resumes an intelligible pattern and direction. Transitions bring out the best and worst in humans.

Like the old worry stone you could carry around in your pocket to rub to soothe your concerns, I would offer a few "pebbles" worth carrying in your pocket during this transition.

Christina Baldwin's book, *The Seven Whispers*, is a collection of spiritual practices for our time focusing on seven meditative phrases. Following are three of these I offer as invitations to your spirit and points of orientation for you and the faith community you belong to, if the way ahead is not clear:

1. *Move at the pace of guidance.* In a fast-moving world, awash with distractions, living at the pace of guidance invites us to combine the practices of "measured movement and listening." When we move at the pace of guidance, we take time to listen and question before moving on. Moving at this pace slows us long enough to wonder where God is and what God may have for us, contrasted against what we have decided for ourselves. Moving fast can cancel out guidance that can smother spirit. When spirit is starved for oxygen, our ego takes over. Today's news is a running commentary on when ego is in the driver's seat.

2. *Surrender to surprise.* There is always a gap between what we think will happen and what actually happens. This gap is surprise. Surrendering to surprise means making room for interruptions and leaving enough space for something you have not considered. It is the practice of "balancing structure and openness." Openness to surprise might go a long way toward reducing the rage and anxiety that seem to be escalating in our culture. Remember, surprise is a "donation to our growth."

3. *Love the folks in front of you.* This third pebble challenges how lazy we can become about love. Loving who is in front of us invites us to relinquish our judgements and move beyond our tendency to see people based on what they can do for us rather than becoming genuinely curious about them. Christina Baldwin recounts in her book a story about one person making a difference: "If you don't think one individual can make a difference, you've never spent the night in a tent with a mosquito."

Who we are and how we behave have a tremendous impact on the quality of life we create around ourselves. As we become people who no longer live in the place we came from, we need to replace the sense of place with a willingness to know the stories of who is in front of us. Perhaps this accounts for the renewed interest in personal story.

Knowing a person's story can soften our reactiveness and judgment of each other. Loving who is in front of us is the practice of putting the reins on stereotype and judgment while taking interest in the story of that person in front of you.

These three "whispers" are gentle invitations or pebbles to place in our pocket. They can be medicine for these days of transition and also guides as we reorient from the lostness and emptiness that is a normal stage of transition. As Rumi said,

> *My boat strikes something deep.*
> *At first sounds of silence, waves.*
> *Nothing has happened;*
> *Or perhaps everything has happened.*
> *And I am sitting in my new life.*

Is There More Than One Theologian in Your Church?

Barry Howard

A few years ago, as I welcomed a first-time visitor to our worship service, he said to me abruptly: "I am looking for a church where the preacher preaches the Bible and doesn't talk about theology and all of that kind of stuff." I knew then I was in trouble because I don't believe you can preach the Bible or talk about God without talking about "theology and all of that kind of stuff."

As a Baptist who believes in the priesthood of every believer, I think that every pastor and every Christian should be a theologian in the truest sense of the word. I propose that our churches will be healthier if our people are equipped to be good theologians.

What is theology anyway? Is it a discipline for sophisticated concepts and complicated descriptions of God? Not at all. Theology is a good word. My esteemed theology professor in seminary, Fisher Humphreys, offered a simple yet practical definition of theology to his students: "Theology is thinking about God." And Dr. Humphreys continued that "everyone who thinks about God is doing theology."

There are many other definitions of theology. Dictionaries generally define theology as the study of God. Theologians Stanley Grenz and Roger Olson say that "theology may be defined as the intellectual reflection on the act, content, and implications of Christian faith." Dale Moody, who was a long-time professor of theology at Southern Seminary, often described Christian theology as "an effort to think coherently about the basic beliefs that create a community of faith around the person of Jesus Christ."

Of course, there are different branches of theology: systematic, historical, ecclesial, evangelical, orthodox, and reformed—just to name a few. But these days, as a pastor, I tend to think of theology in two important categories: folk theology and academic theology. Both are extremely important to the health of the church.

Folk theology is the theology of lay people. It is forged out of the experiences of life, the study of scripture, and reflection on God. Across the years in multiple churches I have been blessed to serve alongside committed Christians who are excellent folk theologians, individuals who faithfully empower the ministry of the local church. They have never been to Bible college or seminary, but they have a rich and insightful knowledge of God that has been forged through personal study of the Bible and their ongoing experience in living the Christian life.

In college and seminary I was privileged to study under extraordinarily devoted and respected academic theologians who had given their entire lives to "thinking about God" with all the vast resources of higher education. Each of them demonstrated a deep personal faith in God, but they also had the remarkable capacity to think about God, speak about God, and write about God with a vocabulary that is much more specific than the dialect of most folk theologians.

For the church to be at its best, we need both academic theologians and folk theologians. We need academic theologians to assimilate the resources of geography, archaeology, biblical languages, and history into a coherent system of beliefs. In the light of good academic theology, we need a church full of folk theologians to keep our congregations reflecting and conversing about the dynamics of our personal faith in God.

In his book, *Thinking About God*, Fisher Humphreys surmises the relationship between folk theology and academic theology as follows:

> All Christians think about God. This means that all Christians have a theology; they all have some ideas about God. This is a good thing because, just as war is too important to be left to the generals, so theology is too important to be left to the academic theologians. We are all entitled to think about God, even if we are amateurs. Of course, just as civilian leaders are wise to consult the generals about war, so all of us are wise to consult the academic theologians about theology.

As a pastoral theologian who thinks about God in the context of local church ministry, I have the privilege of equipping and encouraging members of my congregation to think for themselves about God. I want to help my church members to understand that when they think about God as they are informed and inspired by the Bible, they are doing theology. When they think about God as they hear and reflect on a sermon, they are doing theology. When they think about God as they articulate their prayers, they are doing theology. And when they think about God as they wrestle with the challenging circumstances of life, they are doing theology.

Perhaps Paul was advocating sound theology when he wrote, "Finally, brothers and sisters, whatever is true, whatever is noble, whatever is right, whatever is pure, whatever is lovely, whatever is admirable–if anything is excellent or praiseworthy–think about such things" (Phil. 4:8 NIV).

Theology is "thinking about God." Because our God is a big God, and because our collective insight is wiser than one individual's insight, I want to cultivate more than one theologian in my church. I want a church full of folks, Christians of all ages, who are thinking about God every day.

5 Things Churchgoers Need to Know About the Great Commission

Barry Howard

What did Jesus' appointment calendar look like on the days after his resurrection?

Following his earth-shaking exit from the tomb, Jesus appeared to 10 of his disciples who were meeting in Jerusalem, he walked with Cleopas and his friend on the Emmaus road, he directed the disciples to a huge catch of fish, he instructed Peter to "feed my lambs," and he later met his disciples on a mountain where he gave to them what we commonly call the Great Commission.

In 2018, the Barna Group released the results of a survey indicating that 51 percent of churchgoers are not familiar with the Great Commission, a bothersome bit of data for anyone concerned about advancing God's kingdom. Of greater concern, perhaps, is that among those who are familiar, many have a limited view of this core assignment. Many presuppose that the Great Commission is given to pastors. Or they rationalize that the commission is given to an advanced group of Christians such as missionaries, deacons, elders, or other lay leaders.

Matthew 28:18-20 is the most common Scripture referred to as the Great Commission: "All authority in heaven and on earth has been given to me. Therefore go and make disciples of all nations, baptizing them in the name of the Father and of the Son and of the Holy Spirit, and teaching them to obey everything I have commanded you. And surely I am with you always, to the very end of the age" (NIV).

Having lived in a community adjacent to a naval base for 12 years, I understand the act of "commissioning" to be serious business, a charge to deploy with radical loyalty. When an officer is commissioned, that he/she takes a vow to serve and is given a mission for life. When a ship is commissioned, it is given a name and a strategic assignment.

Following the Resurrection, when Jesus charged his disciples with the strategic assignment known as the Great Commission, his words became for them—and us—their *modus operandi*. Here are five things every churchgoer needs to know about the Great Commission:

1. *The commission is to make disciples.* First, disciple is a unique word that implies "more than a follower." It refers to a student who learns from a mentor or a master teacher. The Greek word for disciple, "*matheteuo*," is similar to our English words "apprentice" and "mentee." It refers to a deeper, ongoing learning process. Second, the call is to make "disciples," not just "decisions." We often talk about leading others to make a decision for Christ. While volitional decisions are crucial to beginning this journey of following and learning from Jesus, leading others to make "decisions" without providing an orientation to the "disciple life" is both counterproductive to the Kingdom and confusing to the supposed convert or confirmed.

2. *The directive is "as you go."* In the English translations, we emphasize more of an imperative to drop what you are doing and "go." While some will be called to be pastors, evangelists, and missionaries who veer from their career path to follow the call to vocation ministry, the overwhelming majority will engage in incarnational ministry through their chosen career path. In the Greek translation, there is more of a sense of sharing this good news "as you go." In other words, we are to be engaged in the enterprise of disciple-making "as you go," "wherever you go," and in "whatever you do."

3. *The mandate is communal.* This assignment is given to the group, not just to a single individual. Great Commission work is team work with significant individual contributions and overarching group cooperation. No one person fulfills the Great Commission alone, but rather by investing his/her best gifts in kingdom service. There are no insignificant tasks in working toward this mission. In the local church, for example, team members include those who tend the nursery, sing in the choir or on the worship team, preach and teach, spend time in the prayer room, drive the bus, and more. On the mission field, team members include those who make financial contributions, translate the language, plot logistics, teach life skills, and articulate the story of the good news. No one church or denomination can fulfill the commission alone, which means that, to maximize progress in implementation, churches of different stripes should collaborate around the mission—not compete with each other.

4. *The scope of the mission is international.* Jesus charged the disciples to take the mission to all nations and ethnicities. Later, in Acts 1:8, he elaborated further by extending the mission to Jerusalem, Judea, Samaria, and the uttermost regions of the earth.

5. *Jesus promised to be with the disciples in this work.* Jesus assured his disciples that he would be with them as they engaged in their mission, even "until the end of the age." Before his ascension, Jesus informed the disciples that even when his physical presence had departed, he would send his Spirit to comfort, teach, and strengthen them. And the Spirit continues to empower and embolden those who engage in this mission in our day.

At its core, Christianity is not assent or affirmation of a doctrinal formula. Rather, the Christian faith is rooted and grounded in a relational commitment to learn and follow the way of Jesus. For sure, Christians believe in grace, forgiveness, and salvation through Jesus Christ. But Christians also believe that the Jesus way of life is the best, most effective, and most fulfilling way to live.

Eugene Peterson in *The Message* translates the commission found in Matthew 28 simply and succinctly: "Go out and train everyone you meet, far and near, in this way of life, marking them by baptism in the threefold name: Father, Son, and Holy Spirit. Then instruct them in the practice of all I have commanded you. I'll be with you as you do this, day after day after day, right up to the end of the age."

Easter people take the Great Commission seriously. And Easter people join hands and hearts with those like and unlike themselves to engage in the mission.

PART 2

Shared Vision

A healthy church has a shared vision that all of its members seek to embody. When a church's vision is fractured its ministry's impact weakens, both in its members' lives and in the community God has given it to serve. Having a clear and focused vision invites us joyfully to align all our resources—spiritual, mental/emotional, physical, financial, and structural—toward shared Kingdom work.

Are You Ready for the 2020s?

Bill Wilson

The 2020s are here, and while I am not interested in speculation, I believe it is important to stop and assess what our current trends suggest we will be dealing with in this new decade. Following are some initial and limited thoughts about what is before us. First, here are some of the challenges we face:

- *The contraction:* There will be a stunning number of congregations that close, sell, or radically transform themselves by the end of the decade. Some suggest that by 2030, up to one-third of our current congregations will no longer exist. The primary financial and attendance support for many congregations today comes from persons over age 75. As they pass on, a void will result that will be difficult to fill and nearly impossible to overcome.

- *The retirement tsunami:* Most American denominational groups are in the midst of a tsunami of retirements of clergy and key leaders. Boomers born in the 1950s are exiting the congregational and denominational stage in record numbers. As the "bulge in the snake" of those born between 1946–1964 exits the leadership scene, the ensuing opportunities and crises will become clearer. By the end of the 2020s, the last of the Boomers will be retiring (those born in 1964 will turn 66), and the leadership transitions of most denominations, churches, and religious institutions will have taken place.

- *The pipeline:* Theological education is in the beginning stages of a massive downsizing and resulting shift in methodology. Enrollments in traditional M.Div. degree programs are already plummeting, and efforts to stem these declines by offering two-year programs have had only modest success. There simply are fewer and fewer college graduates interested in spending three to four years in a full-time graduate school setting. Online alternatives and a shrinking student population will continue to force traditional institutions to adapt. This will have profound impacts on church staffing models.

- *The spread of conflict:* As most congregations continue to contract, and as our culture continues its descent into incivility, more and more congregations will be visited by significant conflict. Scapegoating is a common response to loss, and as losses mount, nearly always there will be a group that sees clergy leadership as the issue. Sadly, forced terminations will continue to rise, and the resulting loss in momentum and trust will accelerate the demise of many congregations. Add to this the likelihood that the decade will bring into focus a litany of knotty issues that many churches have avoided in the past: sexual orientation, justifiable war, sexual exploitation, pervasive violence, political polarization, immigration, civil religion, etc. These will require an ability to address thorny issues that most congregations are simply not able to manage. Our traditions of conflict avoidance and/or our emulation of the toxic political culture have weakened our ability to disagree without demonizing those with whom we disagree. Fragmentation and polarization will continue their growth in congregations.

So, what are some signs of hope in the decade of the 2020s?

- *The gift of clarity:* As their metrics continue to slide, some congregations will accept the invitation to re-examine why they exist, rather than simply assume they have a right to exist. This will return them to the primary call of the church in the Book of Acts and re-engage with their original reason for being. The resulting clarity will energize and invigorate those who have survived the great contraction, and give them a message that resonates with a culture in search of real meaning. As simple as this sounds, it will be very challenging for traditional churches that have become encrusted with decades of local traditions and 20th-century consumeristic expectations. The old adage that "every Sunday is Reformation Sunday" will ring increasingly true.

- *The leadership of Jesus:* As congregations are faced with their demise, some will recognize that they have inadvertently wandered far from being shaped by the Jesus of scripture. As they rediscover his core message and mission, doing so will enable them to differentiate from institutional culture and traditions and refocus themselves around his radical and challenging core message. Realigning and recalibrating every aspect of their corporate life around that message will revitalize those who choose this path.

- *The growth of diversity:* As America's demographics continue to diversify, so will those churches that survive the decade. Think of diversity in any arena (gender, sexual orientation, race, ethnicity, economic, worship style, methodology, missiology, etc.) and it will probably mark those churches that thrive in the coming decade.

- *The surge of the new:* One trend that will continue is the surge in multisite locations and church planting. As facilities become available due to closures, larger churches that are well differentiated and relentlessly focused on a clear mission will continue to step in and expand their growth by multisite methodology. The unfolding culture in American congregational life in the 2020s will become increasingly hostile to 20th-century expressions of faith but more engaged by church starts that begin as cell groups or church plants focused on community, discipleship, and service rather than facilities and staff. Innovation and entrepreneurial thinking will continue to guide these expressions of faith.

- *The emergence of turnaround leadership:* With the overwhelming majority of churches in America in decline (nearly all those started prior to 1980 and with attendance less than 1,000), a new skill set in lay and clergy leaders will emerge. Rather than think of turnaround as simply a reversal of numerical decline, the real turnaround for most congregations will be to move from irrelevance to relevance in the lives of their constituents and their communities. These leadership skills will be birthed and honed in the midst of intense and tense seasons of spiritual discernment among congregations that proactively seek a new way forward. For some, it will be a smaller but more authentic expression of the faith they will come to embrace and celebrate. For others, it will result in substantial growth. The new metric for thriving churches, however, will be faithfulness to the gospel mission rather than cultural or corporate metrics that violate gospel tenants.

The 2020s are here. Buckle up; it's going to be quite a ride.

When You Pastor the *Titanic*

Bill Wilson

What if you knew that your congregation was on a collision course with its demise? What would you do? Who would you tell? How would it change the way you lead? Would it affect your sense of urgency? Would it help you better distinguish between minor and major issues?

The painful truth of the 21ˢᵗ-century traditional congregation is that it faces a very grim future without significant intervention. More than the usual hyperbole or alarmist rhetoric, the crisis is real. David Olson of the American Church Project (www.theamericanchurch.org) has documented the painful truth carefully. Olson, using realistic counts of attendees, reveals that traditional, established congregations that are more than 40 years old are in steady and persistent decline. Some are in dramatic decline. This tends to hold true regardless of theology, worship style, denomination, or locale.

Ominously, the percentage of the American public actively attending local congregations of any type is dropping precipitously. Despite self-reporting that suggests more than 40 percent of U.S. citizens are active attendees, the truth appears to be radically different. Olson's studies reveal that less than 20 percent of Americans attend a Christian church on a given weekend.

Other researchers confirm the facts in a variety of studies. The only growing segments for most denominations are new church starts, megachurches, or ethnic congregations. That leaves the vast majority of American Protestant congregations that have been in existence more than 40 years facing a very uncertain future. So, how do congregational leaders lead when facing such fierce headwinds?

In watching congregations attempt to deal with these realities in healthy ways, I have come to appreciate the following practices:

- *Initiate some honest assessment.* The starting point for creating a hopeful future is a realistic assessment of where you are. Many clergy and lay leaders live in denial of the truth about their congregational life. Someone will need to have the courage to point out the obvious, raise awareness, and wrestle with complex issues.

- *Resist the blame game.* One of the reasons clergy are hesitant to point out the truth of declining metrics is that they know there is a high likelihood that the congregation will point an accusing finger at them. My observation is that, when confronted with the painful truth about their metrics, most congregations react with predictable knee-jerk reactions and seek a quick fix to a deeply complex set of issues. If leaders can agree to hold off on blaming and instead focus on understanding and prayerful analysis, then honest and helpful conversation is a possibility.

- *Develop new metrics that fit today.* Our measurements tend to fall into the "nickels and noses" variety. We think the only measure of spiritual health or success for a congregation is bodies in the seats on Sunday mornings and dollars in the plate. We are woefully ill-prepared for the realities of the 21st century. Such metrics are a holdover from the churched era when congregational involvement was a given and our faith traditions were the exclusive option for the religiously inclined. Dramatically new ways of measuring success and engagement are needed and available for thoughtful congregations.

- *Engage in Spirit-led proactive planning.* Many congregations and leadership groups have neglected proactive planning and fallen victim to reactionary planning. We fail to look beyond the next quarter or 12 months, and find ourselves in a reactive stance, juggling whatever the culture or the economy or demographics or anxious congregants throw at us. Far healthier are the leaders who insist that their congregation invest resources and time to look ahead anticipating rather than reacting.

- *Reclaim your heritage.* Living in the mid- to late 20th century has spoiled us. The church of Jesus Christ has always had its best days when facing the steepest odds or under the most intense persecution. We have grown lazy and sloppy in our outreach, discipleship, and stewardship. Our heritage as God's people on mission reminds us that: "when we are weak, then we are strong." Many of us will have the chance to live out that historic lineage in the near future.

- *Lead.* When we are in a crisis, we need leaders. Don't go at it alone, but don't think your congregation can navigate these turbulent waters without clear leadership from you.

The Titanic? Really? Perhaps I am being a bit melodramatic. But honestly, I sense that this is the truth we all need to face and wrestle with. Business as usual for established churches is going to lead us to a world of declining resources, dwindling congregants, and the loss of vision and passion. Many of you are already there. Now is the time to speak the truth, reclaim our hope, and launch a realistic and thoughtful plan for our future as God's people.

High Anxiety

Bill Wilson

Anyone *not* feeling anxious? God's people in the 21ˢᵗ century suffer a serious malady. We mouth the words of faithfulness, but we are dominated by anxiety and frustration. For every time we parrot "God is good, all the time, and all the time God is good," there are dozens of times we obsess about our stock portfolios, job security, terrorists, or some political crisis. The great gap between our rhetoric and our actions is at the heart of the dysfunction of many local churches and individual Christians.

Living as though the words of scripture or the teachings of Christ are irrelevant for our day and age is a shortcut to conflict and chaos. The church was designed by God to operate under one overarching assumption: We are God's people, and as such, we live distinct and independent from whatever culture we find ourselves in. When we lose sight of whose we are, we become something dark, ugly, and unholy.

Some people have called us "resident aliens." Others use biblical images of "a city on a hill" or "a people set apart." The core truth is that we are to be unique, "in" but not "of" this world. This is not an invitation to disassociate from the culture around us, but to live in it and transform it, offering an alternative view of reality and of the future. God's people are to permeate the world with a deep and abiding love of all people and all of God's creation. Our place is not locked up in a building or isolated from culture, but fully immersed in our "world," living as salt and light to those who think that life is limited to what they can see.

Peter Steinke's book, *Congregational Leadership in Anxious Times,* has an intriguing subtitle: "Being calm and courageous no matter what." Does that describe you? Your church? If not, you probably suffer from what is commonly called "mission drift." You have veered away from your call and your mission. You need to be reminded why you are here.

In the midst of our anxiety and our wandering from our divine mandate, local churches can find their way toward health by spending more time on their mission and their resulting vision of their future. I often ask congregations three simple questions, just 11 words. How you answer these questions is critical to your future:

1. Who are you?
2. Why are you here?
3. Where are you going?

Usually, after the biblical rhetoric and God-talk fades, when I press for answers that are specific to that congregation, a blank look emerges and most members have to say: "We are not really sure."

Our highly anxious times demand that we seek and find clarity around these issues. Nothing will cut through the confusion of the age, the discord within your church, and your disconnection from your community like clear answers to these questions.

If you don't know where to begin, start with the origin of the church. Read the Book of Acts. Spend several days in chapter 2, then keep reading. I'm increasingly convinced that understanding and appropriating Acts is the key to our life in the 21st century. If you want to be a healthy congregation, your future is tied to the words you will find there.

Peter Steinke recounts the story of three bricklayers who are working on the same project and they are asked what they are doing. The first one answers, "I am laying bricks." The second one replies, "I am building a wall." The third one says, "I am building a cathedral."

In bewildering and anxious times, congregations and clergy need the third bricklayer's vision: focusing on the character of God, the mission given us, and upon what is possible as God's people. When we get clear about these things, we emerge as light in the darkness of our day. We become the ones who manage the ups and downs of the stock market, the insanity of the political arena, terrorism, our health, and a myriad of other issues with a deep peace and joy that passes any and all understanding.

We regularly entreat clergy and congregations to please "don't waste this crisis." Whatever your crisis is, God is inviting you to manage it in a way that distinguishes you from our culture. When we allow the spirit of Christ to guide us, we exude and personify faith, hope, and love. Using anxious times as an opportunity for witness and faithfulness affords us the chance to accomplish our prayer: "Thy kingdom come, thy will be done, here on earth as it is in heaven."

Might it be so in your life and in your place of worship.

What's Right with the Church?

Doug Haney

Sometimes a book ends up in your hands at just the right time with just the right words. Reading that kind of book is like meeting with a mentor or friend. You read a bit and think. Maybe you write something in the margin. It becomes a conversation.

A book like this ended up on my desk about 30 years ago. I had served enough churches that I had faced some challenges and some discouragement. I was coming to grips with my own limitations. I had even had a conversation with a trusted counselor about doing some coursework to prepare to take the MCAT to apply to medical school. I wondered if I really should continue being a minister of music.

Fortunately, there were many voices who encouraged me to find a way to do more than survive, but to thrive in local church ministry. Among those voices was a book by William Willimon, *What's Right with the Church?* You see, part of my struggle was that I had been taught to love the church in theory, but I didn't have much experience in loving the church in practice. My error was loving everyone but not *every one*.

Willimon's book helped me to begin to reframe some of the resistance I had experienced from church folk. (I'm sure it had nothing to do with my "I have a graduate degree in music and we're only doing great music here" attitude.) There was much to appreciate, to value, and to love about particular people and places. To quote Robert Webber, "All worship is local." Yes, I could honor the gifts and callings bestowed on me. But when I was at my best, I would find ways to honor the story and traditions that made each church unique in God's kingdom.

After Bill Wilson invited me to be a consultant in worship and music with the Center for Healthy Churches, I began to learn about "Appreciative Inquiry" or "AI." This approach to organizational development was developed by David Cooperrider and others at Case Western University in the mid '80s. Cooperrider was a graduate student doing some consulting at the famed Cleveland Clinic when he made a discovery. Using an interview approach with positive questions, he focused the attention of the medical staff on success stories and what was effective. Cooperrider reported in *The Power of Appreciative Inquiry* that the "inquiry itself resulted in quantifiable increases in people's attention to and valuing of the behaviors they had set out to explore."

AI is an approach to organizational development that assumes in every enterprise there is something good and right happening. AI asks generative questions such as "How can we do more of what is working?"

Asking "what's right with the church" is not simply positive thinking. It does not mean being naive or oblivious. But if we acknowledge that the way we see reality often shapes that reality, perhaps it is worth rethinking how our very questions influence the answers we seek and the paths we follow. So, let's end with some questions:

- Can you remember the thrill of the early days of your ministry?
- How can you do more of that which brings life and energy to your work?
- Can you reframe your view of your life as one of discovery and challenge?
- Can you become a student again and learn what this place, these people, and God can teach you?

Treasures New and Old

Guy Sayles

Jesus once said: "Every scribe who has been trained for the kingdom of heaven is like a householder who brings out of his treasure what is new and what is old" (Matt. 13:52). A householder managed a large estate on behalf of its wealthy owners: handling its finances, providing food and clothing for family members and workers, supervising servants, and overseeing the education of young children. The job required skill and wisdom. Nothing could be wasted: the householder was the steward of things both new and old.

My great-grandmother, Laura Beth Linkfield, was that kind of householder. She was a champion organizer of church bazaars and rummage sales, and she devoted her talents to her little, rural independent Methodist church outside Huntington, West Virginia.

In two of the "out buildings" on her place, Grandma collected merchandise to be sold at the annual bazaar and sale. As a child, I delighted in rummaging through all that "rummage." The buildings were chock-full of treasures: old clothes from which I made pirate and cowboy costumes, used tools that made me think I was a master craftsman, and old radios and televisions that I turned into radar stations and spaceships.

There were new treasures, too: shelves lined with Mason jars of vegetables, pickles, preserves, and jellies that the women of the church had canned; Laura's creamy apple butter, a jar of which "mysteriously" disappeared every time I visited her; and handmade quilts, baby blankets, scarves, and shawls.

When the day of the sale came, the lawn of the church was covered with tables laden with the treasures. The men made and sold barbecue. Musicians picked and sang. Children ran and played. Everyone talked, laughed, and spent the day in the crisp autumn air. Laura and her neighbors were householders like Jesus described: they used new and old to benefit their church.

We have a similar task: to use all of God's treasures—"new and old"—to serve the rule and reign of God. We need ancient wisdom and time-tested truth; history and tradition have a lot to teach us. It's not wise to discount the past. After all, we're not the first people to try to offer God authentic worship or to face the challenge of living faithfully in a challenging culture.

C.S. Lewis warned us about "chronological snobbery," or the wrong-headed and wrong-hearted idea that the newest and latest are also the smartest and best. Sometimes, in fact, what we most need is stored in the treasure house of memory. Near the entrance to Winchester Cathedral, there's a sign that reads: "You are entering a conversation that began long before you were born and will continue long after you're dead."

Notice, though, that Jesus accented, not the old, but the new: "treasures new and old." Even more than the invaluable lessons of the past, we need to open our eyes, ears, and hearts to the surprising new things God is doing *now* in the world through Jesus.

Since Jesus was, and is, restless for the revolution he called the "kingdom of God," his followers can't acquiesce to a status quo that allows injustice, violence, inequality, harshness, and condemnation to stand. In Jesus, the often unsettling and always-new will and way of God are breaking into the present moment.

Such divine newness challenges those people who want churches to maintain or even return to familiar patterns and routines. Too many seasoned church leaders pine for church as it was "back in the day."

- Never mind how much more diverse communities have become and how different are our expectations about the roles of women and men.
- Ignore the exponential rise in two-income households and the shrinking number of available volunteer hours.
- Pretend that family schedules haven't become bewilderingly complicated and tightly jammed.
- Overlook the fact that the culture, even in the South, long ago stopped accommodating the church's programs by not offering recreational or extracurricular activities on Wednesday nights or Sundays.
- Don't consider how incredible innovations in communications have shortened people's attention spans and increased their demands for visually oriented learning.

Never mind all these things and you end up with a church perfectly designed for the 1950s or the 1980s.

Church leaders should ask instead: "How can tradition help us to recognize and receive the newness of God?"

If this new thing looks, sounds, and feels like Jesus, it's a gift we can gratefully receive. We face vast challenges: socioeconomic inequities, gender and sexuality issues, racism, and xenophobia among them.

There are new treasures in the storehouse. Through his Spirit, Jesus is speaking. He promised: "I still have many things to say to you, but you cannot bear them now. When the Spirit of truth comes, he will guide you into all the truth" (John 16:12-13).

Shifting from "Why" to "Why Not"

Jim Kitchens

Over the past several years, I've had the opportunity to work as a consultant with numerous congregations around the country, trying to help them look directly into the adaptive challenges we all face.

When I talk with them, they know the way they did church 20 years ago isn't working anymore. They understand they need to do things differently. Almost everyone agrees things need to change. We just don't know what those changes ought to be or how to make them.

Each church presents a unique case—based on factors such as size, average age of its membership, financial resources, and the part of the country in which it is located. However, one of the things with which every church needs to wrestle is the role we give to our policy manuals.

Given our inclination to think about worst-case scenarios, these manuals often turn into long lists of regulations. We add amendments only when someone does something bad. In response, we make another rule everyone has to follow, adding one more entry to the list of things we can't ever do.

But what if we were to change our perspective on these documents? What if we began thinking of them as encouraging us to listen for the voice of the Holy Spirit and making innovative decisions that respond to the Spirit's nudges?

This shift happened in my own tradition, the Presbyterian Church USA, a few years ago when we adopted a new version of our denomination's constitution. It gave us permission to become a far less regulatory, far more permission-giving church. It gave congregations a whole lot more freedom and flexibility in their decision-making, inviting them to join God where God was already at work in the communities around us. It encouraged us to be open to the life-giving, innovative winds of the Holy Spirit and to dare taking risks for the sake of that mission.

Immediately after its adoption, this new freedom scared many of our churches to death! This new openness meant we would have to discern the way forward for each particular request presented to us, rather than having a set of rules that would excuse us from having to do that often-messy work.

So, what did churches do? Many groups with whom I have worked will say they want the freedom to do whatever is best for a church's or pastor's ministry. However, they continue to take a regulatory approach to their work. They talk a new ballgame, but they still play by the old rules.

I once recommended that a group with whom I was working take all their policy manuals out into the parking lot and burn them. They were taken back by the suggestion, but it made the point that they needed to let go of their older, more regulatory policy approach and develop new policies more open to the Spirit's leadership.

If you're not quite ready to burn your policy manuals, let me make a gentler recommendation. If you want to be open to the future-facing leadership of the Spirit more than to the precedents of the past, then turn the Holy Spirit loose in your church's life.

One of the best ways we can turn the Holy Spirit loose is to change our way of reading those policy manuals from "I don't see where it says we *can* do that" to "I don't see any place where it says we *can't* give it a try."

Making the shift from the language of "shall," "must," and "cannot" to the language of "why not" will help us notice where the Spirit is at work among us in innovative and life-giving ways.

Will this permission-giving approach create some messes along the way? Sure, but so does our current regulatory approach. Will it be hard to say "yes" to one group but "no" to another in a very similar situation? Sure, but the work of true discernment always includes having the courage to say either "yes" or "no," based on which answer will better enhance the church's mission.

The wind of the Spirit is always blowing through the church. Let's risk unfurling our churches' sails into that wind and see where God wants to take us.

Taking the Right Hill

Guy Sayles

In his raw, painful, but finally redemptive memoir, *The Night of the Gun*, the late journalist David Carr describes his fits-and-starts, zig-zagging journey from more than a decade of drug addiction, broken relationships, and personal shame to sobriety, a stable and loving family life, a successful career, and a feeling of contented happiness. He's unsparingly honest about his failures and regrets, and he's realistically hopeful about the possibility of new beginnings. He says: "The answer to life is learning to live." And, from his struggles he offers us hard-won lessons about how to live and, surprisingly, about how to lead.

Even when mired most deeply in the muck of his troubles, Carr managed to work intermittently as a journalist. Editors and colleagues recognized the dogged determination he brought to investigating cases of public corruption, and they respected his way with words: direct, tough, and aphoristic.

As Carr slowly gained more freedom from the power of his addictions, his career found greater traction. He became editor of the *Twin Cities Reader* and, eventually, of the *Washington City Paper*. He says of his leadership style that he was "a parody of a boss, someone who knew how to motivate people to take a hill." He added, however, that he was not "great at picking hills."

Both capacities are important for effective leaders, including church leaders: motivating people to take a hill and discerning which hills to take.

Strictly speaking, of course, leaders can't actually motivate other people; lasting motivation always originates from within. People motivate themselves as they respond to the possibilities and responsibilities they have. Sources of motivation vary and are most often mixed. Among them are duty, habit, a sense of grateful stewardship, eagerness to learn, the fulfillment of using one's gifts and talents, delight over an exciting opportunity, the joy of seeing others grow, and the satisfaction of working alongside people who share a common commitment.

While leaders can't directly motivate others, we can create a climate in which people are more likely to discover and develop their own motivation. It's a relational climate in which people respect, enjoy, and care for one another. It includes genuine enthusiasm, authentic celebration, abundant gratitude, generous affirmation, and worthwhile challenges. In my own development as a leader, I regret that it took me longer than I wish it had taken to learn about the contagious and positive motivational energy of laughter and playfulness. Our work is serious, but serious is vastly different from somber.

Pervading a motivational climate is a sense that something wonderful, crucial, or transformational is at stake. By the example of our own passionate commitment, leaders communicate that the kind of faith community we are attempting to be and the ministries we are doing together matter, and they matter for kingdom-of-God reasons.

Leaders need the capacity and skills to motivate people to take a hill, and we also need the ability and practices to help congregations discern which hills to take. We often say of pastors that we want them to "have *a* vision," by which we mean that we want them to see the future of the church, articulate that vision with compelling words and images, and guide the church—strategy by strategy and goal by goal—to turn that vision into reality.

It's wiser to expect "visionary" pastors to have the capacity to see with insight and foresight and a commitment to value and encourage the seeing of others. The best kind of vision comes, not from a solitary individual, but from a "visionary community—a church in which people with a shared commitment to God's purposes pray, study, discuss, debate, and yield to the insight-giving Spirit in order to discern God's present work in, and future call of, their congregation.

Leaders of visionary communities will need to nurture their own capacity for vision by taking time to reflect prayerfully and thoughtfully on the voices they hear and images they see in their minds and hearts, because those voices might be whispers and those images might be glimpses of God's unfolding call to them as leaders. They will also invite other participants in the congregation to take time and space to allow their own perceptions of God's presence and purpose to emerge. When we've been individually attentive to the movement of the Spirit, we are more prepared for meaningful conversations about the opportunities and needs we face together.

Pastors in visionary communities also need to teach and model the skills of listening vulnerably to one another and to the Spirit and of speaking honestly about one's own understanding of God's call. Such open listening and hospitable speaking make it more likely that the hills we take—our visions and dreams—will be the higher ground of faith, hope, and love.

Discernment: Getting Ready to Hear God

Jayne Davis

I hate to admit it: My hearing is not what it used to be. Voices in the room sound a bit more muffled. Reading lips is an emerging skill. Some days I truly believe my kids are speaking more softly just to mess with me. Maybe you're there, too, finding it a little bit harder to tune in to the voices that you want to hear amid a growing sea of noise around you.

Discerning God's voice is a lot like that. It is challenging to listen for the Spirit's guidance while other loud and persistent voices clamor for our attention and competing motivations lure us in opposing directions.

The good news, though, is that, just as there are ways to mitigate the noise around us to enhance our physical hearing—sitting closer to the speaker in a meeting, turning up the volume on the television—scripture shows us that there are things we can do that enable us to hear God's voice more clearly.

Discernment didn't just happen for folks such as Moses, Samuel, and Elijah. They got ready for it. They didn't always know at the time that they were getting ready, but they did things that put them in a position to hear God—actions and attitudes that created an environment in their lives that was more conducive to discerning God's voice.

If you're seeking direction from God—in your personal life or in your ministry—consider the following ways to get you ready to hear:

• *Be curious.* In Exodus 3, Moses is curious and goes to investigate the burning bush. He leans into the moment. Discouragement, worry, boredom, cynicism—these are all great enemies to curiosity. They keep our eyes cast downward. They filter the divine wonder out of conversations and experiences and reduce them to less than ordinary, simple life moments that may well be "burning bushes" in our path. In the Exodus story, when God sees that he has caught Moses' attention, God calls to Moses.

Burning bushes are never what we imagine they will be. They are unexpected, out of place, not obviously divine—and they require a response from us. How is God trying to get your attention? Are you curious enough to lean in and see where it leads?

> Earth's crammed with heaven,
> And every common bush afire with God;
> But only he who sees, takes off his shoes,
> The rest sit round it and pluck blackberries,
> And daub their natural faces unaware
>
> —Elizabeth Barrett Browning, "Aurora Leigh"

- *Pay attention to patterns.* God persists. If God wants to get our attention, he won't give up easily. That's good news for those of us who are a little slow to take a hint or worry that we'll only get one chance to discover God's will. In 1 Samuel 3, God calls to Samuel four times as he sleeps in his bed. Three times Samuel shares what he hears with Eli, the priest, before Eli understands the divine nature of the encounter. When they finally comprehend that the repetition is holy, God speaks.

  God's hand was on Samuel from before his birth, and God would not give up easily on guiding Samuel's life. That same hand rests on us. God wants to lead us, and we can count on him to persist. Where is the repetition in your life? In your ministry? Who can help you pay attention to the pattern?

- *Come out of the cave.* In 1 Kings 19, the prophet Elijah is weary and afraid. The people have broken their covenant and are trying to kill him, so he has run away. "I have had enough, Lord," he says. Have you ever been there? Feeling alone? Exhausted? Defeated? When moving forward feels too risky? Fear greatly diminishes our ability and our inclination to hear what God has to say about what's next. God reminds Elijah of two things at this point.

  First, Elijah must be in this for the long haul. He needs to prepare himself for this journey, and so God puts food and water before him to strengthen him and get him ready. Second, Elijah cannot hide in fear. "What are you doing, Elijah?" Come out of the cave. Truth is, if there is no one trying to "kill us," we are probably not investing ourselves in much of a vision from God. Discernment is a journey that requires stamina and courage.

- *Know who you are.* Mission and identity: the clearer we are on these two things, the more we'll be able to distinguish God's voice from the cacophony of constituencies that aim to stroke our egos or prey on our vulnerabilities in order to get their way. Before Jesus began his public ministry, he was tempted by Satan for 40 days in the desert. Henri Nouwen contends that Satan tried to distort Jesus' understanding of who he was with the lie that we are loved and have value because of what we do, what people say about us, what we possess. Prove that you can do something and turn these stones into bread. Jump off this building and let them catch you, then they will say good things about you. Worship me and I will give you everything you want. But Jesus could not be moved from the truth of who and whose he was.

  We are not nearly so steadfast as Jesus. We are lured by the siren call of accomplishment, affirmation, and acquisition that we too easily wrap in holy language. God's voice will be elusive when our identity is locked up in what we do, not whose we are.

Discernment doesn't just happen. We have to get ready for it. Be curious. Pay attention to patterns. Come out of the cave. Know who you are. God wants to lead you, and he will persist until you are able to hear.

Confession from a Consultant

Bill Wilson

It's time for a confession. Let me tell you a consultant's dirty little secret: congregational strategic planning is frequently a waste of time and can be counterproductive. There, it's out. Now, it's time to explain.

Many congregations, for a variety of reasons, choose to engage in strategic planning. Some opt to conduct the process internally, while others hire an outsider to help. Denominations and judicatories are getting in on the action, selling scads of books, workbooks, and assessment tools to help the process.

Since consulting with congregations is all the rage, there are many variations on this theme. Most take some form of corporate planning and apply a thin veneer of spirituality to a secular model. Behind these plans is a paint-by-number approach to your future that, if followed, promises to produce a set of core values, a mission statement, SWOT (strengths, weaknesses, opportunities, threats) analyses, strategic initiatives, SMART (specific, measurable, achievable, relevant, time-bound) goals, and the like.

Some vary the theme and design a process that produces the same thing in every church that uses the plan. This sort of prescriptive planning is used by those who know what your future should be and have a not-so-subtle agenda of turning your church in a direction that they have predetermined. If you get hooked into one of those plans, expect unnecessary conflict and unhealthy upheaval.

The truth is, far too many of these generic plans are a waste of time and energy because they give only lip service to the question of divine guidance. Oh, there is the obligatory prayer emphasis, but genuine spiritual discernment is lacking. Without this, the planning becomes an exercise in stating the obvious/inevitable, and wastes a valuable opportunity to deeply consider the future God has in mind for you.

A spiritual discernment process is very different from a corporate strategic planning model or a biased approach to your future. Spiritual discernment begins by admitting we do not have the solutions. It invites thinking, praying, and reflecting at a level that most of us studiously avoid. Spiritual discernment is messy, often slow, and extremely complicated. Most churches want neat, quick, and simple. Sorry, but neat, quick, and simple work in this area—as in most of congregational life—will lead to be shallow, predictable, and counterproductive.

My wise friend and colleague Steve Scoggin recently reminded me of the following time-tested pattern of spiritual discernment for individuals and organizations:

1. Spiritual discernment begins with *disorientation.* Something happens to knock us off our feet. Some event or series of events conspires to turn our world upside down. It may be an unpleasant experience such as a death, or a beloved pastor's departure, or some

crisis. Whatever it is, our life and world are shaken and we experience high anxiety. Throughout scripture, disorientation is the portal God uses to break into ordinary lives and do extraordinary things—for example, Joseph, Moses, Esther, Mary, Paul, Peter, and others. God's people are constantly finding themselves thrown off balance and unable to manage things using old frames of reference.

2. The next phase of spiritual discernment is a time of *reorientation*. On the heels of our crisis, we look around for something or someone to hold on to that will help us make sense of our shaken world. We find that the promises made by culture, leaders, politics, money, possessions, and an array of false gods are empty. We turn once again to the One who is the same yesterday, today, and tomorrow. All of our self-made structures, programs, and hollow leadership models collapse under the weight of the issue before us. In their place we rediscover our reason for being as a congregation. Our pride gives way to brokenness and humility as we reconnect to our mission and purpose. We lean into our future with a willingness to lay aside those things that have distracted us from our true calling.

3. Finally, a spiritual discernment process leads us to a *new orientation* to life and ministry. We reorder and reprioritize our life as God's people so that we are on his mission, not ours. We find a depth of meaning and fulfillment that has been missing. We sense passion and engagement rather than lethargy and apathy. Because we have taken seriously the voice and movement of the Spirit, we no longer rely on others to prescribe our future, but we create that future as collaborators with God in an ongoing process of regeneration and renewal. Our time spent in re-visioning our future has produced a new spirit of openness to God's leadership. We begin the hard work of aligning every part of our life with our new vision.

We need congregations that resist the temptation to cut corners and go for easy solutions to complex issues. Instead, what if we journeyed along the narrow and arduous way of spiritual discernment? I believe we will find that spiritual journey leads us to become the people God intended us to be. That is a very good place!

Listening for the Still Small Voice

Jim Kitchens

When we at the Center for Healthy Churches do a visioning process with churches, we always start by explaining to the congregation that the work we are doing together is more profound than corporate strategic planning or the visioning exercises with which they may be familiar from their workplaces. The primary difference is that the visioning process into which we are inviting them is a prayerful engagement in spiritual discernment.

Rather than leading the congregation to ask, "What is it we want for our church in the years ahead?" we instead ask them to be open to the question, "What is God calling us to become in this next season of life together?" The focus is not on what *we* want, but on what *God* wants for us.

Most of what I know about spiritual discernment I learned at a School for Discernmentarians led many years ago by Chuck Olsen and Danny Morris. These two ministers—one Presbyterian and one United Methodist—dedicated most of their ministries to helping Christian leaders listen more carefully for the voice of the Spirit in their church boards and judicatories.

Olsen and Morris started from their experience that when American Christians make decisions about the lives of our congregations, we far more often enter into a parliamentary process than into the rich Christian tradition of spiritual discernment. We are more apt to turn to Robert's Rules of Order than to scripture and tradition to find our way forward.

If we want to be more open to the Spirit in our decision-making, they suggested, we will need a guide to help us along the way. Just as a deliberative body needs a parliamentarian to lead it through its decision-making process, a body seeking to discern the will of God needs a "discernmentarian" to help it notice the movement of the Spirit in its conversations. And so, they developed their School for Discernmentarians.

Olsen and Morris gleaned most of their insights for that school from the discernment practices of the Jesuits and the Quaker tradition of "making a minute." They merged the two traditions' insights into an easily followed discernment process that can help us be more attuned to the voice of the Spirit as we dream together about the future God already has in store for us.

One of the most important steps in that process (detailed in their book, *Discerning God's Will Together*) is what Quakers refer to as the process of "shedding." If the goal of discernment is "listening for God's voice: nothing more, nothing less, nothing else," then we need to let go of all the other voices clamoring for our attention as we enter that process. The voice we typically most need to silence is the voice that expresses our own desires. Shedding, then, is primarily the process of silencing the voice that speaks when we ask the question, "What do *I* want?"

Quakers engage this step by wrestling with the question, "What would I have to let go of in order to be open to nothing more, nothing less, nothing else than God's will?"

Imagine what going through a shedding process together might mean if your church wanted to undertake a discernment process about its future? What if you invited people to ask themselves even the question, "What is the one thing I'm going to find it hardest to let go of as we listen for God's voice together?" When I have asked people to engage this question, I have received responses such as these:

- I'm open to our changing lots of things, but you'd better not touch the pews in the sanctuary.
- I'm willing to be open to what God wants us to do, but I sure hope it doesn't make us change the kind of music we sing on Sunday morning.
- I want us to do what God wants us to do, but I don't want it to make me feel uncomfortable.

Naming the one thing that is most likely to get in the way of our being fully open to God's will for our church is helpful for a discernment process in at least two ways:

1. Each of us can catch our self when our "hardest" issue comes up in the congregation's conversation. We can remind ourselves to breathe deeply and hold our issue more lightly as the conversation continues.
2. When other people say, "I'm totally opposed to that"—and we remember that what they are opposed to is what they said they would have the hardest time letting go of— we can discount their resistance just a bit.

There is no perfect way to be attuned to the "still, small voice" of God when we do our visioning work together, but actively engaging a shedding process can go a long way toward helping us silence the voices that make it difficult to hear God's clarion call.

Creatively Outrageous Congregations

Bill Wilson

I recently heard an interview with George Lois, a leader in the advertising world in the 1950s who helped revolutionize the industry. His innovations transformed advertising and made several of his clients into household names. I found his comments about creativity both interesting and applicable to modern congregational life.

According to Lois, creativity can solve almost any problem. "The creative act, the defeat of habit by originality, overcomes everything. And I really believe that. What I try to teach young people, or anybody in any creative field, is that every idea should seemingly be outrageous."

His thoughts resonate with what we are learning about congregations that not only survive but also thrive in the 21st century. Let's think about two of them.

1. "The creative act, the defeat of habit by originality, overcomes everything."

Every congregation must manage the polarity of traditional habits and originality. We live somewhere along a continuum between the two. Habits are both gift and curse to the follower of Christ. Our habits define us and give our life structure and depth. Conversely, our habits can blind us to new thoughts and growth that require a break in our routines.

Congregations desperately need to provide an anchor in the lives of people who find themselves caught up in overwhelming change. Having a place that worships an unchanging God and stands as a reminder of what really matters is a fine role for a church. However, worshipping an unchanging God does not mean congregations are to worship an unchanging methodology. Those that do are cursed by sameness. Such congregations are apt to be trapped in habitual and robotic planning, repetitious events, and a sameness that deadens and does disservice to our God who is the author of creativity and originality.

Healthy congregations engage the part of their brain that God intended to be used for creativity and originality. They do not disdain new ideas because they are new, but filter them through the truth of scripture and the spirit of Christ. Creativity and originality are sadly lacking in too many congregations that have come to equate only the habitual with the holy. Nature teaches us that God is the source of an amazing diversity that defines everything, from people to plants to planets. Why don't our churches embody more of this aspect of God? How is your congregation doing at managing the polarities of creativity and habit?

2. "Every idea should seemingly be outrageous."

Most congregations need to be introduced to some aspect of seeming "outrageousness." Far too many of us equate different with bad, and so do our churches. Notice that the qualifier for outrageous is "seemingly." Some of the most meaningful and memorable moments in our lives start out seemingly outrageous: "Let's get married." "We're going to have twins!" "What if we relocated our church?" "I think God is calling us to Haiti."

In the Bible, God repeatedly shows up with outrageous ideas and invites his people to live into them: "Leave the land you know for a land I will show you." "Place the baby in a basket." "Cross the Red Sea." "Leave your job and follow me." "Pray for those who persecute you." The list is endless. We serve an outrageous God who invites us into seemingly outrageous acts of faith and service.

Appreciative Inquiry is a powerful, strength-based tool that enables a congregation to think strategically about its future. As part of a process of planning, we invite a congregation to imagine and create "provocative propositions." In the exercise, members of the congregation are invited to imagine a future that is only possible if God intervenes. The idea is to break out of our limited imaginations and dream God-sized dreams.

The results are nearly always inspiring and energizing. People begin to break out of the meaningless repetition that weighs them down and then start to glimpse the future God has in mind for them. The ideas are seemingly outrageous, but as we unpack them, they become innovative and inspiring catalysts for change. Finding that sweet spot between outrageous and walking by faith is a very spiritual place for God's people to be. How is your congregation doing with that balance?

It bears remembering that simply being creative and changing for the sake of change or just being outrageous are no guarantee of being in alignment with God's dream for you or your congregation. However, doing so in the process of seeking to be faithful to the call to bring the Kingdom to earth is an important component of a healthy congregation.

When we engage our creativity and fold in a sense of audacity and boldness, then we are becoming more like the early church than we may know. When that happens, we have a chance to not only survive, but also to thrive.

The Courage to Become

Bill Owen

I'll never forget August 3, 1995. My family and I were in Destin, Florida with good friends. We vacationed there regularly during the child-rearing years. We did the same thing every summer. We had our place to stay, our spot on the beach, and our list of restaurants we loved.

The image has never left me: the water was literally "rocking" in the toilet! I was searching for a "safe" place for us in the condominium.

Hurricane Erin was making landfall on the Florida panhandle. For most of that week, we followed its route from its origin in the Atlantic Ocean across the Florida peninsula, projecting along with the "experts" the path it would take. All along, we convinced ourselves that this year would be like every year. We could expect our experiences in the past to be so again.

The weather channels predicted a Texas coast event. However, authorities in the Destin area encouraged all residents and tourists to evacuate. Despite the warning of Southeastern Conference basketball expert Joe Dean the night before at a local restaurant, we still decided to stay put and do nothing.

At 2:00 a.m., Erin turned due north, straight toward Fort Walton Beach, leaving us just to the east of landfall at 8:30 a.m. on August 3.

We were scared all day long. Hurricanes come early and stay late. They aren't like tornadoes. Suffice it to say, though shaken, we were not hurt. A section of the roof from our condo struck our van. Thankfully, it was still drivable and we made it home.

I will never make that mistake again.

Today's church finds itself in a similar position. Warning signs are all around us. The winds of change are literally "rocking" the things with which we are most familiar. We can no longer ignore or simply talk about it.

Statistically, the signals could not be clearer. Sunday morning church attendance is in decline. Denominational structures are weakening. The church's influence in society is waning. At best, there's growing ambivalence about our place in the larger community.

What are we to do? The church can be encouraged today by this familiar story, particularly the courage of Peter. "So Peter got out of the boat, started walking on the water, and came toward Jesus. But when he noticed the strong wind, he became frightened, and beginning to sink. . . Jesus immediately reached out his hand and caught him" (Matt. 14:22ff).

It takes courage to break out of whatever ruts we might find ourselves in. Just like Peter, if the church is going to change, we must take decisive, sometimes uncertain, steps out of the boat onto the water and forward into the unknown.

At the Center for Healthy Churches we're committed to a process that meets every church where it is. We believe every church has within itself all that is needed to face the stiff challenges of an unknown future. We believe every church has . . .

• the courage to become
• the courage to remember the stories that shape them
• the courage to see the present needs around them
• the courage to dream of a God-sized future

It begins with and is sustained by a period of spiritual discernment—a practice of concerted and consistent prayer for God's will and not our own. It continues with people growing in faith, striving to be all God has called them to be. It's about being committed to Jesus even in the teeth of the storm. It's about joining together in collaborative focus on the best of who they are. It's about bringing core positives to bear on the current needs of the community around them. It's about making authentic connections with any and all outside the "boat."

No one is saying that this is simple work. No one is saying that we might not "sink" like Peter. But fortunately, we too have Jesus' redeeming presence and support, his hand reaching out to us, if we sometimes fail or lose our way.

Memory or Imagination?

Bill Wilson

Some call it a battle, others a wrestling match. Let's go with something a bit less confrontational and call it a challenge that will impact whether or not you survive.

I'm describing one of the foundational polarities every church must confront and manage. Simply put, will your life together be primarily shaped by your memories or by your imagination?

No one questions whether both are important. Our memories and the past are a vital component of a healthy and vibrant faith and church. Our imaginations and the ability to innovate and adapt are a vital component of a healthy and vibrant church. Neither can exist in an appropriate way without the other.

However, the default position of the vast majority of congregations and parishes is to lean most heavily upon the familiar, the known, the former. Our imaginations grow weak from lack of use as we loop repeatedly back to what is comfortable and predictable.

Jesus confronted a religious system steeped in tradition and ritual. While honoring those who had gone before him, he also peeled back the layers of meaningless repetition to reveal the original intent and then breathed new life into that truth. Worship was not about Sabbath rules but about revering almighty God and offering one's self wholly to God. Sin was not so much a matter of external habits as a habit of the heart. The love of neighbor was not limited to "people like us" but extended to those very different from "us"—even lepers and Samaritans!

In each case, Jesus paid homage to the memories and traditions, but landed most emphatically on the power of imagination to rethink and reframe an eternal truth in a new and innovative way. The resulting earthquake that rocked the established religious order still reverberates through the church that tries to follow his lead.

Imitating our forefathers and mothers, we calcify eternal truth by wrapping it in temporal traditions and practices. We too often cling to memories and set patterns rather than engage our imaginations and creative capacities. For example:

- When confronted with the challenges of a culture that no longer regards Sunday as sacred space to be set aside for religious activities, we whine and complain about Sunday attendance rather than adapt and adjust to the new lifestyles that we ourselves have adopted. What is valuable and timeless is the worship of God and the fellowship of faith. What is temporal and open to imaginative reframing is when, how, and where that worship and fellowship take place.

- When confronted by a pluralistic and diverse community, we revert back to primitive thinking about race rather than see this new world as perfectly suited for Jesus' message of inclusion and Christ-centered unity in the midst of diversity.

- When facing dwindling financial resources and cumbersome facilities, we double down on guilt-laden stewardship and "clubhouse thinking" about our buildings rather than imaginatively exploring new streams of revenue and using our facilities as community assets rather than private quarters.

- When hiring and assigning staff, we repeat patterns from earlier eras that no longer result in effective outcomes. We fail to reimagine new models of staffing positions and tasks that shift the church culture away from "paying for professional services" toward leading a focused team on a missional adventure that includes everyone taking part as God has gifted and called them.

If your church or faith community is going to have a future, and if you want that future to be more about thriving than simply surviving, then you must get this balance right.

Are you going to be primarily driven by memory or imagination? You will need both.

Every church I served on staff was birthed in the 1800s. I understand the power and value and place of memory. I have profound respect for and appreciation of traditions and past practices. I want to honor those who sacrificed mightily for me to have the privilege of ministering in the 21st century.

And yet, I know that a significant part of what got those churches through the challenges of previous eras was the willingness of past leaders to engage their imaginations and push past the limitations of their memories. Like Jesus seeking to reform a tone-deaf religious machine that has lost its way, every generation must confront the temptations of our church to lean on what was and to lean away from what will be.

If your church constantly allows your memories to overrule your imaginations, you will die. It is that simple. Inviting God's creative Spirit to invade and inhabit our minds and hearts is the first step toward vibrancy and sustainability. Walking by faith and not by sight has always been our challenge.

Blessings to you as you seek to live by faith in the One who gave you an imagination and expects you to use it.

Thanksliving

Bill Wilson

Thanksliving: Christian humorist Grady Nutt introduced us to this delightful word in his epic book *Agaperos* a generation ago. In each chapter he blended two ideas into one integrated and complete whole. In doing so, he taught us to play havoc with spellcheckers and discover a world that we too often overlook.

"Thanksliving" has become a bit of a mantra for me. Granted, some days it has been more a question than a statement, but gratitude has served me well as a guiding attitude. Cultivating a lifestyle of gratitude rather than simply observing a designated season of thanksgiving seems to align well with the words of Jesus and Paul: "Give thanks in all circumstances" (1 Thess. 5:18).

In our work with congregations seeking to strategically engage their future, we have found it helpful to use the underlying philosophy of a process known as Appreciative Inquiry. AI begins with the assumption that there is, at the core of a church, a positive set of experiences and capacities. Discovering those and cultivating an attitude of gratitude that pervades the entire process is key to imagining and participating in God's positive dream for the future.

To call out those positive traits, we usually ask a series of questions:

• What attracted you to your church?
• Why do you stay at your church?
• When did your church become the "body of Christ" for you?

These simple questions, and the conversations they engender, inevitably lead to a deeper conversation focused upon gratitude that is filled with hope.

It's interesting that there is nearly always a discernible and measurable shift between the responses to the question of "what attracted you?" and "why do you stay?" Many people originally came to their church in response to a ministry, program, or personality. No surprise there, since most of our current members came during the programmatic era of congregational life.

Almost inevitably, however, what keeps people connected to their church is much less likely to be a program and much more likely to be a relationship. Generally, what keeps people connected and what enables a church to become "my church" almost always centers upon people. If a member of a church never develops deep and powerful personal relationships with others, then congregational involvement soon becomes just another organization competing for a slot on their already-full calendar.

Assimilating and retaining congregational members is a high priority issue for observant congregations. As one large-church pastor put it to me, "Nearly as many people are exiting our back door as are entering our front door."

In the end, what people will remember most about a minister or a church is not likely to be the spectacles or high-profile events that we are so enamored with. Instead, their gratitude will be directed toward those who called them by name, knew them deeply, and helped them discover their place in this world.

I recently was in a worship service in which a member of the vision planning team shared her testimony of the value of her church to her across her 22 years of life. It was a beautiful word of thanksliving as she recited the names of nearly a dozen men and women who had nurtured her through the ups and downs of her life. Choir leaders, Bible school teachers, chaperones, and random church members made up her list. Interestingly, despite being in a gorgeous sanctuary that was part of a beautiful campus, she did not mention buildings. I was impressed that, while a minister or two made the list, the vast majority were fellow parishioners not on the payroll.

Thanksliving for a congregation means being cognizant and overtly grateful for the people around us. They may be flawed and imperfect, but in the end, they matter most.

Healthy churches will devote their current and future energies toward strategically building up their capacity for transformative relationships. Whenever we are tempted to think programmatically, we should always ask: "How is this going to help us connect to people in Jesus' name?"

Most churches would do well to focus for a season upon growing deeper rather than wider. I'm often tempted to declare to a church contemplating its future: "What if we agree that for the next year, there will be no new programs and that our entire focus will be on going deeper?" I actually think such an approach would yield more long-term congregational growth than we can imagine.

Being thankful and appreciative for the multitude of ways your church has supported and sustained your spiritual formation is a start. Let that gratitude permeate every part of you, and experience thanksliving. Then, imagine and live into a future that is more focused upon people than things or events. God will be pleased, and lives will be transformed.

Dream with God

Bill Wilson

I've made a transition in recent years in the way I think and talk about God's will. For many people, the will of God is a mysterious, elusive, and frustrating concept. Too often, we have made it into a game that borders on God playing "keep away" with us. We speak of God's will as though it is something he hides or does not want us to know.

Some people confuse God's will with luck or coincidence or happenstance. Others are sure that if they could just decipher God's will, then their life or their family or their marriage or their church or their career would be straightened out and all would be well. At times of tragedy or death, some blame God for things that are far from his intentions for us. Others reduce God's will to pragmatic decisions about whom to date, what school to attend, where to eat dinner, what to do on vacation, etc. God's will has become a source of conflict and confusion for many people.

Like much of our confusion, our misunderstandings of God's will for us stem from our lack of biblical literacy. The Bible is rather clear that God's will is knowable and available to all. Many times I have suggested to someone seeking God's will that he/she take Matthew 5–7 and simply spend time reflecting on and doing the things Jesus explicitly speaks to in the Sermon on the Mount. Those pages are full of God's will for his people. As the Lord's Prayer suggests, God's will is inextricably connected to God's kingdom coming on earth as it is in heaven. God's will is bound up in all those things that bring God's kingdom to reality among us. If you are confused about this, then nothing about life as a Christ-follower will make sense to you.

I think our language proves to be a hindrance at this point. Thus, a few years ago I shifted to no longer talk about God's will for people or a congregation, but rather to speak of God's dream for us. Before, when I would ask a couple preparing for marriage what they thought God's will was for their life together, their eyes would glaze over and they would mumble some religious pabulum that nearly put me to sleep. Now, when I ask them to tell me about God's dream for their life together, their eyes light up and they engage their imagination around the amazing possibilities God has for them. The same is true with congregations, clergy, deacon bodies, sessions, trustees, elders, and/or church staffs.

Talk about God's will, and familiarity breeds a degree of contempt. Ask church leaders what they believe God's dream for their life is or invite them to dream with God about their future, and energy emerges as they envision possibilities and activate a part of their imagination that has been dormant for far too long.

Healthy churches dream. Healthy clergy have visions. Healthy Christians have healthy imaginations. One of the most important conversations you will ever have with your children, your spouse, your congregation, or any group seeking to live with meaning and purpose is when you ask: What is God's dream for us? Throw that out at your next deacon retreat or Sunday school lesson or sermon-planning event. I hope such a conversation is a regular and deliberate part of your life.

The pace of life is such that many of us neglect carving out time to think, dream, and imagine under the Spirit's guidance. To try and do church without an overarching divine dream guiding us is to reduce congregational life to the mechanical work of trying to balance budgets, count attendance, run programs, marry and bury, and manage facilities. No wonder our churches and ministers are burning out with frustration over such a small and boring agenda.

What is God's dream for you? It is the essential question for us. Why not set aside a season to dream your dreams and then align them with the divine dream for you and your congregation?

Start by looking to the biblical witness and church history for stories that inspire and invite us to imitate. Take stock of the amazing assets God has blessed you with. Look honestly at the community around you and the overwhelming opportunities before you. Then, dream together. Make it God-sized and more than you can do on your own.

The result will be clarity of purpose and energy for making such dreams into reality. Perhaps you will be able to pray "Thy kingdom come, thy will be done on earth as it is in heaven" and actually know the joy of seeing that dream come true around you.

Navigating the Land of Giants

Bill Wilson

The story of the Israelites' thwarted entry into the Promised Land has always made me curious. The 12 spies cross the Jordan and reconnoiter the land before them, returning with a mixed message. Ten of the spies are convinced the giants in the land will devour those who challenge them. Caleb and Joshua, however, are confident that God's provisions will suffice. "Let us go up at once and occupy it, for we are well able to overcome it" (Num. 13:30). Their minority report falls on deaf ears, and the children of Israel turn back in fear and wander in the wilderness for decades.

Later, we hear the rest of the story. In reality, the inhabitants of the land trembled in fear of the Israelites (Joshua 1–2). "Our hearts melted and everyone's courage failed because of you, for the LORD your God is God in heaven above and on the earth below" (Josh. 2:11). Due to their faithfulness, Caleb and Joshua are rewarded (Joshua 14), and a lesson is taught that God's people have been forgetting for centuries.

When the giants look most menacing, God's people can take heart in God's strength and power. "Be strong and courageous" is not just an inspiring phrase from Joshua 1; it is an invitation to a lifestyle.

Do you need convincing that there are giants in the land? Does your congregation need to be awakened to the fact that business as usual will probably lead you to extinction in a few generations? Perhaps your fear is ignited by David Olson's research that reveals only 17 percent of Americans attend a worship service of any sort on an average weekend. Perhaps it is David Kinnamon's findings that two-thirds of our youth will abandon local church life during their 20s. Perhaps it is the fact that 4,000 Protestant churches will close their doors permanently this year. Perhaps it is the sense that we live in a land that no longer values our traditions and methods. Perhaps it is your own children telling you how irrelevant church seems to be to their life.

Whatever it takes to awaken you to the giants in the land, you may be tempted to come to the same conclusion as the 10 spies: "We're in trouble, and the best way to proceed is backward!" Instead, what would it look like to live in the spirit of Caleb and Joshua as we seek to navigate our way forward through the land of the giants? For this journey, we need at least these items:

- *A map and compass to guide us:* God's people, when they have been at their best, have always been clear about their purpose and reason for being. Jesus struggled to convince the disciples that the life of faith was as simple as bringing heaven to earth in all that we say and do. Over the years we have picked up additional interests and tasks that now divert our attention from our primary goal. A fuzzy mission will prove deadly in this new landscape. In our new reality, we will need to say no to many good things in order to say yes to the best things God has in mind for us.

• *Adequate provisions:* We launch out on this journey knowing that we are opting out of a life of excess, but knowing that we will need critical supplies if we are to be successful. Every congregation I know is in a conversation about what is essential to the mission and what is a luxury. We face hard choices about what to take with us on the adventure ahead. What is essential? What can we live without? What is mission critical and what is a carryover from the past?

To make it in this new world, we will need to jettison some of the baggage we have accumulated. Some of us will be very sad and find it hard to let go. But if we are to survive, we will have to make sacrifices.

• *A strong and courageous spirit:* Who will be our Caleb and Joshua? Granted, the future will be challenging and marked by struggle. It will also be inspiring and filled with great meaning. Whiners need not apply. Those accustomed to getting their own way will be disappointed. Fair-weather believers will want to scurry back to Egypt. Naysayers are not needed.

As we face our own giants, a leaner, more focused and dedicated church is emerging. Despite the challenges, I believe there has never been a better day to be God's people living out our divine mission. The way through this land is the way of Joshua and Caleb: "Be strong and courageous. Do not be terrified; do not be discouraged, for the LORD your God will be with you wherever you go" (Josh. 1:9).

Why Visioning Efforts Fail or Succeed

Bill Wilson

I have had the privilege of working with numerous congregations to clarify their identity and lean into the future proactively. When that has gone well, one consequence has nearly always been true: The fresh vision requires a significant shift in the organizational life of the congregation.

David Cooperrider, one of the founders of Appreciative Inquiry, says: "If people do great work with the processes of inquiry and dreaming, then rarely, if ever, do the older command and control structures of eras past serve the organization. The new dreams always seem to have outgrown the structures and systems."

Of course, this is where many visioning processes get derailed. When the visionary rhetoric of a vibrant future collides with the realities of established precedents, facilities, job titles, or traditional methods, the result is conflict. The organizational inertia usually favors maintaining the status quo, and so the congregation talks a good game for a season, but eventually settles back into whatever patterns predated the visioning process.

How might we anticipate the impact of a fresh vision and welcome the inevitable shifts it will demand? Consider these suggestions:

• Design your visioning process to be as inclusive as possible.

The best processes are radically congregational, engaging as many people in as many formats as possible. Doing so is messier and more time-consuming than a top-down model, but in the end, it promotes ownership and buy-in. This will be invaluable when it comes to implementation of the uncomfortable parts of the plan.

• Help your congregation learn to distinguish between essentials, icons, and opinions.

Essentials are the parts of the congregation that are non-negotiable and not up for debate. You'll find these in scripture (see Acts 2). If we changed these, would we cease to be the church? Not included in essentials are: buildings, existing staff models, styles of most anything, schedules, budget models, or most organizational charts.

Icons are those things in our church that have deep and powerful symbolic meaning to us that disguise themselves as essentials. Some of the icons I see most frequently are: facilities, liturgies, staff members, traditions (especially around holidays), and organizations. Icons hook us emotionally and make us illogical. We can lose our icons and still be the church. Watch what happens to a congregation whose sanctuary burns. Almost always, while the smoke is still rising from the rubble, someone says: "Our church is so much more than a building." Every building of every church in every part of the world is iconic, not essential to being God's people. But that doesn't keep us from being irrationally devoted to them.

Opinions are our feelings about any and every part of congregational life. When we turn our impressions and opinions about a staff position/program/schedule into fact, we lose crucial objectivity. I recently heard someone proclaim in an implementation meeting: "We cannot do church without our Wednesday night activities!" Really?

• Once the differences between essentials, icons, and opinions are clarified, work hard to make these words come alive:

Nimble—Congregations that are effective in ministry in the 21st century will be able to respond quickly and nimbly to opportunities. The old structures that prized lengthy deliberation and glacial progress must give way. Beware of overcompensating and becoming unmoored, but know that pace matters.

Lean—Vibrant congregations are pancaking their organizational structures and simplifying their decision-making life. The cumbersome models that strangle us are a product of the post-industrial models that dominated the last 75 years of congregational life. Vibrant congregations are morphing those structures into leaner, less redundant models. An annual church business meeting is plenty. The decisions and work of the congregation must take place in smaller settings where teams/committees/task groups are empowered to act.

Collaborative—One of the most predictable outcomes of a healthy visioning process is the recognition that the gifts of all the congregation are required for fulfilling the mission of the church. Staff must adjust to laity as partners in ministry, rather than subjects. Laity must step up as engaged in their call, rather than hiring staff to do the work of the church. Staffing models that assumed an over-functioning paid staff and under-functioning laity need to be rebalanced.

Leadership—Your new vision will require real leadership. Many congregations will need to define leadership (I'd suggest following Jesus' example) and allow their leaders to lead. This is easier said than done, but does not change the fact that it is essential.

Most congregations don't start out to reorganize staffing models, worship styles, Bible study groups, or leadership structures, but they soon find that the old wineskins of the past cannot always hold the new wine of 21st-century ministry. The good news is that this constant reformation is at the heart of what has kept the church vibrant for centuries. Let it continue!

The One Word of Advice
Every Church Could Use

Matt Cook

When is the last time you noticed a vibration in your car? I'm not a car guy. If my car starts and gets me where I need to go, I might not notice some small things that need fixing. When I'm driving down the road and my car starts to shake, however, that typically will get my attention.

"So, what is it?" I asked Karl, my trusty mechanic. "Is my car about to explode?"

"Well the bad news is that this is a dangerous issue, but the good news is there's actually nothing broken and it won't cost you that much to fix this. The problem is that your tires are just poorly aligned," he said.

A couple of hours and a relatively low auto repair bill later, I was back on my way, problem solved.

When is the last time you noticed a vibration in your church? At the Center for Healthy Churches we get a lot of requests for different kinds of help, for example:

• "Our church is declining in attendance. Help!"
• "Our church is in conflict. Help!"
• "We're searching for a senior pastor. Help!"
• "We want to make a difference in our community. Help!"

At first glance these requests for help might strike as you very different. In every case, however, they share a common need that will help that church move readily into a vibrant future: *alignment*.

We talk about four different aspects of congregational alignment at CHC: staff, structures, facilities, and finances. In a car you want all four wheels to be pointing in the same direction, and that's also true for churches.

Take the problem of declining attendance. Nine out of ten churches in the United States are plateaued or declining, a situation fostering huge anxiety for most of them. And yet very few of those churches are finding ways to align all the various aspects of their identity with their desire for growth. The composition of their budgets, structures, facilities, and staff are largely the same as they've been for decades despite the enormous cultural changes around them.

If your desires for growth do not align with the way you're organized, then you will be left with conflict. The minister or staff team who believes the church should be growing will experience emotional conflict. Congregational conflict will arise when there is a highly desired outcome but no real success in achieving that outcome. People want their church to grow but don't often understand that making growth happen requires more than just a decent website and a few hours a week of the pastor's time. In a day when fewer and fewer people place a high value on God, faith, and church, it will require a far greater degree of congregational alignment to reach new people than many of our congregations currently experience.

That is not to say, however, that numerical growth should be your congregation's highest priority. There are any number of things you might focus on that would be greatly enhanced by a higher degree of alignment. Does your church want to help the poor? Does your church want to help people experience the presence of God through silence and solitude? Maybe your church wants to engage deeply in global missions.

Every one of these goals is a worthy focus for a congregation, but they all beg the same question: Is your church aligned to achieve these goals? Or are you just living with the incessant vibrations that come from a hope that's out of alignment with the reality of your budget and structures, or worse, out of alignment with the energy and engagement of both your staff and lay leadership?

But here's the good news: this problem can be fixed. There's nothing wrong with your church that can't be fixed by what's right with your church. The healthiest congregations learn to align their programs, budgets, and leadership structures (and often even their facilities) with the most dynamic elements in their core DNA.

Ironically, some of the congregations that might not necessarily consider numerical growth as a major aspect of their identity still end up experiencing some measure of growth when they align themselves in this way. When congregations are well aligned, passion and creativity flow, creating a natural magnetism that is almost always far more effective at drawing people in than growth strategies born out of a desire for institutional survival.

So, what are you waiting for? That vibration isn't going to take care of itself. Help your church find a better alignment. It will cost you something, but compared to the much higher cost of ministerial burnout, congregational conflict, and the disengagement of Christians in the work of the Kingdom, it's a small price to pay.

Jesus on Strategic Visioning

Bill Wilson

Building a congregation's life around a clear vision and purpose is an easy thing to believe in. Aligning that purpose with biblical teaching and witness is an agreeable notion. I seldom encounter a leader or leadership group who resists the idea that the path toward a vibrant and engaging congregation is to embody God's mission in clear, dynamic, and powerful ways.

The problems emerge when we begin to talk about the "how" of living out God's call to be his people on a mission. Like barnacles on a ship, our preferences, traditions, icons, and cultural accommodations have encrusted the mission and threaten to smother it.

I've been thinking about using Jesus as a model for how to live out a clear and compelling mission. In his life and practices, perhaps there are some insights for us in our struggle to stay true to our calling. How about the following for a list of healthy habits of congregations on a mission?

- *Solitude:* Jesus knew the value of time spent with a compass rather than a calendar. He repeatedly frustrated those who prized efficiency. From the beginning, he was prone to pull back from the limelight and reconnect with the divine dream and mission. Rather than allow others to sway his agenda and trajectory, he clearly defined who he was and what he came to do. The wilderness was his friend, and solitude was a regular habit. Planning and preparation claimed a healthy portion of his time.

- *Relentless adherence:* For the Kingdom vision to take root, Jesus found it imperative to avoid every temptation to water down or diverge from the vision with which he had been entrusted. Repeatedly, he declined opportunities that would have compromised the mission. Instead, he demonstrated an iron will that held fast to the calling despite popular acclaim or the threat of rejection.

- *Right people:* Jesus chose men and women to help him carry out the mission with an eye toward their visible and invisible gifts. He taught a diversity of gifts in the Kingdom, and his followers were a living example of that lesson. He paid attention to individuals and pushed them to become what they had been intended to be. Missing in his actions was an insistence upon lockstep behavior or thinking. When he spoke of unity, it was a unity of purpose, not style. In the diversity of the disciples and other followers, he found a powerful combination that turned the world upside down.

- *Repetition:* On a regular and consistent basis, Jesus taught and retaught the basics of the Kingdom dream. Using parables, he helped those around him visualize what it would look like for the Kingdom to actually come to earth as it was in heaven. Whether it be a story featuring a waiting father, a good Samaritan, a lost coin or a bridal celebration, he repeatedly reinforced the new way of living and being God's people.

• *Reinforcement:* Not content with mere theory, Jesus illustrated his prevailing vision with real-life examples. Blind men, innocent children, lepers, wayward women, and demon-possessed men all served as vehicles for him to reinforce and drive home the core teaching of this new kingdom.

• *Celebration:* Along the way, there were victories that needed to be celebrated, and Jesus focused on those successes to build a growing sense of movement among his followers. When bodies were healed or lives redirected, the resulting exclamations and joyful dances served notice that this was going to be a kingdom whose end result was abundance and joy. The Gospels are permeated by glimpses of joy and laughter.

• *Integrity:* Jesus insisted that all of his life with his disciples be congruent with his teaching. He was the one who noticed the beggars, the blind, lame, and diseased. He was the one who stayed true to a life of simplicity and singular focus. When others wanted to crown him king or build him a temple, he redirected them to the deeper meaning of his coming. Even when the mission led him to the garden and the cruelty of the cross, he remained true to his calling and his divine mission.

If our churches were willing to exercise these habits in our quest to live out the mission God has entrusted to us, perhaps we would ask these types of questions:

• How much time do you spend in quiet solitude reconnecting to the vision?
• Are you willing to say no to lesser things so that you can say yes to the mission?
• Are the right people leading the effort?
• How often do you simplify, repeat, and reinforce your reason for being?
• Does this journey make you smile, laugh, and resonate with joy?
• Does this mission embrace your whole being?

Lip service to the Kingdom is easy. Missional living? That's another story… a Jesus story.

Is Your Church Enlarging Its Bandwidth?

Larry McSwain

It was a simple question from a Center for Healthy Churches colleague: "Larry, do you have enough bandwidth to help me with a church staff analysis?" Initially, I had no idea what he was asking. "Bandwidth?" I had to catch up with the 20-year cycle of change in language. A central technology of the information revolution was being applied to my "energy or capacity to deal with a situation." That is personal bandwidth.

Think about the explosion in the past decade alone of technological bandwidth that has allowed for the dissemination of information. My wife, Sue, and I spent several days in the car recently enroute to and from visiting family. As we drove the interstates, we accessed the internet, read the news, texted our children, and answered telephone calls from a pastor wanting a recommendation for a youth minister—all on our 4G cell phones. The church office of the 21st century is wherever the staff members have their cell phones on! Expanding bandwidth enlarges the capacity for digital signals, expands the amount of information available in less time, and overwhelms us with its impact. It is a question of capacity.

Every congregation has a certain amount of bandwidth in fulfilling its dreams for the future. The challenge of most of the congregations I know is that they have not adequately engaged in the hard work of discerning the fullness of their inherent potential in the settings in which they minister.

I have been unable to escape the question for congregations. The voices I hear from current research and conversations with church leaders is the language of limitations: we are too busy, we are aging, we have too few people willing to take on new initiatives, we are tired, we are struggling to meet our budget, the culture is no longer friendly to the church, we do not know how to change, etc. We do not have the bandwidth to survive!

The challenges we all face are issues of spiritual discernment. In those moments when communities of biblical faith struggle, the God-led response has always been a prophetic reappraisal of the movement of God's Spirit in our midst. Pentecost is the paradigmatic response as Peter claimed the prophetic insights of Joel in the face of Israel's struggles: "I will pour out my spirit on all flesh; your sons and your daughters shall prophesy, your old men shall dream dreams, your young men shall see visions, Even on the male and female slaves, in those days, I will pour out my spirit" (Joel 2:28-29).

Joel called for a "solemn assembly" of the people to participate in a renewal of the Spirit of God. Is this not what congregations need to do to enlarge their capacities, their bandwidth, for a new future? This is part of what we mean by "healthy" at the CHC. It is an enlarging of our capacities for new visions. How do we do this?

- *Gather in openness to new insights of our strengths and abilities.* Congregational vitality is essentially spiritual, and the presence of the Spirit in our midst has no limitations if we are open to the reality of the new. Congregational capacity is more fundamentally an issue of the imagination than the metrics of bodies, buildings, and budgets. Any congregation is capable of enlarging its bandwidth if it is led by the Spirit. The focus is on what we can do rather than what we can't do. Ask the members of your congregation about their dreams and watch the energy in the room explode.

- *Maximize the diversity of the congregation.* Low-capacity congregations tend to be controlled by an attitude of sameness, an emphasis on group cohesion, or a power group that throttles new ideas. Both Joel and Peter proclaimed the principle of participation by all in the body for the presence of the Spirit—young and old, women and men, servants and leaders, all language and ethnic groups. Processes that involve voices seldom heard can transform the vision of your congregation. Any group with a willingness to try a new idea consistent with the core values of God's kingdom will be affirmed in the Spirit-led church.

- *Enlarge participation at the margins of congregational life.* Enlarging capacity includes expanding the connections with people at the margins: newcomers, teenagers, children, people who live blocks away but we do not know, sister congregations with whom we could build alliances, inactive members, and former leaders limited by mobility and health. About 40 percent of the average church's members keep it alive with their attendance, leadership, financial support, and prayers. Think about the impact if 10 percent more would feel enough inclusion to become involved!

- *Practice the principle that commitment follows participation.* The true capacity of a congregation is the level of commitment to its vision. Focus on commitment without involvement in shaping and accepting that vision narrows capacity because it is someone else's vision. Whenever people participate in shaping what they wish to see happen, they will generate the resources needed to make it happen. It is a matter of maximizing your congregation's bandwidth.

Time to Rethink Everything

Jim Kitchens

When I was the pastor of Second Presbyterian Church in Nashville, Tennessee, one of my friends was the pastor of a thriving tall-steeple United Methodist church in town. It was the sort of church that might lead some of the rest of us to struggle with the sin of envy. Its membership was large, it enjoyed abundant financial resources, and its ministries and involvement in the wider community were having significant impacts.

Nonetheless, the church's leaders were beginning to sense that the vision that had been guiding them for several years was beginning to wear thin. They felt a bit stuck, as if they didn't know what to do next. They decided to invite a well-known church consultant to come in and help them discern whether the Spirit might have a new vision for mission for them.

The consultant, as consultants often do, spent several days at the church engaging in conversations with the congregation as a whole, talking with its staff and leadership, and meeting with as many of the congregation's sub-communities as he could. He asked lots of open-ended questions and listened as carefully as possible during his time with them.

During the week following the consultant's visit, I shared a cup of coffee with the pastor and asked him how he felt the experience had gone. He responded by telling me a story about the consultant's final night in Nashville.

The church's council had held a dinner with the consultant at the church. As conversation picked up over dessert, one of the council members spoke up.

"We appreciate the time you've spent with us this week," he told the consultant. "We know you're going to go home and write a fine report that will tell us all the things you learned during your visit, and I'm looking forward to reading what you will recommend. But I'm wondering if you might have some immediate insight into our situation, something that has already come to you—some quick *bon mot* you could share with us tonight."

The consultant thought for a few seconds, panning the faces in the room, and then said: "Yes, I believe I do. If the only thing you're worried about is whether or not there will be someone here to bury you when you die, then you don't need to do a darn thing. However, if you want there to be a community of faithful followers of Jesus Christ here 100 years from now, you already need to be rethinking everything you're doing."

I recounted this story to the president of one of our denomination's seminaries. Having served a large, thriving church immediately before taking on the leadership of the seminary, the story clearly struck a chord in him. He immediately said he was going to call the editor of one of our leading publications and tell him to print the consultant's last two sentences in the largest size font that would fit on the magazine's main editorial page. "Every church board in America needs to hear those words," he said.

This story has stuck with me ever since and comes to mind when I'm talking with other friends who are pastors, especially the pastors of medium to large, thriving churches.

Too often, we who are leaders of congregations mistakenly think the impact that the spread of post-Christendom in America has on congregations is an issue only for churches that are already in steep decline or are struggling with whether they can keep their doors open for another 10 years, much less 100.

The truth is that the smaller, struggling churches have an advantage over the rest of us: They know they can't wait any longer before beginning to ask deep and sometimes messy questions about the changes they need to make if they are going to be faithful to their call. They can't stick with business as usual. They are dealing with the consequences of this changed landscape every day. It is those of us in the medium to larger churches who too often are lulled into thinking we don't need to take any of this stuff too seriously—at least not yet.

Healthy churches—no matter their size—hear the truth in that consultant's words: they realize they already need to be rethinking everything they're doing. They intuitively get this unique moment in American Christian history in which we all live.

Those of us who work with the Center for Healthy Churches believe that the Spirit is more than ready to discern that "new thing" the prophet Isaiah promises that God is already doing in our midst. We are eager to come alongside and partner with you as you listen for the ways the Spirit is leading you into that future God already has in mind for you. If you're ready to begin that adventure, be in touch.

The Conversation We Don't Want to Have

Bill Wilson

Our current economy, coupled with the ongoing transitions in congregational life and ministry focus, has created intense pressure on church staffing models. With finances tight, congregations are being forced to take stock of the number of professional staff members they require and can afford, and also the focus of those staff members. It is a difficult conversation to broach in most congregations, so we often delay and deny the looming issues. Unfortunately, the conversation then erupts as a crisis at budget or transition time. Proactively leaning into the conversation is a much healthier alternative.

As you consider your situation, here are some guiding thoughts:

• *Clarify your church's mission, vision, and strategy for the immediate future.* Whatever you believe the Kingdom is to look like in the coming season of your congregation's life is what reigns supreme when it comes to facilities, staff, structures, and finances. That clarity is essential if you are to make wise and appropriate choices in regard to your staff. There are multiple options for doing this clarification work. Choose one and pursue it with energy until you are clear and united around a shared agenda for the future.

• *Define the relationship between professional staff and laity.* What is the leadership culture of your congregation? Some churches seemingly hire staff to do most of the work of the church. Others seek a more balanced ministry model of an engaged laity and ministerial leaders. What if you made this choice deliberately rather than by tradition?

• *Analyze staffing expenditures and congregational attendance patterns.* Analyze your congregation's budget, and rebalance the budget so that it fits generally accepted models for operation. Specifically, break your budget into five categories: personnel, facilities, programs, debt, and missions. Assign every line item in your budget into one of these categories. Hopefully, you are debt-free or paying your debt down by using a parallel capital campaign. If so, then the following four categories and their allotment ranges apply to you; if not, you will need to adjust to include the debt service.

Personnel:	45–60%
Facilities:	10–25%
Programs:	10–25%
Missions:	10–25%

One of the key indicators of congregational health is the combined percentage of personnel and facilities. When this number exceeds 70 percent, the ability of the congregation to successfully engage in ministry and missions begins to be negatively impacted.

These percentages are strictly guidelines and need to be evaluated in terms of your context, congregation size, and special circumstances. Even with that, once you know your budget percentages, you can begin to make needed adjustments based upon your ministry vision, rather than in emotional reaction to a crisis.

You will discover all sorts of innovations and alternative ways to engage the question. For example, the "lean church" movement suggests that no more than 33 percent of your budget go toward staff. Lean church priorities of high laity engagement, minimal staffing, and no permanent buildings may work well with a new church start, but most established churches with physical facilities will find it unworkable.

Another metric that lends insight into the discussion is the ratio of weekly attenders to ministerial/professional staff. The generally accepted ratio is one ministerial staff member for every 100 regular attenders. Thus, if your congregation averages 325 attenders, the ratio suggests you can support three ministerial staff members.

This ratio has been around for many years and seems to hold up in current scenarios. However, attendance patterns are shifting dramatically and may impact these figures. The frequency of attendance by those who consider themselves regular attendees is dropping. Do a quick check on the actual attendance habits of your congregation, and you will find that faithful, regular attenders often are present 35–40 Sundays a year. Not only does this have an impact on volunteer positions (class leadership, choir, etc.), but it also means that a congregation must staff and prepare for a larger congregation than the weekly attendance average suggests you have. An average worship attendance of 300 may actually be an active congregation of 450–500, and that has implications for the staffing ratio.

However you choose to approach the issue, there are ways to evaluate your congregation's staffing model that are tied to both metrics and mission. When you do, remember that each staff member is a real person with a real family and a real call to ministry. Any adjustments must be approached in a thoughtful, generous, Christ-like spirit as you move forward.

While it is a difficult conversation, it is one we must have if we are to be good stewards of our resources and our witness.

Everything Breaks Down

Joel Snider

Any homeowner can tell you that concrete cracks, metal rusts, wood warps, caulk fails, paint peels, and sunlight fades everything. Sometimes we can get by with touching up our home's age spots. But, if we own the house long enough, we eventually face a remodeling job.

The process at work in an aging home is nothing less than the Second Law of Thermodynamics. If you don't remember your high school physics definition of this law, I'll summarize it for you in three words: "Everything breaks down."

The Second Law of Thermodynamics explains why we always have to change the oil in our cars, why the interstate is always being repaired, and why home ownership is frustrating. Everything breaks down. Our cars, our highways, and our homes need maintenance or repair. And despite our best efforts, sometimes they need overhauls, repaving, or remodeling. None of them can last forever in their current state.

As a young associate pastor, I learned how the Second Law of Thermodynamics applies to churches. I had responsibility for the weekly training of adult Bible study teachers. I developed a good program and had excellent participation—for about a year. Then attendance decreased slightly until, at the end of the second year, less than half of the original participants still attended. I lamented the situation to a man in the church who happened to be a professor. He shrugged his shoulders and said, "It's the Second Law of Thermodynamics. Everything breaks down."

From there we had an interesting discussion of why programs "age out" and become less effective. Original participants age, die, get sick, move, or have changes in life circumstances. Their initial vision becomes tempered as other interests subtly compete for time or attention. New participants ease into the program with interest, but less ownership. Enthusiasm is diluted. Eventually, the program exceeds its shelf life and becomes ineffective.

Any of us who lead in churches know the frustration of having to retool a once-effective outreach program. Even the best stewardship campaign themes have an expiration date of two to three years. Everything breaks down. Regular maintenance helps, but sooner or later, some programs need an overhaul or remodeling.

Traditionally structured churches currently face the effects of the Second Law of Thermodynamics in several critical areas. One is Sunday School. Bible study that solely focuses on Sunday mornings in age-graded classes simply isn't the final answer for how congregations must train members in the knowledge and use of the Scriptures. Look at attendance figures across a wide range of congregations. How many churches have a Sunday morning Bible study attendance equal to their attendance of 20 years ago?

Communication is another critical area. The printed newsletter cannot carry the brunt of delivering timely information to members. Even email is fast losing effectiveness as a tool. What comes next?

So that we don't lose sight of the big picture, behind all these individual programs is the overall vision of the church. Given enough time, it too will give in to the forces of physics and break down. A once vibrant and inspiring mission can suffer from the effects of old age.

One of the convictions of the Center for Healthy Churches is that intentional maintenance and remodeling of church programs can create new passion and purpose within a congregation. It is possible to create fresh cycles of energy and growth. As with a home or a car, planned maintenance or replacement of a vision is better than the crisis of unexpected repairs.

Consequently, the CHC offers consultations in a variety of the core functions of a church: communications, worship, and children's ministry are a few. We also assist in a "revisioning" process that is designed to help churches find their focus for the next cycle in their lives. Additionally, we worked with author Bob Dale to create a 21st-century revision of his classic work, *To Dream Again* (Nurturing Faith, 2018). Bob's original book helped hundreds of congregations explore ways to break downward cycles and find new patterns for effective futures.

If you are frustrated with a program or process in your church that is less effective than it once was, don't feel defeated. Even the most effective programs have expiration dates. The best ideas have a normal shelf life. Things break down. But with regular maintenance, good programs can last longer. Remodeling a vision can be planned and exciting.

Leading Change at the "Church of Stuck-ness"

Bob Dale

So, is your church stuck and can't move forward? Are you wondering how to lead it out of its well-worn ruts?

Churches are conserving groups by nature. Our communities of faith have a precious message to protect and share. That's our legacy and stewardship. But, since it's also easier to conserve and protect than it is to share faith and expand, we often settle for options with few risks. Holy practices become habitual patterns in churches.

How do you exercise creative leadership at the "Church of Stuckness"? Three kinds of leader partners can help your church get out of its ruts. How can you both identify and bless them?

1. Which of your church leaders show a scouting mentality?

Think of the scouts for the wagon trains that traversed the American western frontier in the early-to-mid 1800s. Those scouts had two roles: they found the way forward, and they protected the travelers. Your church scouts face two leadership directions, too: they assure the congregation is secure while risking new ministries and opportunities. It's a balancing act to find the future without circling the wagons in the face of threats, both real and imagined.

John Colter, the advance scout for the Lewis and Clark expedition, was the first European to see the geysers in what became Yellowstone National Park. He thought he'd found hell, but his scouting mentality wouldn't let him turn back from the scary unknown. His pioneering mindset took him all the way to the Pacific Ocean.

Who in your church has a bifocal "protect and pioneer" mentality to reassure other leaders while seizing the future? Who can relate to the congregation's internal and external tribes? Cultivate a team of leaders with both/and perspectives of your congregation's future. Stabilize, stretch, and move ahead.

2. Who are your congregational leaders with faith's holy unrest?

Let's take a "faith census." In your church, who's being stirred by Christ's Spirit to explore faith's frontiers? Who are your Calebs—those restless souls who are ready to face the daunting challenges just ahead (Numbers 13)? These leaders are ready to exercise faith's muscles and serve beyond the ruts. Let them be contagious.

There was a cautionary sign in St. Joseph, Missouri for those heading west across the frontier in the 1800s: "Choose your rut carefully. You may be in it all the way to

California." Stretch goals challenge us to escape our paralyzing routines and follow our holy unrest into new cultures and eras.

Who, among your leaders, is moving toward God's kingdom? Gather a leader team of believers who are growing steadily. Don't settle for "we've always done it this way."

3. Who are your church's leaders with risk intelligence?

You've heard of "multiple intelligences"—the observation that we're all smart in a variety of ways. Recently, the idea of risk intelligence has shown us how to deal better with uncertainty. This business arena has studied leaders the church has overlooked—financial traders, gamblers, and weather forecasters.

Discovering how to cope with uncertainty, measure the limits of our knowledge, identify reliable sources, learn fast, estimate possibilities, make better predictions, and act on them are the pivot points of effective decision-making. In the words of that late, great theologian Kenny Rogers: "You've got to know when to hold 'em, know when to fold 'em, know when to walk away, and know when to run."

The easiest way to discover your own risk tolerance is simple — if you know yourself. Do you focus on personal and institutional survival and preserving the known? Or, are you a person who thrives on fresh ministry frontiers? Are you stuck, or are you strategic?

Develop a cadre of faith leaders who are wise adopters without being risk averse. Look for folks who thrive on the edges of tomorrow.

Are you ready to believe in your future? To sum up, risk is a secular word for faith. Are you able to "faith" your way beyond stuck-ness and into the future? Remember a simple truth: change begins with your faith and the faithfulness of the team you disciple and develop.

Being Constrained Doesn't Have to Mean Being Stuck

Guy Sayles

One of the most significant "leadership" books I've read in recent years is *A Beautiful Constraint: How to Transform Your Limitations into Advantages and Why It's Everyone's Business*. Adam Morgan and Mark Braden have given us a gift: a beautifully crafted book that is creative, wise, and practical.

Morgan and Braden claim that "we sit at a nexus between an abundance of possibilities on one hand, and the reality of scarcities on the other." Every church leader I know would say "Amen" to that statement. Our restless and questing culture is open in surprising ways to the good news of God's justice, peace, mercy, and love, especially when the people who give voice to that news embody it in the authentic practices of community life. At the same time, churches wrestle with perceived scarcity of human and financial resources, of creativity and innovation, and of willingness to take risks and venture change. This scarcity is the source of constraints.

Morgan and Braden call these scarcity-imposed constraints "beautiful" because they believe that leaders can see a constraint as "a stimulus to see a new or better way of achieving our ambition." Ambition, in this context, is not rooted in pride, but in passion for the achievement of a mission or the pursuit of a noble mission. In the language of faith, it's the determination to trust that God can "make a way out of no way." The God who feeds multitudes from meager resources can make it possible for us to carry out needed ministries in the face of real constraints. When determination and commitment meet limits and constraint, the energy of that clash can provide opportunities for us to see ourselves, our churches, and our communities differently and can create a willingness to consider changes we've previously been unwilling to make.

The authors suggest that leaders become adept at asking "propelling questions" that hold both the constraints and the mission in tension with each other. Examples for churches might be:

- How can we make our church's identity and ministry known when we have very limited money to spend on marketing and communications?
- How can we minister effectively to children and youth when we can't afford any paid staff to lead those efforts?
- How can we make our unused (and expensive to maintain) building an asset for both our church and community?

The key to a propelling question is to include limitation and determination and to refuse to ignore either in our exploration of possible answers. Holding them in paradoxical connection means that our responses will be practical and implementable because we've factored in the constraints from the outset.

A Beautiful Constraint offers us another helpful exercise for seeing our possibilities more realistically and hopefully: "Take the six words that are most important to the organization, and articulate what you mean by them: What do we really mean when we say innovation, or marketing, or customer satisfaction, or growth, or consumer insight, or production, efficiency, or strategic partnerships, or operating discipline, or healthy, for example?"

I can imagine very productive conversations in our congregations if we attempted to describe what we mean by cherished terms such as the italicized ones below:

• What is *worship*? A gathering on Sunday mornings? The musical parts of that gathering? A magnet for outreach? An offering to God? Being "lost in wonder, love, and praise?"

• What is *mission* or *missional*? Providing volunteers, prayers, and financial support to need-meeting and educational partners? A series of programs and initiatives that a church adopts? Joining in God's mission of healing creation and reconciling everyone?

• What is *growth*? Is it numerical mostly? If so, which numbers? What and whom do we count? What are other forms of growth? Growth in maturity, in faithfulness, in risk-taking, in love? How are numerical and other forms of growth related?

• What is *ministry*? Is it what "ministers" do? Is it who ministers are? How are "being" and "doing" related? Are ministers the paid staff or everyone? How are the ministries of everyone and paid staff related? Who is eligible for what kinds of ministry? Why? Why not? How do we prepare and equip ministers for ministry?

• What is *church*? A voluntary association? A nonprofit organization? The body of Christ? The fellowship of the Spirit? How do the various metaphors and images relate to each other? How does the local church relate to the universal church? How—and how much—do denominations and networks matter?

• What is *salvation*? A transaction related to the afterlife? Transformation that affects all of life? A decision or a process or both? Wholeness, forgiveness, freedom? Social? Individual? Since our answer will have many dimensions, how will we describe and declare salvation? How does our view of salvation affect how we understand and practice evangelism?

Conversations about these key words can open our eyes and hearts to renewing our commitment to them. Such dialogues can also broaden our understanding and enrich our practices.

A Beautiful Constraint reminded me that constraints are inevitable; being stuck isn't.

Flipping Orthodoxies

Mike Queen

Every organization, including the church, has deeply held beliefs about "how things are done around here." Larry Keeley of the Doblin division of Deloitte Consulting calls these deeply held beliefs "orthodoxies." He defines an orthodoxy as "a set of pervasive beliefs that often go unstated and unchallenged…They shape strategy and create blind spots… They are the rules, tools, techniques, and behaviors we accept or agree to…They are ingrained ways of thinking and acting—from habit or from previous successes…They are commonly held across the organization."

Orthodoxies are not always bad. Some orthodoxies are essential to define identity and purpose. But knowing when an orthodoxy has devolved from being inspirational and helpful to being a detriment is never easy. We tend to get attached to our orthodoxies, particularly those that have served us well.

During the 20th century there were some generally accepted orthodoxies in most churches, for example: Worship takes place at 11:00 a.m. on Sunday morning, worship services last no more than one hour, clergy all have a seminary degree, Vacation Bible School will be held for one week each summer, and the name on the church sign serves as a helpful identifier. All around us, in both new churches and in reimagined existing churches, these kinds of orthodoxies have been flipped.

This is a much easier process when a church is being planted or is in its earliest years. In older established churches, however, it requires someone with the courage to question the prevailing orthodoxies.

In a *Rotman Magazine* article titled "Flipping Orthodoxies: Overcoming Insidious Obstacles to Innovation," Bansi Nagji and Helen Walters contend that absent a plan, orthodoxies will continually block innovation in any organization. "Overcoming orthodoxies rarely happens in isolation or as a one-off exercise. They are generally far too pervasive and deeply rooted to overturn by decree or exhortation. Rather, you have to design initiatives in such a way that you can identify, discuss, and challenge key orthodoxies."

To that end, they offer five steps toward the goal of flipping unhealthy orthodoxies. Here they are adapted for the church:

1. *Be ruthless about finding them.* The very process of naming orthodoxies in your church can be quite threatening. Even the most open-minded person will hold some of them dearly. A good way to identify them is to engage younger people or those who are new in the congregation. They will not be as blinded by tradition or habit. Remember, some orthodoxies need to be cherished, but those that no longer serve the greater

mission and vision of the church must be identified and held up to honest, truthful scrutiny. They must be named.

2. *Ask "why not?" on a regular basis.* As the authors have noted, "Asking 'why not?' isn't simply the prerogative of whiny children; it's a useful exercise to insure you're not slipping into bad habits or missing important opportunities." When my former colleague, Jeannie Troutman, announced to me that she wanted to replace our traditional VBS with something else, I said, "You can't do that." She asked, "Why not?" Vacation Bible School had become an orthodoxy at our church. In three years she transitioned us from a "free" VBS with 75 to 80 children to "fee-based" Camp Jonah and Camp Creation with more than 400 kids learning about God and God's love for them. Ask "why not?"

3. *Widen your field of vision.* You can learn a lot from others. As a pastor, I quit going to big conferences. Instead, I began to visit other churches that were doing innovative mission and ministry. Those visits inspired me to see church and congregational life in new and different ways. What I learned from others reshaped the trajectory of my entire ministry.

4. *Be a credible heretic.* People who challenge "the way things have always been done" are often seen as heretics. To be credible, says Jeff Semenchuk, "You have to acknowledge the orthodoxy and the good reason it existed in the first place, and then you have to be willing—in an open, positive, sometimes playful way—to challenge that."

5. *Recognize those who dare.* This tends to be easier in business than in the world of the church. We need to learn to celebrate those people who launch new ministries—even those that fail. This one strategy will encourage others to dare and to take risks.

Nagji and Walters conclude that leaders everywhere need to dare to imagine a different future that encompasses more than just business as usual. If the process of overturning orthodoxies is not deliberately adopted by the church leadership, old patterns are certain to re-emerge.

None of this is easy. There is a fine line between a winning formula and hardwired assumptions that constrain a church. But through careful assessment and conscious choices, you can discern between self-imposed limitations and the true cornerstones of your church and its mission.

Worth Fighting Over

Bill Wilson

As part of the work of the Center for Healthy Churches with congregations that are engaging in the process of imagining their future, we invite them to first look back and connect with their past. One effective tool for doing this is to create a timeline that includes significant events from the life of the church, the community, and the world.

Recently, one church we worked with did an exceptional job in noting when significant events occurred in the life of the church. Along with the obvious major events, members of this work group also noted how innovation had been a constant part of their story. They dutifully recorded, for instance, when indoor plumbing was first installed at the church. Next came the year in the early 20th century when electricity was added. Other notable advancements included the first time a sound system was put to use. Their timeline also included: air conditioning in the 1950s, the first paid youth minister in the late 1960s, the first church bus in the 1970s, the first international mission trip in the 1980s, the first web page in the 1990s, screens in the sanctuary in the 2000s, and the first live streaming worship broadcast in 2016.

As we traced the church's history of innovation, we asked: "What was the response to these innovations?" In every case there was substantial opposition, with multiple stories of bruised feelings and damage among the fellowship. One elderly member remarked that he had never seen as bitter an argument at a business meeting as the night the church voted to install air conditioning in the building. That night, six families stormed out of the church and never returned, angry over the reckless extravagance of air conditioning.

Remember, what seems indispensable to us today was at one time considered a luxury or a waste or folly.

We would do well to reconsider Arthur Schopenhauer's dictum: Every truth passes through three stages before it is recognized. In the first, it is ridiculed. In the second, it is opposed. In the third, it is regarded as self-evident.

We regularly see two primary change scenarios that inflict great harm among congregations:

1. Congregational leaders force change/innovation too quickly and without adequate relationship bonds. Armed with good intentions and a substantial surplus of knowledge, these leaders assume that others will take their word for needed change. Pushing forward without allowing others to come to experience a similar learning curve, such leaders incite havoc among the body with their steamroller tactics. Nearly always, the resistance organizes and the conflict escalates. Seldom is the end result a good one.

2. A leadership group has the mistaken notion that they can achieve 100 percent agreement with their suggested change. Inevitably, they end up paralyzed by their need for unanimity. In such cases, a small minority holds the majority hostage and creates great discord in the body. Even a cursory glance at the literature regarding change reveals that 5 percent of any group will fall into the category of "never adopters." Jesus does not call us to make everyone happy; he calls us to be faithful to the gospel.

Rather than fall victim to these two extremes, perhaps we could all agree on some insights into change/innovation as we seek to live out our divine mission:

- Dramatic change is one of the hardest things for a human being to endure. At the very least, let's approach it with reverence and respect.
- Resistance and opposition to your suggestions is not to be taken personally, but should be expected, planned for, and welcomed.
- To those who have taken a vow to resist all change, please, instead, take your cue from the biblical record. Throughout scripture, God is constantly doing a "new thing." Jesus threatened tradition with his radical notions about worship, discipleship, and holiness. Why would you expect any less from your church's leaders? In the end, you really do want to side with Jesus, right?
- While our core message will never change, the methodologies for practicing our faith will be in a constant state of change for the rest of our life. The changes we will go through in our near future (for a glimpse, read *Physics of the Future*, by Michio Kaku) will make our squabbles over screens and technology look laughable, for example.
- Let's admit that not every innovation, piece of technology, software, or new idea is equally valuable. Remember shuffleboard inlays in the fellowship hall, or the dozens of roller skates you purchased for the throngs that were going to come to the gym and skate?

What if we filtered all change/innovation through this question: Does this enable us to more nearly fulfill our mission as God's people? What if that question mattered more to us than air conditioning, indoor plumbing, or screens?

The Oxbow Lake Church

Bill Wilson

A friend was recently talking about an organization that is struggling to adapt to some very necessary changes. While not a church, the observation she made about that group's inability to adjust to a changing world rings true for many of us.

Her observation focused on the constituents' resistance to change. They have a 50-year history of doing what they do in a specific and familiar pattern. While that way worked well in a simpler, less complex world, it has struggled to find customers in recent years. When suggestions about innovation are made, the reaction is defensive and dismissive.

My friend's analogy was helpful: "If they are not careful, they will become an oxbow lake organization."

An oxbow lake is formed when a meander in a river is cut off from the main channel and forms a lake. The name comes from the lake's unique U-shape, which resembles the bow in a yoke of an ox. Some oxbow lakes are large, while most are not. Nearly all suffer a similar fate. Without a current to move the water along, sediment builds up along the banks and gradually fills in the lake.

I know about oxbow lakes. I love flying over the Mississippi River and seeing the evidence of the many shifts the river channel has experienced over time. It is fascinating to see how the great river is never at rest, always reinventing itself in the midst of floods, droughts, and development. It's probably not too much of a stretch to suggest that the metaphor fits the current challenges local congregations face.

Without meaning to, many of us run the risk of becoming oxbow lake churches. Think about it: disconnected from the movement of the main stream, the oxbow is cut off and stands outside the life and energy of the river. It becomes irrelevant to the commerce and activity of the river, relegated to recreational activities.

My friend was seeing a group that has grown comfortable and lost the capacity to innovate and be creative. With the change in the currents of culture, the organization faces a bleak and "cut-off" future.

What are some signs that a congregation may be facing an "oxbow lake" moment?

- When a congregation decides that their survival must be on their own terms, they risk becoming an oxbow church.
- When a congregation decides that change is their enemy and not their friend, they risk becoming an oxbow church.
- When a congregation puts their own agenda ahead of the Kingdom agenda, they risk becoming an oxbow church.

- When a congregation assumes their ways and patterns are synonymous with God's they risk becoming an oxbow church.
- When a congregation loses the willingness and ability to self-critique, they risk becoming an oxbow church.
- When a congregation disengages from the movement and energy of the Spirit at work in their community, they risk becoming an oxbow church.
- When a congregation thinks more about their past than about their future, they risk becoming an oxbow church.
- When a congregation spends most of their money on itself, they risk becoming an oxbow church.
- When a congregation's staff devotes most of their time to servicing the needs and requests of its members, they risk becoming an oxbow church.
- When a congregation walks by sight, rather than faith, they risk becoming an oxbow church.

Oxbow lakes are formed by the unrelenting forces of deposition and erosion. Over many years, the river deposits massive amounts of material in areas of lesser movement. Simultaneously, erosion works to break down riverbanks as the river continually seeks the most direct route from one place to another.

Congregations must guard against our own forces of deposition and erosion. Our deposits might be all our preconceived notions about how church must be done. Those deposits create barriers to the fresh wind of the Spirit as they form immovable attitudes and obstacles. Wise leaders watch for, name, and deal with such dangerous deposits.

Anyone who has lived near a stream knows that erosion will eventually win out over our efforts to control it. Many churches can attest to the fallacy of ignoring or trying to manage the movement of God's Spirit across the ages. Wise leaders constantly listen for, look for, and invite fresh expressions of our timeless story of God's redeeming love for the human race and all of creation.

Let's work to make sure no one ever labels us an oxbow lake congregation.

PART 3
Thriving Ministry

A healthy church has a thriving ministry. There is a sense of excitement and passion among its members. People experience meaning and purpose as they are given the opportunity to share their gifts. They experience God's deep generosity and grace and are glad to give of themselves and their resources. They understand that their church has all it needs to accomplish the mission God has given it.

12 Healthy Trends Emerging in Revitalizing Churches

Barry Howard

There are a lot of adjectives that can be used to describe churches: vibrant churches, mega churches, healthy churches, dying churches, transitioning churches, and emerging churches—just to name a few.

While some people may propose that vitality and relevance only exist in new church starts, there are many churches typically considered to be traditional churches, flagship churches, or big steeple churches that are undergoing a healthy process of revitalization.

There are a multitude of reasons that contribute to the need for revitalization. Almost every church is faced with generational attrition, a more mobile constituency, cultural shifts, increased diversity, and adjudicatory or denominational restructuring. Additionally, many churches have been adversely affected by natural disasters, congregational conflict, unpleasant leadership transitions, and changing neighborhoods.

Churches should be careful not to fall prey to quick-fix strategies of church growth or canned programs that often cause more harm than good. Most churches actually need to focus on church health, which leads to the right kind of growth. There are no shortcuts to revitalized church health. I have observed that healthy congregations grow in healthy ways, and unhealthy congregations tend to grow to be more and more unhealthy. Revitalization is the process of restoring a healthy vision, good congregational morale, and a sustainable model for engaging in mission and ministry.

What is a revitalizing church? A revitalizing church is a congregation wisely and discerningly upgrading its mission and methodology to contextually engage and serve its culture and community. A revitalizing church recognizes that the matrix for assessing effectiveness is no longer based on "budget, buildings, baptisms, and butts in the pew," so a revitalizing church is in the process of devising a new scorecard for evaluating mission and ministry. Although every church is unique, there are some common characteristics that seem to be prevalent in revitalizing churches.

Here are 12 healthy trends that I am noting in revitalizing churches across a diverse spectrum of denominations and geographic locales:

1. A revitalizing church is cultivating a strong sense of spiritual community, while simultaneously experiencing declining interest in church as an institution.
2. A revitalizing church is notably trending toward serving rather than being served.
3. A revitalizing church is nurturing a worship culture that promotes engagement more than entertainment.
4. A revitalizing church is becoming more readily identified by its location than its denomination, often revising its name or brand to enrich its welcome.

5. A revitalizing church embraces the full giftedness of men and women in service and leadership.
6. A revitalizing church is developing ways to streamline decision-making by empowering committees, councils, ministry teams, and ministers with specific responsibilities on behalf of the larger body.
7. A revitalizing church is developing a high tolerance for healthy change, maintaining its core message, but upgrading it methodology.
8. A revitalizing church is strategically multigenerational, valuing the perspectives of several generations rather than being monofocused on a single demographic.
9. A revitalizing church respects diversity and is becoming more comfortable with diverse ethnic, economic, political, and theological streams within the community.
10. A revitalizing church is adapting to a culture of mobility, offering a variety of worship and study opportunities on campus, off campus, and online.
11. A revitalizing church treasures the past but is invested in the present, and does not waste energy competing with images of its former glory or being haunted by its past mistakes.
12. A revitalizing church develops strategic ways to cultivate and mentor future leaders.

While I am sure there are other factors that describe and shape churches that are on a journey of revitalization, these 12 healthy trends seem to be emerging in the churches I am observing and the church I am serving.

Churches that become satisfied with a mythical status quo and remain highly resistant to new winds of the Spirit can easily become entrapped in a time warp, and they risk being vacuumed into a black hole of irrelevance. Churches that undiscerningly "throw out the baby with the bathwater" and sell their soul to popular culture lose their capacity to be salt and light, and their Kingdom influence goes down the drain.

However, churches that are committed to living out the time-tested values of scripture with a passionate sense of mission will find ways to share the good news with fresh relevance and to dialogue cross-culturally with transformative grace and radical hospitality.

Revitalization is a challenging and ongoing process. And most churches need an experienced and trustworthy networking partner to walk alongside them during the journey of revitalization. If your church needs to begin the process of revitalizing, I recommend contacting the Center for Healthy Churches to discover more about the resources it can provide to equip clergy and congregations for healthy revitalization.

We live and serve in an opportune season for missional innovation and cultural engagement. Rather than being anxious, this season calls for courage. "For God has not given us a spirit of fearfulness, but one of power, love, and sound judgment" (2 Tim. 1:7).

If a church wants to thrive and not merely survive, a continuing revitalization process is essential.

Empowering "If" in Local Congregations

Bob Dale

In the Industrial Age, national and regional denominations had a religious monopoly, producing and providing programs for local churches. Pre-planned activities and structures, like gumballs, were placed in the chute in Nashville, Atlanta, Birmingham, Memphis, or Dallas, and they rolled all the way to your congregation's door. Ministry was simple and stable.

Then, a cultural watershed happened. Our world tipped into the digital age with younger generations. Traditional ministries stopped working. Programs-in-a-box no longer fit new times or new needs. Mechanical methods didn't serve living communities or causes. Consequently, denominations were stymied, and dependent churches didn't know what to do next. Doing church "wholesale" waned.

But many congregations are still thriving. They are thinking and acting locally. Is religion becoming "retail"? one may ask. Interestingly, the same culture that's closing old doors for denominations is opening new doors for local churches and their community ministry partners.

"Ifs" are easier to deal with in local contexts, a huge advantage for our churches. Let's explore seven local "ifs." In other words, how can today's churches respond to "if" and thrive?

1. *If faith overcomes fear* . . . Transitions are scary. They push us out of our comfort zones. When large-scale cultural watersheds occur and the familiar ends for us, our world feels chaotic. In our present era, change is constant and fears have become contagious. It's challenging to practice faith when fear has us by the throat. We need local companions to shrink our fears and make our journey easier. God's Spirit calms us and helps us move ahead, if we practice faith that's stronger than our fears.

2. *If "out of the box" creativity builds on "inside the box" clarity* . . . Struggling organizations often wander off course, becoming less and less defined. In their anxiety, they may simply flounder faster rather than stopping to find their "why" and "who." As a result, they keep on doing "how" and "what" by rote and become more lost. Clarity anchors churches. Clarity emerges when we look into our own mirrors and see ourselves "face to face" (1 Cor. 13:12). Local creativity can then be generated freely, if clarity of vision and direction is already established.

3. *If ministries and missions are launched in neighborhoods first and then to nations* . . . Acts 1:8 guides us to minister to our neighbors first and then reach out to more distant needs. A century ago we did missions from a colonial mindset. We sent our

representatives to the nations and called what we did missions to foreigners. We concentrated on the Great Commission but neglected the Great Commandment. Our churches cooperated globally, but we competed locally. Now, in a more connected world, churches can begin outreach nearby and then extend our outreach to faraway places, if we love our neighbors as we love ourselves.

4. *If leadership batons are shared across generations . . .* For the first time in human history, six generations are alive simultaneously. But, we find few congregations with all generations worshiping inside their walls and serving outside in their communities. In fact, most congregations are led by older members. Gutenbergers still out-number Digital Natives in the majority of our church's pews and planning groups. Culturally speaking, top-down leadership is receding, and side-by-side leadership is ascending. Churches can enrich and empower our leader circles, if we bridge generations.

5. *If diversity is embraced . . .* In traditional churches, "from here" members were typically valued more than "come here" members. We liked our own. We sang "red and yellow, black and white, all are precious in His sight," but we didn't practice our lyrics with energy. Now, in a global world with many backgrounds, cultures, and outlooks, variety is everywhere—even at 11 o'clock on Sunday morning. Diverse ministries can become portals for redemptive relationships and innovative outreach, if we act on "God so loved the world."

6. *If while recognizing different congregational sizes, we affirm that God's kingdom has no limits . . .* In the old industrial perspective, bigger was better. Large churches were lauded, and megachurches became ideal models. We sometimes forget that God's kingdom focuses on obedience rather than numbers. We drifted away from the view that every size church is vital in God's eyes. "On earth as it is in heaven" calls us to value every believer and all churches. We can welcome God's kingdom, if we say "yes" to God's absolute reign in our lives and congregations.

7. *If training is tailored to local needs and opportunities . . .* Denominational programs were "one size fits all" in earlier days. Those uniform resources have diminished. Now, training for growth and discipleship can be customized to specific settings and needs, if we know our contexts and seize our opportunities.

"If" is a tiny word. But "if" has huge ministry potential. It's time to explore "if."

Hope: A Trait of Thriving Congregations

Matt Cook

In the 1950s Curt Richter, a professor at Johns Hopkins University, conducted a somewhat morbid experiment. He placed wild rats in a container of water and forced them to swim as long as they could before drowning. Most of the rats swam for only a few minutes before they gave up hope and sank.

In round two, however, Richter made a small adjustment to the experiment. After a short initial period when the rats would be left alone, he would come in and remove them from the water and then put them back. These rats swam for hours. One even swam for almost an entire day before it sank. The difference, according to Richter, was simple: hope. "After elimination of hopelessness," wrote Ricther, "the rats do not die."

Since 2019, the Center for Healthy Churches has been involved in a project at Belmont University helping churches find new ways to thrive in the 21st century. I say "new ways" because, for many churches, the old ways aren't working any longer.

The growth of the American church is one of the great success stories in Christian history. People think the U.S. was a Christian nation at the founding of the republic, but that is revisionist history. By most accounts, less than 20 percent of the population was connected to a congregation immediately following the American Revolution. Early in the 19th century, however, a highly democratized and deeply American style of religion began to catch on, resulting in a period of growth that lasted for a century and a half. By the 1960s, the United States had among the highest rates of religious adherence of any nation in the world.

And then things changed. For half a century now, the American church has been experiencing numerical decline. Yet, even amid the doom and gloom, there are certain places where congregations aren't sinking—they're swimming. What's the difference?

There are several different traits that we're seeing where churches are finding ways to thrive despite the institutional decline of American Christianity. At the top of the list, however, is this one simple thing: hope.

Congregations that believe they can make a difference in the lives of people and on the world around them aren't simply watching the death of Christendom as if there is nothing that can be done. These congregations are creating new forms of congregational life and new ways of partnership that are creating newness of life in individual adherents and in the communities where they minister.

Furthermore, these congregations aren't finding such hope by imitating the latest and greatest strategies from the largest churches around them. They are mining a virtuous mixture of the deep wisdom of scripture, the timeless resources of their particular traditions, and their own unique congregational DNA. Every existing congregation has a story of a season of ministry that not only made a meaningful impact on the world, but also revealed the passions, gifts, and strengths that God placed within that congregation.

What about your congregation? When is the last time your church looked around and saw possibilities rather than problems? When is the last time your church decided to jump into the deep end of the pool rather than fearfully treading water in the shallow end?

The congregations that are thriving as Christendom dies around us are the congregations that are focused on the possibilities of a vibrant future rather than fearfully trying to maintain the present or recreate the past.

3 Signs of a Healthy Church

Bill Owen

After 40-plus years of working in and alongside churches, I believe church health may be the best lens available to assess the culture of today's church.

It doesn't matter how sophisticated the strategy, how talented the staff, how plentiful the resources, or how ideal the location, if the culture isn't healthy. An unhealthy culture leads to mediocrity, or worse, failure.

In *The Advantage*, Patrick Lencioni puts it this way: "The health of an organization provides the context for strategy, finances, marketing, technology, and everything else that happens in it, which is why it is the single greatest factor determining an organization's success. More than talent. More than knowledge. More than innovation."

How would you describe the "health" of your church? Even the most experienced leaders have trouble answering this question. It's tough because church health is hard to measure on a chart or graph.

The truth is that every church leadership team, led by the pastor, is responsible for the health of the church. Church leaders are the cultural architects. And by intention or neglect, every church takes on the cultural characteristics of its leaders. Here are three signs of a healthy church culture:

1. *Clarity of vision:* Healthy churches know who they are and where they are going. Clarity seems to be the area where pastors and leadership struggle the most. Healthy churches effectively communicate and align themselves around what Simon Sinek calls the "Golden Circle."
   - Why do we exist?
   - How do we behave?
   - What do we do?

Lencioni adds three more questions to the mix.
   - How will we succeed?
   - What is most important, right now?
   - Who must do what?

Healthy churches rally around clear answers to these fundamental questions. As "culture" suggests, this doesn't happen in one meeting or via one sermon series, but over time, constantly embedded in the life and direction of the church.

There may be no greater challenge for churches today than effectively communicating a clear and consistent vision.

2. *Conflict transformation:* If there are people present, so is conflict, at some level. Speed Leas' *Levels of Conflict* is helpful in assessing where your church may be on the scale.

Leadership teams know that transforming conflict always takes place in a culture of trust. Low-trust environments are the breeding ground for division and discontent, suspicion and drama. Nothing fractures a fellowship more than the lack of trust.

Healthy church culture begins with a cohesive leadership team. Pastor and staff model open, vulnerable, and trusting relationships. It's their default mode of operation.

Lencioni says, "When team members trust one another, when they know that everyone on the team is capable of admitting when they don't have the right answer, and when they're willing to acknowledge when someone else's idea is better than theirs, the fear of conflict and the discomfort it entails is greatly diminished."

Healthy churches don't run from conflict: they embrace and transform it, beginning with the leadership.

3. *Authentic community:* Every week churches offer opportunities for people to connect with one another through services of worship, times of prayer, opportunities for Bible study, and points of ministry.

Yet fewer and fewer people, who only know one another on a surface level, gather in half-full buildings hoping to some way make a difference in their own lives and the lives of others.

Healthy churches are about relationships with depth, relationships that move beyond just "being nice" to "speaking the truth in love." People in healthy churches trust one another on a fundamental, emotional level. They are comfortable being vulnerable with each other about their weaknesses, fears, and behaviors.

"I'm sorry." "I was wrong." "I need help." "I made a mistake." "You're better at that than I am." "I forgive you." These are the statements made in authentic communities of faith.

Healthy churches are constantly striving to nurture this kind of transparency and trust. Healthy churches believe that every person grows best when connected to others in a culture of welcome and hospitality, of acceptance and trust.

What signs do you look for in assessing your church's health?

Some Things Never Change

Larry McSwain

Looking backward is occasionally necessary to understand the present or future. I first worked as a congregational consultant in 1971. As a young seminary assistant professor teaching Church and Community, I was invited to meet with a small church in inner city Louisville, Kentucky.

Before the meetings I scoured census data and drove through the church's neighborhood. It was a predominantly poor, African-American community while the church was an all-white, aging, middle-class group, all of whom commuted into the neighborhood.

I told those church people what they should do to reach their community and concluded, "Your church will not exist in five years if you do not change." I gave no appreciative inquiry nor listening conversations as to why they were still there—just judgment from an inexperienced "know it all." (That is the way a lot of consultants function even today!)

Well, 20 years later the church was still worshiping and serving a small gathering of older families who drove into the city to keep the doors of their church open because they were family and they needed what it offered.

I learned from that experience that a Baptist church is difficult to kill, even when you try. Some things just do not change! Why?

- *The church is a collection of humans.* These "treasures in earthen vessels" often forget that the uniqueness of a church is the power of God's Spirit within it. Living in a community of people requires order, organization, and stability for people to negotiate their relationships in positive ways. Change has a way of threatening the "ties that bind," as the expert congregational observers who understand Family Systems Theory readily note. It is only natural to depend on the same format of worship, the same style of preaching, the same set of respected leaders, the same agendas for education, and the same ways of ministering. But sameness ensures boredom and loss of vitality.

- *Inertia stifles vision.* Past success is a barrier to future change. Every congregation with which I have worked had a significant portion of people who viewed a significant past set of events as the most important time in the life of the church. The best they can imagine for tomorrow is a re-creation of an era in the past. But seldom do the same approaches of the past fit today's contexts and needs for ministry.

- *A divisive conflict has immobilized the members who remain.* Conflict is a part of every congregation's life. There is the "good," "healthy" conflict that is a part of growth and energy. There can also be the "destructive," "ego-assaulting," "mean" conflict that divides people and inevitably "splits" a congregation. When those kinds of conflict happen, the focus of the remaining congregation turns inward. We write rules and regulations to guide behavior so such an event will never happen again. Trust is lost. Risk is too costly. Stagnation is the consequence. And in these settings, change is slow and difficult. If you want to see Exhibit A for stability, read the bylaws of your church. They are usually written to protect against new voices, new ideas, and risky ventures. Their language often addresses a past conflict that no longer exists.

• *Tunnel vision blinds people to the changes in the environment.* Every congregation has a founding story that shapes it identity, core values, and future hopes. But the context in which that story was first written tends to change radically every 12–20 years. So the settings in which churches live change faster than the changes in the people within the congregation. The people within become increasingly different from their neighbors because the people within seldom change.

• *Generational differences favor the folks who have been around the longest.* The healthiest churches I know are churches that have been able to adapt to the values of their children and grandchildren in ways that keep those generations in the same church. Stability favors the long-term, older, more affluent of the congregation who love their church so much they are going to keep it just like it has always been. The result is a declining, aging congregation of people who like each other but want their clergy to re-create a church that will look like it did when they were younger adults.

The good news is that even when a congregation seems to be set in concrete, the Spirit of God can breathe new insights and understandings for a new future that is dynamic and attractive to new people who change even the most entrenched of congregations.

Living in the Flux of Constant Change

Larry McSwain

Stability is the focus of most Christian congregations. Two thousand years of tradition in belief and practices are not easily altered. The world in which that tradition is sought is in constant flux. How we followers of Jesus maintain our commitments while adapting to ever-shifting realities is the major challenge of healthy congregational life! In my experience of study of culture and congregations, there are several primary catalysts most congregations must understand.

1. *The impact of immigration:* A major driver of change is the alteration of population characteristics within a neighborhood, city, state, or nation. Birth/death rates and immigration are the two key sources of such change. The United States has been a country of immigrants throughout its history, but the diversity of immigration sources has shifted dramatically since 1965 when quotas for legal immigration shifted from primarily European sources to more international ones. The result is a decline of Caucasians in the U.S. from 89.5 percent in 1950 to the following in 2010:

• 63.7 percent Caucasian
• 16.3 percent Hispanic/Latino
• 12.2 percent African American
• 4.7 percent Asian
• 1.9 percent mixed race/ethnicity

Current predictions for 2050 indicate the following:

• 47 percent Caucasian
• 28 percent Hispanic
• 13 percent African American
• 9 percent Asian
• 2 percent mixed race/ethnicity

Obviously, there are communities in which the degree of such change is more dramatic—coastal cities, agricultural communities requiring seasonal labor, and border areas. Since Protestantism is by tradition overwhelmingly Caucasian and African American, such churches in highly transitional settings face the most dramatic impact from changes in demography. My family lives in such a setting.

We have lived in the same upscale, relatively new suburban community for the past 15 years. We have only to look at the schools, restaurants, and houses of worship near us to understand how much change has occurred.

Within a 10-mile radius, we can attend any number of houses of worship: Primitive Baptist, Orthodox Indian (in a former Baptist church facility), Bahai, multiple synagogues, dozens of Korean-speaking churches, neighborhood mosques, a Hindu temple, one of the largest megachurches in the country, and all of the usual denominational groups (Baptist, Methodist, Presbyterian, Episcopalian, Lutheran). In sum, there is a brand of religion for any faith in the world.

My dentist is Chinese, my wife's dentist is Korean, her eye surgeon is Indian, my barber is Vietnamese, her hairdresser is Romanian, our dry cleaner is Indian, the store cashiers are international from all over the globe, and we can enjoy any kind of international food one might want at a nearby restaurant. Our grandchildren in elementary, middle, and high school have as many non-Caucasian classmates as Caucasian ones.

Doing church in such a setting differs radically from the way it could be done in the typical neighborhood of even 20 years ago.

2. *The growth of mega-churches:* Interestingly, the model of most U.S. mega-churches was imported from the ministry of David Yong-gi Cho, retired pastor of the Yoido Full Gospel Church in Seoul, South Korea. That model began with multiple weekly worship services with upbeat contemporary music, small group Bible studies, and expansion into satellite locations. The largest worldwide megachurches are more like mini denominations than congregations. There are now at least 1,500 of these congregations with an average of 2,000 or more in weekly attendance in the U.S. The largest one attracts more than 40,000 worshippers each week. The top 10 percent of churches in size attract more than 45 percent of the weekly participants. No wonder thousands of small and middle-sized church leaders feel such frustration with their metrics of decline! Only 55 percent of weekly worshippers can be found in 90 percent of the churches.

3. *The embrace of technology:* The way we receive information, participate in social conversations, communicate events, or convey meaningful experiences is changing with mind-bending speed. Technology is reshaping the willingness of people to participate in the repetitious. If I can review last week's worship service via video on my phone or tablet, or worship with the sermon on video to 30 locations, the importance of gathering together is diminished. When only the latest entertainment technique will attract followers, increasing numbers of churches will find themselves living in the past or attracting a small crowd of older adults.

4. *A cultural revolution in thought and practice:* Most of institutional Christianity developed in the last 500 years of an era of Western history we call "modern." The modern era was built on the power of words that carried the authority of truth, whether in speech or written words. Thus, doctrine, belief, and defined practice of what was correct was readily understood by believers of multiple traditions. Each had its own truth—Orthodox, Roman Catholic, Baptist, Methodist, Lutheran, and a host of others who fought each other to win the masses. In today's post-modern world, authority is defined by the individual and thereby makes consensus on anything difficult. The young are the first to be impacted by cultural change whether in music, theology, dress, or language. Thus, the power of generational difference with which all leaders must work becomes a major congregational challenge.

5. *The loss of civil speech:* Unfortunately, the bombastic argumentation of talk radio and numerous television programs focusing on politics have replaced dialogue with argument for finding truth. Division becomes easier than unity, and diversity among people more difficult than finding a like-minded group. The tenor of congregational discussion around issues of controversy becomes the basis of unhealthy conflict.

These are just a few of the changes today's leaders must face in doing ministry. How do we manage them? By living courageously in a community of Jesus-followers who are open to change in all arenas of life by loving interaction with each other and commitment to the Holy Spirit who unites all with a common vision.

Connecting the Dots

Bill Owen

Every week it seems someone is blogging about the obstacles the 21st-century church faces—the rise of the "nones," the decline in frequency of attendance, budget creep, culture wars, etc. These challenges are consistent across America's faith families. You may find yourself in a changing neighborhood or singing a sad song for lack of leadership. Like others, you may be struggling to reach a younger generation or striving to motivate a fresh corps of volunteers.

Today's church requires leadership that sees beyond the boundaries of limitation.

In a blog on church revitalization, Amy Butler, former pastor of the Riverside Church in New York City, reminded congregational leaders to "make it our priority to perpetually reframe the narrative from scarcity to abundance...When congregations speak in narratives of decline and death, desperation and fear, we are crippling our ability to think in new ways and take action toward the next expression of our lives together."

Well said, and it needs to be said again and again. We need a fresh narrative to move us beyond the boundaries that confine us. What I find most interesting, especially in my work with churches, is how often we set our own artificial limitations without even knowing it.

Too many churches today are stuck in the muck of "we've always done it that way," as evidenced in:

• a ministry staff based on decades-old programming
• a budget document that has been tweaked, cut, and adjusted but never aligned to a fresh vision to meet present needs
• an allocation of resources (money, time) that goes to propping up ineffective strategies and thus shutting down creativity
• an aging leadership group (deacons, elders, staff...) that bemoans the lack of young adults but fails to invite their voices into the discussion

These kinds of limitations prematurely shut down possibilities and restrict vision.

You may be familiar with the "nine-dot puzzle." If you have paper and a pen near you, you might try it right now. Make a grid of three rows of three dots each and try to connect all the dots by drawing only four straight lines that are connected (without lifting pen from paper).

If you are anything like me, the first time you try this puzzle you will try several different ways to connect all the dots but not be successful. You then begin to wonder whether the test is really to see how long people will keep trying a seemingly impossible task! The key to solving the nine-dot puzzle is to refuse to see the outer line of dots as a boundary. This allows you to draw above and beyond the rows and connect all the dots quite easily.

By design we are trained to see patterns, and part of seeing patterns is detecting boundaries. Much of the time, this is really valuable. But when you are trying to solve problems or see possibilities, it is counterproductive and stifles innovation. To move beyond self-imposed boundaries in today's church, we need the following types of leaders:

• *Leaders who listen:* They are in tune with the Spirit and in touch with the community in which they serve. Churches today have no choice but to turn their attention and resources outward. There is no excuse for not knowing your context: Who is my neighbor? What problems do they face? What gifts can we bring to bear?

• *Leaders who collaborate:* Stay open to new ideas, new ways of doing things. Ideas don't always come from experts. Sometimes the greatest innovations come from unexpected voices. Bring new voices to the table of decision-making and problem-solving inside the church. One younger member suggested that perhaps in every area of decline we face "we should take everything we do and either scrap it or completely rebrand it." Collaborating with outside groups (complementary non-profits, universities, and think tanks) often brings new perspectives and ideas to the innovation process. This is no time for the church to go it alone. We should be moving beyond our walls and partnering with others who share common goals.

• *Leaders who embrace failure:* Knock failure off its pedestal. Commit to a culture of trial and error. Innovation always comes by way of reiteration. It's okay if this doesn't work this time. Many of the greatest innovations were unintended results and, oftentimes, created by accident. Breakthroughs such as the discovery of penicillin or the power of microwaves were the unintended results.

Healthy churches and organizations today think outside the box, boldly crossing boundaries that otherwise keep us stagnant. Healthy leaders promote this culture of innovation and creativity in the face of such challenge.

Stop, Look, Listen

Bob Dale

It's no secret: America's denominational structures are steadily losing momentum. Downsizing missionary staffs, shrinking giving levels, selling properties, and disappearing financial reserves are common. These challenges aren't new, and they're consistent across America's faith families.

Religious leaders are anxiously looking for practical solutions, but our structural silos are empty. May I offer a modest "Stop, Look, Listen" approach for finding fresh futures?

Stop: For starters, our theological anchors hold. The gospel is powerful, God's kingdom continues to unfold, and ministry is still needed. Albert Einstein wisely observed that we can't solve today's problems with the same thinking that first created those problems. Our future demands that we adopt new ways of thinking and ask new questions.

Look: Focus your "living eyes." Discovery is often a matter of having our eyes see what's already before us. Remember the encounter on the Emmaus Road? Over the journey, the disciples finally developed insight and saw the Living Lord (Luke 24:31).

Traditionally, our Baptist structure has mirrored the Industrial Age that invented it a century ago. Our structure is centralized, compartmentalized, and specialized—essentially a mechanical assembly line. As a friend once observed, "They put a gumball in the pipeline in Nashville, and it rolls all the way across the country to my church." Baptists built a machine that produced organizations, programs, and church rhythms. Now, the machines are rusting out.

Actually, this pervasive mechanical way of thinking began to wane in the 20th century, and it's too late for superficial overhauls. Currently, industrialism is being replaced by a more organic approach, a living mode of thinking. But Baptists and some other denominational groups haven't heeded this deep change yet. When God is a life-giving, growth-oriented gardener, inventing a new machine is not apt to redeem our world. We need more greenhouses, not mere garages.

What does a living, organic mindset look like? What if we lived out Jesus' stories of seeds, soils, sowers, seasons, vines, wineskins, and harvests? What if we really believed that Christ's church is alive and ripe for future seasons?

Listen: Sharpen your "seasonal ears." We also need faith-full ears. Jesus pointed to the wisdom of attentive listening (Luke 8:8, 14:35) for the harvest. New, seasonal questions– not more data–will show us God's direction.

Living communities naturally move through seasons. God's creation is always on the move, and we are healthiest on the edges where partners join hands during new growing seasons. Each season has its own unique opportunities. What can seasonal ears hear about the future from living churches? Consider these questions:

- When growth stops, how can we use winter's fallow seasons?
- During dormant periods, what can we discover about our strengths and blind spots?
- What is healthy and needs to be stewarded?
- Since fruit only grows on new wood, what is ready for pruning?
- How are we preparing for new growth seasons?
- What new seeds and new seedbeds need to be considered next?
- When seeds germinate, how can we learn to marvel at spring's beginnings?
- How faithful have we been in planting good seeds in good soils?
- Like the sower in the parable, when have we generously risked many seeds in faith?
- How do we appreciate timing and patiently wait for God to awaken new life?
- How does our evangelism appeal to nonbelievers and various people/ethnic groups?
- When growth needs cultivating, how can we nurture summer's potential?
- To counter the accusation of "dipping and then dropping them," how can we cultivate disciples and leaders?
- How are we nurturing faith formation across entire lifespans, across generations, and in family clusters?
- How are we linking inreach and outreach, belief and behavior, discipleship and missions?
- When harvest ripens, how can we treasure fall's yields?
- How have we carefully gathered God's harvests *and* called for more harvesters?
- How have we preserved the best of the harvest to seed new seasons?
- How do we guard against eating our future potential?

Our ears can tune into the cadences of living churches' ministries. We can hear opportunity in Creation's turning of seasons. Change happens naturally when seasons overlap and boundaries open. The Book of Acts demonstrates how the Spirit's seasons unfold.

Thinking theologically, congregational life and ministry were central in the New Testament. Across history, faith families elevated structures until churches faced denominations. That organizational model is now correcting. In an organic world, living churches anchor faith, and churches invite denominations to look and listen with them. Together, new and creative partnerships are emerging.

Healthy living congregations—small and large, young and old, rural and urban, poor and affluent—remain our best faith labs. Churches and denominations can focus on organic growth; they can work seasonally for God's kingdom. The future of living congregations—if we stop, look, and listen—is limited only by our faith and imaginations. Living, organic churches and their denominational partners with living eyes and seasonal ears can serve well.

pay it forward
SEBTS → TWFBC → SC

From 4-Way Stops to Roundabouts

Bob Dale

I was surprised. Driving into an intersection with a 4-way stop at one of Springfield, Missouri's most notorious traffic bottlenecks, cars were moving ahead smoothly. What was going on? Then, I saw something new: a roundabout!

A traffic roundabout is a circular intersection where drivers travel counterclockwise around a central island. With entrances and exits but without stop lights or traffic signals, drivers slow down, yield to others, move together in the same direction, and find their lanes easily in roundabouts. Traffic moves ahead steadily and easily. No wonder some roundabouts are called "calming circles."

Compared to traditional stop-and-go intersections, roundabouts increase traffic capacity by 30-50 percent—a huge improvement. What can churches learn from roundabouts about maintaining ministry momentum? Consider the following three suggestions:

1. Maximize ministry momentum.

Ideally and theologically, congregations are God's heavenly colonies on earth, witnessing and ministering actively. But, practically and operationally, congregations can become 4-way stops where movement is blocked and momentum is stymied. At ministry intersections where everything brakes to a complete halt, congregations stop, miss ministry opportunities, and are slow to regain their forward motion.

What if congregations functioned more like roundabouts than 4-way stops? What if a congregation's key leaders yielded to the larger flow of ministries and traveled into the future together?

If your church operated like a roundabout, how would ministry pick up speed and move ahead more easily?

2. Choose leaders on the move.

Let's explore our mixes of ministry leaders, those people who accelerate or slow congregational progress. How would "center" leaders, "edge" leaders, and "bridge" leaders best approach ministry roundabouts together?

- Center leaders traditionally anchor a congregation's core callings. They tend ministry flames and preserve the congregation's redemption stories. But sometimes they also guard crossings, insist too zealously on rules, and withhold permission to move ahead.
- Edge leaders usually inhabit the congregation's margins, seeing "next" ministries first. Crucially, as early adopters of innovations, edge leaders are their congregation's eager explorers and first drafters of new ministry chapters. But sometimes they lose patience

with slower paces of action, become congregational pests, and leave if changes aren't made in short order.

- Bridge leaders are the connectors and living links between a congregation's centers and edges. Vitally, they serve as reporters of ministry's new possibilities, as hosts of discernment conversations, and as cultivators of congregational grapevines. But sometimes they ally with one faction over the other, lose their neutrality, and politicize their congregation's processes.

But when center, edge, and bridge leaders navigate roundabouts together, the congregation doesn't get stuck and its ministries move forward smoothly. Ideally,

- Center leaders guide the congregation's progress toward central missions from valued traditions and keep ministries moving through the roundabout in the same direction.
- Edge leaders point to "traditioned innovation," driving toward exits that lead from where we are now to new and promising ministry ventures.
- Bridge leaders manage entrances to the roundabout, keeping "center" and "edge" leaders in conversation and steering toward the congregation's next steps in ministry.

3. Create new congregational traffic/organizational patterns.

- Major on neighborliness inside and beyond our congregation. The Great Commandment (Matt. 22:38-40) reminds us that community is basic for Christian living. We're on our faith pilgrimages together. Look for ministry experiences and local mission projects that enrich fellowship, collaboration, and respect. Sweating together fosters unity.
- Cultivate balance and continuity among congregational leader teams. Leader diversity strengthens congregations' clergy, lay teams, and committees. Ideally, teams have three clusters of leaders: those who are doing the jobs, those who are preparing to step into responsibility next, and those who have already done the jobs and are coaching the other two groups. Our best ministry teams include "now" and "new" leaders in the game, "next" leaders on the bench, and "near" leaders with experience. Blend them, and let them teach and support each other with different skills and generational perspectives.
- Simplify and streamline congregational structures. Hierarchies are a legacy of the fading Industrial Age's top-heavy structures. Consequently, many congregations have structured work groups with nothing much to do. Prune deadwood, and travel lighter.

As congregational leaders, look for green light ministry roundabouts at every opportunity. Reduce as many 4-way stops as you safely can. Slow, yield, and move into your congregation's best future together.

When Your Building Is Simply Too Much

Jim Kitchens

One of the most common conversations I have with churches of all sizes is one I've come to call "too much church, not enough people." These churches have physical plants built for a time when the congregation's membership was far larger than it is now. The current congregation rattles around in a building with way too much space and is mildly depressed by their situation.

As membership declined over the years, the building—once an asset for an expanding ministry—has turned into a liability that threatens to drown the congregation in maintenance costs.

Building maintenance is deferred from year to year, and the building becomes increasingly in need of repair. The deteriorating physical plant—and the resulting impression visitors take away from their first visit—quickly becomes an elephant in the room that everyone knows needs to be addressed but everyone is scared to name. Some of the church leaders tell me they are "one broken furnace" away from a financial emergency—and possible closure.

All options look like negative ones. The church can try mounting a capital campaign, but the leaders sense that repairing the building won't generate the needed buy-in by the congregation. They can let go of essential personnel or programming to meet the mounting building costs, only to see the congregation continue to shrink. Or they can simply let the building fall down around them, knowing that option most often leads toward the church's death.

Dealing with these issues is lonely work. The pastor and laity don't have anyone with whom to talk or ask for advice. They don't feel they have the skill sets they need. They don't see any models or templates out there in the wider church for how to proceed. Declining staff levels in regional and national denominational headquarters means there's often no one to come to their aid.

My long-time colleague Deborah Wright and I have worked with the Presbyterian Foundation to develop a better model: building a collaborative learning community made up of pastors who share the "too much church, not enough people" dilemma and working with them to crowd-source one another.

We've brought together pastors from around the country to hear about the particular issues and options with which they are wrestling and the tools they need to do their work faithfully. We listen to the questions they have, including the ones they don't quite yet know how to form. We invite them to tell stories of success and failure as they experiment in their particular contexts. The group has already identified several different ways their churches are making faithful decisions, for example:

- Developing "tentmaking buildings" in which space is rented to other churches or nonprofits that share the congregation's mission goals
- Becoming a "building-less church," selling their property and using the resulting assets to support new forms of missional groups within their membership
- Developing a "ministry/worship center" in which several other congregations nest in their facilities and share worship space
- Concluding that it is time for them to become a legacy church, to bring their ministry to a close, and to work with others to make remaining assets available to develop newer forms of Christian community, thus dying well in resurrection hope
- Enabling their pastor to become "bi-vocational in place" by developing a second use of the buildings that provides the pastor a supplemental income stream
- Working with developers to build on unused portions of the property or to take down the current buildings and build an entirely new facility that includes space for the congregation (often to build senior or low-cost/mixed-income housing)
- Turning their church into a community center in which the worshiping community still has a stake

What if you were to start a similar collaborative learning community to address these issues in your own context? Starting the conversation is not that difficult. Think about other churches near you that you sense may also be wrestling with these issues. It can be a cluster of churches in your own denomination, or it may be an ecumenical table you gather. It may be a local conversation, or it can be a regional or national one—especially with the availability of inexpensive or free videoconferencing services. Invite other pastors to join you in a conversation.

Get together. Tell your stories. Help each other form important questions. Share resources you've already discovered. Make a list of the additional resources you need. Generate a list of leaders (other clergy, judicatory staffs, non-profit managers, developers or real estate agents) you want to contact to ask about the resources they may have already developed or the insights they have to share.

Those of us who are consultants and coaches with the Center for Healthy Churches think of ourselves—first and foremost—as a collaborative learning community, helping one another listen for how the Spirit is leading Christ's church into the future. We also believe that whatever the Spirit is saying to the American church today, it is bubbling up from below in communities like these. We know how important it is to have a supportive community of friends and colleagues with whom to share this discernment. We would be honored to work with you as you figure out how to create a community of your own.

Do We Have to Talk about This?

Phill Martin

Good policies and finely tuned processes can be the backbone of the healthy church. Policies and rigid process can be the noose of death for congregations. But wait… Are these statements a clear contradiction? Let's think about the difference.

Policies often have an origin in the law, regarding employment or protection for members or staff. Best practices can avoid fraud in the accounting processes or ensure consistent handling of important ministry tasks. However, the language used in the policy and the language used to communicate implementation of the policy or process can make all the difference in a negative versus a positive outcome.

Processes can "do the thinking" for ministry. A good system can ensure that welcome of the first-time visitor happened and follow-up occurs in a healthy manner. A good system can ensure that money received in ministry is secure income and reduces the risk of theft. A good check-in system can ensure the safety of children and provide confidence for parents. A clear sexual harassment policy with an outline for reporting can protect both victims and the accused. A process done correctly can ensure that what is "right" happens.

Policies and processes at their best are proactive rather than reactive. The congregation that says, "We have never had that problem, so we don't need a process" is at risk. The congregation that overreacts to an event of misbehavior by creating rigid policy rather than dealing with the misbehavior may err to the extreme. This practice may run the risk of limiting ministry or of detraction from A-level staff. Here are three questions to ask about your church:

1. *Do your policies and processes reflect the values of your congregation?* Does your church have a value statement about ministry to its surrounding community, but your facility and security policies place a huge "no trespassing" sign at the door? Using other congregations' policies as a model is okay, but filter them through your congregation's values.
2. *Do your policies and processes reflect the culture of the staff?* Do your staff work in a high-trust environment or merely exist in low trust? Whereas laws regarding time structure vary by states and exempt and non-exempt employees have different reporting requirements, a church's implementation of these policies can help to create either a culture of trust or implied distrust. Clear communication and constant training over time are critical.
3. *Do your policies and processes facilitate ministry or control ministry?* In a planning session have you ever heard the response, "Well that would be a great idea, but our financial policies state that…" This may be a strong indicator that your policies need a review.

Often the difference can stem from the origin of the policy. At times, policy is written from an overreaction to a situation or as a means of responding to something that happened in the past. An example of this might be the policy one congregation adopted to eliminate all outside use of the church facilities. The policy emerged when a short-term after-school event was poorly supervised and resulted in damage to a game room. The policy, written a decade earlier, still stands in sharp contrast to the church's value statement to impact the greatest needs of the community—one of those being unsupervised elementary children after school.

At other times, the process is unwritten and not understood by all but has just become "the way we do things around here." Sometimes these processes can be the greatest deterrence to trust and efficient ministry; they are controlled by unspoken political power in the church's systems.

Does your church have a process to review policy and process? Just because it was a good plan five years ago or two pastors ago doesn't mean it is a good plan for today and tomorrow. Here are some suggestions about when it is a good time to start reviewing policy and processes:

• When you hear about major changes in law, such as the new current tax law, accounting rules, or healthcare requirements
• When you have significant ministry leadership change
• When a new senior pastor or a new mission minister comes on board
 (A new minister may see old processes as limiting and have creative ideas to improve or streamline, or may find the current guideline helpful.)
• When changes occur in ministry teams or committees
 (Don't let the lack of understanding of policy and process outlive the individuals responsible for their implementation. If you have a three-year rotating system of leadership, each year one third will have a new learning curve to understand and support the established process. It is okay to ask, "Why do we do it this way?")

Good policy and finely tuned processes are the friends of healthy churches. It is worth the time and effort to put them in place and constantly review them to ensure they are serving good ministry outcome.

Evangelism Implosion

Bill Wilson

It's time to talk about the obvious: We have a problem with evangelism. Let me explain what I mean.

"We". . . all of us, regardless of theology, denomination, setting, or worship style are struggling with this issue. I work with churches from all points on all spectrums, and I have yet to find one that would argue with this statement.

"Have a problem". . . The ability of a church to reach the nonbelieving, unchurched community is at the heart of the design of the church Jesus left us to implement. When that pipeline of new converts is cut off, our days are numbered. It's simple math and basic health. Nearly all our conversion growth is among our biological offspring, and the vast majority of it occurs prior to age 18.

"With evangelism". . . The abrasive American evangelism methodology from the mid- and late 20th century has left us leery and reticent about evangelism. Most churches have no real strategy for reaching others.

We need a fresh appreciation for, understanding of, and plan for sharing the Good News with a world in need.

I find it helpful to consider evangelism through the simplistic ministry lens of my father, myself, and my son.

My father graduated from seminary in 1955. The prevailing method of evangelism in the churches he served was *the revival*. Growing out of the Great Awakening and the citywide crusades of the early 20th century, evangelism took place at the church in a revival. Gradually, the era of local revivals waned, as they became less and less effective.

I graduated from seminary in 1980. The primary method for evangelism during my early ministry was *personal witnessing*. Evangelism Explosion, CWT (Christian Witness Training), the Four Spiritual Laws, and other methods were developed as a script to guide conversations with strangers toward a life-changing decision on the spot. Gradually, these methods fell victim to shifts in culture and an awareness of their limitations.

My son graduated from divinity school in 2012. The church culture he entered is generally missing a coherent evangelism strategy. In its place has emerged a nebulous *"missions emphasis"* that seeks to engage church members in projects near and far with those in need. The good works and real help are done in the name of Christ, with the hope that the recipients will somehow become Christians as a result.

I have participated fully in all of these methods and found meaning in all. I have also found each of them severely limited in its ability to reach and appropriately convey deep meaning to nonbelievers. None of these methods adequately embody what our churches need if we are to live out our call to preach the good news and make disciples.

When I work with a congregation that decides to revisit evangelism with a 21st-century methodology, here is what often happens.

• It quickly becomes apparent that a general lack of clarity and literacy with regard to scripture and theology is a foundational problem. You cannot talk about something with others that you do not understand. The first step toward a coherent evangelism strategy is usually a strong discipleship strategy for existing Christians.

• Confrontational evangelism is rejected for relational evangelism. The injury done by confrontational evangelists to the kingdom of God is hard to overestimate. As a result, any congregation starts its efforts to reach nonbelievers with a significant handicap of guilt-by-association that must be overcome. Emphasizing relationships leads to another insight for most churches: we don't have very many relationships with nonbelievers.

• These churches gradually discover that others are wrestling with similar issues, and that there are some excellent resources available. Many find *Just Walk Across the Room* by Bill Hybels and *The Celtic Way of Evangelism* by George Hunter especially helpful. Groups such as Fresh Expressions offer creative and healthy ideas. There are many others.

• It soon becomes apparent that some of the primary times people make significant shifts in their faith-life are clustered around crises and pain. Thus, a beginning point for churches that want to impact the nonbelieving community is to offer relevant and ongoing help in these critical fracture moments. Life crises such as addiction, poverty, death, divorce, single parenting, mental illness, medical issues, homelessness, hunger, and incarceration become significant foci of the church. This means funding, staffing, facilities, and intention that are far more extensive than offering a basement room to an AA group.

• These churches are becoming increasingly aware of who lives in their neighborhood, and taking responsibility for them and all of their life needs. Mission projects become much more than "turkeys, trips, and toys." Missions means seeking to establish life-changing and ongoing relationships and conversations with neighbors or with a specific community.

Our evangelism implosion is real. I pray you will embrace evangelism in a way that honors Christ's intent, your church's DNA, and your context. God bless you on that journey.

Loving Our Neighbors

Jim Kitchens

In each of the Synoptic Gospels, Jesus enters into conversation with a crowd about the traditional summary of the Torah: "You shall love the Lord your God with all your heart … and your neighbor as yourself."

In Luke's gospel, a man seeking clarification (if not also self-justification) poses a follow-up question to Jesus: "And who is my neighbor?" Jesus doesn't respond directly to his question. Instead, he explodes the crowd's potentially self-serving categories about mission by telling the parable of the good Samaritan. From the perspective of God's realm, he insists, a neighbor is any person in need whom we meet on the road, even if we tend to think of him/her as "other."

If Jesus were having the same conversation with us today, though, I think it might go in a slightly different direction. I imagine him focusing on the more traditional understanding of neighbor as someone living in your immediate geographical area. I see him asking us a follow-up question: "How can you love your neighbor if you don't know your neighbor?"

Most of us might start to protest, saying that our churches really do love our neighbors and even want to serve our neighbors. But the truth of the matter is that many of our churches don't know our neighbors or what our neighbors' needs, hopes, and dreams might be.

Maybe that's because the neighborhood has changed around us, as demographic shifts mean members who used to live nearby have moved to other parts of town and different populations have taken their place in the immediate area of the church. Maybe we've been in our particular location so long that we have simply quit paying attention to our neighborhood—we no longer "see the forest for the trees." Or maybe we think we still know our neighbors, without actually having paid attention to the subtle cultural shifts that have taken place over the years. Whatever the reason, if we want to be faithful in carrying out God's mission, we need to get to know our neighbors again. There are any number of ways to do this:

- *Take a neighborhood walk.* Send teams of church members out onto the sidewalks around your church on a weekday and again on a Saturday. Ask them simply to notice and record what they see. Are the houses and other buildings in good repair or are some looking a bit shabby around the edges? Are people out walking on the streets, or does the neighborhood feel deserted? Who do you encounter on your walk? What ethnicities, ages, and kinds of family units do you see? Are there different businesses in the area than you remember?

- *Strike up a conversation.* Invite church members to spend some time sitting in a neighborhood coffee house, or laundromat, or anywhere else people from the neighborhood congregate. Ask them to start up a conversation with the people at the next table, asking what they think about the neighborhood and what issues concern them most. Inquire about needs they have that could make their life better if they were met. Ask them what they know about your congregation. You may be surprised by some of the things they know—and even more so by some of the things they assume about you.

- *Talk with community leaders.* Invite the principal of the school closest to your church to tell you about the children who attend and their families. Have the chief of police tell you about neighborhood issues they notice most often. Ask the city council member who represents your part of town to tell you what requests for service he/she most regularly receives. Do the same with the head of the welfare/social services department. Ask each of them what your church might do to help address the unmet needs they have identified.

- *Look at the demographic data.* There are several sources for demographic data about your immediate surroundings. Your denomination may have information that will help you better understand your neighborhood. You can use publicly available data such as census reports for the zip codes in your immediate area. You can purchase relatively inexpensive reports from "data mining" vendors who not only pull together a lot of information about your neighborhood but also will help you understand it. Mission Insite (mission-insite.com) is a commonly used vendor that—in addition to hard numbers—can tell you about your neighbors' religious preferences, their lifestyle choices, and their values and dreams.

You certainly can imagine other ways to hit the sidewalks and learn who your neighbors are. Knowing your neighbors and their real needs is an important first step toward loving them in the way Jesus calls us to do.

Why a Building-use Policy Matters

Bill Wilson

I know firsthand how utterly boring and laborious creating a building-use policy can be. Every church I have ever served has entered into a major building project. The debate around building use has been a constant. It also has evolved dramatically for me.

As a "low on the totem pole" staff member, I remember sitting in a meeting of the Property Committee as the members debated the use of our new facilities. I promised God that if I ever got out of that meeting, I would give myself to a lifetime of ministry in Siberia.

There was a relatively simple agenda in the room: How can we make sure that our building is only used by people like us who will take care of it? How can we make it so expensive for outsiders to use that they stay away? Influential members and our custodians were complaining that we had too many of "them" using our facilities at our current prices.

We established a pecking order of who could use the building: members first, other churches second, and outsiders a distant third. To accomplish this, we dramatically increased the fee structure. Predictably, outsiders gradually stopped asking to use our facilities.

As a pastor, I came to understand that this question of building use is at the heart of our mission as God's people. Rather than being a nuisance and a dreaded task, it is essential to shifting our mindset from maintenance to mission. Jerry McClung was my inspiration.

Jerry was a gentle, wise, and profoundly insightful layman at a church I served. He had been the church clerk for 50 consecutive years. When Jerry spoke, we all listened. In the debate about whether to build and renovate space, the necessary question of whether we were doing this simply for ourselves intensified. Jerry, in a video that was used to raise funds for the project, looked into the camera and said: "This building is not a monument to a crucified Christ, but is an instrument to be used by the people who have been led to him."

That spirit began to permeate the congregation: instrument, not monument. Eventually, we had Jerry's quote framed and put on the wall to help us remember that our facilities were tools and instruments for ministry—not a monument, memorial, or museum.

As we debated our building-use policy, we deliberately made it economical and attractive for outsiders to use our space. We had the finest multipurpose facility in the city, and found ourselves hosting school events, social events, civic clubs, government functions, family functions, and a host of other groups. Many people came onto our campus and found a warm welcome. More than a few eventually found their way into our fellowship. True, we had to add custodial staff, and we constantly debated the flood of "outsiders" on our property. Emotions ran high when conflicts emerged, but we remained true to our mission and vision of being radically hospitable to our community. Gradually, I learned that policy which supports vision is very different from the reverse.

Here are three more examples of how this seemingly inconsequential debate actually matters a great deal:

• I heard Leith Anderson describe how those persons in his megachurch in Minneapolis approached the use of their large campus. Reaching the unreached was their highest priority. When it came to their building use policy, they decided to align it with their congregational vision. The result was a pecking order that reflected their vision. Specifically, outside church groups were not allowed to use the property, congregational members had limited privileges, and non-church groups and entities were given complete and minimally expensive access to the property. Anderson then told us that the Minnesota Vikings football team's headquarters were near their property, and used Wooddale's facilities for all their team meetings. Not coincidentally, a dozen players and their families had become active in the church.

• The leader of a congregation in the heart of a large southern city realized that the area around them was gradually being redeveloped into high-end condominiums and apartments. Young adults were flooding the formerly desolate downtown. The church had a very restrictive wedding policy that essentially barred non-members from using it. Realizing the opportunity, after intense and heated debate, the church leaders restructured that policy to make it possible for young adults to have a place for their weddings. The resulting flood of interest provided a unique opportunity to minister to and with those couples.

• A church had a preschool deliberately structured to attract only high-income families. Surrounded by an ocean of need, when they added that congregation space, the leaders rewrote their policy to make it accessible and affordable to those who most needed it. Gradually, their exclusive school grew to become a tool to impact their community.

Your building use policy says something important about you. Make sure it communicates the spirit of a crucified Christ, and not that of a self-absorbed congregation.

A New Digital Covenant

Joel Snider

Have you ever . . . Sent a text that the recipient misinterpreted? Wondered how to decipher an angry-sounding email you received? Congratulated someone on Facebook for an accomplishment, only to discover the news was still confidential?

If you haven't had one of these experiences, you've had one similar. We can all share stories of digital communication gone wrong.

Members of faith communities today often ask, "How will we relate to each other as Christians in a digital world? How will we treat our brothers and sisters in Christ in the ever-changing cyberworld?" Many people assume they know the answers, only to discover that not all members of the fellowship share the same convictions.

How do we come to a common understanding of appropriate digital communication? A church may adopt an official policy on the subject, but policies are only enforceable with employees. How does the broader membership agree on principles of Internet conduct?

While exploring this idea, I discovered the concept of a digital covenant between members—a common commitment to how we treat each other in the virtual world as part of Christ's church. I don't have a finished product, but here are some suggested principles:

• *Use digital communication for information, but not for emotions.* Seven percent of interpersonal communication is verbal; the remainder is nonverbal. The recipient can't see your facial expressions, hear your tone of voice, or read your body language in an email or text. In fact, 93 percent of your digital communication is hidden and, therefore, easy to misinterpret. If your message has emotion behind it, go see the person or pick up the phone and call.

• *Use caution when copying someone on an email.* This is for information, not leverage. Do not copy someone in an effort to pressure the primary recipient. Consider using this practice at work, too.

• *Do not share another person's information digitally until they do.* I know an instance where a person posted this prayer request on Facebook: "Pray for my neighbor whose father died tonight. She dreads calling her children at college to tell them their grandfather is gone." It seemed innocent enough until the Facebook user's daughter saw her mother's post, made the connection, and texted one of the grandchildren: "I was sorry to hear about your grandfather." It was an unfortunate way to hear about a death. Therefore, be respectful. Either ask directly if you can share the information or wait until after the other person posts a message.

• *Ask for permission to post pictures of children.* A couple shared a video of a funny moment in their child's life. One of the recipients posted it to YouTube. The parents asked them to take it down, and they refused. They were addicted to the number of hits they were getting. The parents found that even though their child was the subject, they had no legal standing to have the video removed from the Internet. Get permission to post pictures or information about another parent's child. If a friend asks you to remove a photo or information about them, respond in Christian charity and comply.

• *Remember that the world is your audience.* Randi Zuckerberg, former spokesperson for Facebook, says that when you share information digitally, think "Who among the recipients do I trust the least?" This question sounds cynical, but contains much wisdom. Don't say anything in an email that would embarrass you if it were forwarded.

• *Remember the permanence of the digital.* Digital communication is quick and convenient and allows us to stay in touch with more people we could never see or call. The ease of writing and deleting lulls us into thinking messages come and go. Google's search ability is quick, and its memory is permanent. A tweet or post that may seem funny in the moment can have lasting embarrassment.

• *Remember that "whatever you do, in word or deed, do everything in the name of the Lord Jesus" (Col. 3:17).* We don't have permission to stray from the mind of Christ just because we are angry or participating in sports—or because we are on the Internet. Paul mentions no exclusions to "everything."

These are starting points for a covenant about how we treat each other in the digital age. Consider having a church discussion about the idea. Develop your own principles, and then pledge together to treat others on the Internet in a way that honors Christ.

By the Numbers

David Hull

How large is your church? For many years the primary way of measuring church size was to look at church membership. In Baptist churches we began to track Sunday School attendance as a measuring stick.

Membership numbers are not really helpful since Baptists are not very good about adjusting our rolls over the years. Some denominations do better about this than Baptists. Total membership numbers tend to be very inflated for churches that have been around for a number of years. Instead of membership numbers, tracking attendance is the best way to know the size of a church. In addition to counting Sunday School attendance, churches now often count worship attendance. Usually this worship attendance is a head count, rather than a posting of attendance by individuals. So, how large is your church?

In recent years we have observed that even our most faithful members are attending worship and Bible study on Sundays less than they did a few years ago. Opportunities pull our people in different directions on the weekends. Very regular attenders who used to make three out of four Sundays a month may now feel good about being present for two Sundays a month. This new attendance trend obviously affects average attendance; however, you are counting it. A congregation of 1,000 people who come three out of four Sundays a month averages 750. A congregation of the same number who come two Sundays a month averages 500 in attendance.

Another attendance trend is happening, too. People connect to the life of the church in other ways than just Sunday School and worship. In fact, it is common for churches to offer various opportunities through the week that enable people to experience spiritual growth, enter into prayer, and have Christian fellowship in a community of faith. Sunday morning is not the only time this occurs. A Tuesday night young adult group or a Thursday morning Bible study are ways to connect people to spiritual growth through the ministry of the church, but these groups may not be counted in our traditional ways. We need a new way to measure the lives that are being touched through the ministry of our churches.

To address these new attendance realities, some churches have now introduced a new way of counting. Various names are used, but let me give an example with the name TouchPoints. Each quarter a church will track the total number of people who have attended Sunday School and various other groups where attendance is taken and where spiritual growth, prayer, and fellowship occur. Attendance is taken throughout the week in addition to Sunday mornings. (Worship is not included in TouchPoints since most churches do not keep track of individual names in their worship attendance numbers.)

Instead of just concentrating on average attendance, this gives us a way to measure the *total number of people* who have been touched over the last three months through the ministry of the church. People are just counted once, even if they were present every week and involved with several different groups.

Churches that track these numbers should not be surprised to find that their Touch-Points number of total people in a quarter will be more that 50 percent higher than their Bible study average attendance for that same quarter. Churches can continue to track these numbers quarter by quarter. In the second year of measurement, you can see if you are touching more people than in the same quarter of the previous year. Perhaps that will be a metric for a church to utilize, even in a day when average attendance may be declining.

Church leaders may not have much impact on college football home games or lake homes or traveling soccer, baseball, and volleyball schedules, but we can give our best efforts to make sure we are reaching out to as many new folks as possible to touch their lives with the love of Jesus. TouchPoints is one way to keep track of this outreach as we determine if new people are being connected into the life of the church.

The Sunday School director in my first pastorate taught me an important lesson. He asked me one day: "When Jesus told his parable about the lost sheep, how did the shepherd know that one sheep was missing? Out of 100 sheep, how did he know that one was astray?" He answered his own question: "Because he counted." Unless we count, it is hard to look at 100 sheep and know that one is missing. Numbers do matter because people matter! Healthy churches find the best way to count.

So, how large is your church? How are you counting?

Frequency of Attendance

Bill Wilson

Have you ever heard of a perfect attendance pin for Sunday School? Many of you have never seen one. There was a day when it was a regular feature in churches all across America. If a person attended Sunday School every Sunday in a year, he or she was awarded a pin, or was awarded an attachment that hung below the original pin to denote *another* year of perfect attendance. People took great pride in amassing multi-year pins that honored their spiritual fortitude and persistence. (For examples, see http://www.lifeway.com/Article/News-Illinoisan-celebrates-75-years-perfect-Sunday-School-attendance.)

Gradually, the expectation that weekly attendance at church was a given has eroded and been replaced with a hope that people will attend church "regularly." The definition of what constitutes "regular attendance" has been redefined downward as competition on weekends has increased. Some churches are coming to realize that very active and loyal people are attending church much less frequently than before. As a result, average weekly attendance is in serious decline for many.

Several pundits have offered their take on why this is happening, and their explanations are often tinged with criticism and a thinly veiled sense of condemnation.

In 2014, the Center for Healthy Churches worked with 50 different churches from 16 states and 8 denominations. The churches ranged in size from 32 weekly attenders to 5,000. In nearly every situation, we engaged our clients in a conversation about frequency of attendance. Rather than conjecture about why people are attending less frequently, we decided to ask them where their people are when they are not attending church.

Here are the 10 reasons, listed alphabetically, most frequently mentioned by those we polled:

1. *Athletic events:* College and professional athletic events evoke intense loyalty. For those who travel to Saturday night games, showing up on Sunday mornings is a stretch. Many professional athletic events take place on Sundays and force a choice between attending church or the game or a tailgate event.
2. *Commitment:* Many church members told us that the depth of their commitment to weekly attendance is eroding. There are multiple reasons, but at the heart of the matter is a sense that what is offered on Sunday mornings is not meaningful or valuable enough to make the effort to attend.
3. *Exhaustion:* On several occasions we heard younger families say that they find themselves exhausted by a six-day workweek, overactive social life, over-engaged children, and a host of other stresses. Several mentioned that Sundays are now their only day to be together as a family. Occasionally, they choose to spend the morning together.

4. *Holidays:* The number of Sundays that are now part of holiday weekends has risen dramatically. One church counted and discovered that 26 Sundays in the previous year were impacted by a holiday or vacation week. Long weekends and breaks invite travel and time away from home.

5. *Illness:* Several senior adults shared with us that they are living with chronic illness that inhibits their ability to attend weekly worship. In previous years, they would not have survived such a serious illness. Now they find their ability to get out and participate severely restricted.

6. *Children:* The array of activities for children offered only on weekends is overwhelming. Athletic travel teams, academic conferences, chess tournaments, cheering competitions, parties, and trips have proliferated in the last 30 years. Many parents tag along and find themselves far from home on Sunday mornings.

7. *Parents:* Related to #5 above, several median-age adults recounted that they miss Sundays because they are caring for aging and/or ill parents. We frequently heard about rotation systems among siblings to care for an invalid parent. Taking your turn for a weekend each month keeps you out of your church.

8. *Travel:* The proliferation of travel as a high-value activity for Americans impacts weekend activities. The ease of travel in our day is a huge shift from 50 years ago.

9. *Vacations, timeshares, second homes:* Many people admitted they spend multiple weekends a year on vacation or taking advantage of second homes or timeshares.

10. *Work:* Nearly every gathering evoked stories of people who work, or travel for work, on Sundays. The official estimate is that 1 in 3 Americans regularly work on Sundays.

What are we to make of these statistics? We will explore the implications more in the future. For now, we must grapple with the illusion that Sundays belong to the church and that loyal members will be present four or five Sundays a month. Here are some possible strategies to explore:

• Measure your impact rather than simply counting your attendance.
• Count participants over the course of a month/year rather than attenders by the week.
• Investigate the possibility of having Bible study and worship on alternate days and locations.

The Case of the Declining Congregation

Bill Wilson

It is becoming a consistent scenario in our work with conflicted churches: Anxious congregations overreact to symptomatic issues and cause great harm to people and ministry. In its simplest form, it looks something like this: A congregation begins to notice that attendance at weekend Bible study and/or worship is declining. Assuming that a decline in attendance means their church is in trouble, desperate measures seem called for. A move to change ministerial leadership is carried out. Following a bruising internal conflict, the attendance decline accelerates as the church implodes.

Sadly, some version of this scenario is probably playing out in a congregation near you. It is hard to list all the ways such actions harm the body of Christ and the work of the kingdom of God. The damage such a scenario wreaks upon a community of faith, the lives of clergy, and the future of the church is breathtaking.

Ironically, ignorance about causal factors for such a situation is widespread and pervasive. Key facts that are at the root of the issue are often overlooked.

Take, for example, the decline in attendance. While it may be a foregone conclusion that declining attendance is synonymous with fewer people active in the life of a congregation, such may not be the case.

I recently helped a church examine its attendance records. Over the course of a decade, Sunday morning average attendance had steadily declined. Much hand-wringing had commenced, and several initiatives to address the decline had been launched. Those remedies had little positive result, but only served to raise the anxiety in the congregation about attendance. Interestingly, during that same time, congregational membership had steadily increased. How could this be?

A closer look revealed a previously unseen culprit. While more and more people joined the church and were blessed by its ministry, the frequency of attendance by those who considered themselves active members began to slip. Thus, a growing church saw a decline in attendance. Here's how that happens:

A church grows from 400 to 600 active members over a decade. That's 50-percent growth. During that same decade, the frequency of attendance by the active members declines from an average of three Sundays a month to two Sundays a month. The result? The average attendance remains the same (300) for the decade. While there are 50 percent more people active and attending, they come less frequently and the church appears to be plateaued or declining.

This congregation rightly identified the culprit, and it was not under-performing clergy. In fact, we made a list of contributing reasons for the decline in frequency of attendance. Here is what we came up with:

- Youth sports leagues and competitions taking place on weekends
- The proliferation of vacation home/timeshare ownership
- Collegiate and professional athletic weekend events
- One-third of Americans now working on Sunday morning
- The dramatic increase in "holiday" weekends
- Illness
- Aging parents requiring care
- Ease of travel
- Lifestyle fatigue
- A decline in commitment to regular Bible study and worship attendance

After we compiled this list, we had to admit that scapegoating or simple admonishments would not solve attendance problems. Instead, we must rethink how we connect with people and accomplish the mission of the church.

This group immediately agreed on an obvious truth. They could no longer rely on a simple headcount of attendees at Sunday morning events as the sole measurement of their impact on people's lives and the community around them.

New metrics were necessary to fully grasp the breadth and reach of the church. For example, when this church's leaders measured the number of people who attended Sunday School over the course of a year, they found a significant growth curve, in spite of a stagnant average weekly attendance. When they began to imagine how they might measure impact, they quickly realized that the multiple ministries that congregants engaged in during the week needed to be included in their numbers. Rather than being in decline, this congregation was actually growing and expanding.

Gradually, the brewing conflict over declining Sunday morning attendance shifted into a vibrant conversation about how to engage a congregation and community outside the traditional confines of Sunday morning ministry. Such adaptive or "both/and" thinking is at the heart of a healthy and thriving church.

The Unbalanced Church
Bill Wilson

When a congregation wants to become, stay, or remain healthy, one of the key questions it asks has to do with the balance between its internal and external focus. One excellent congregational exercise to help with this question is to gather a group in a large room, and on one end of the room create an imaginary continuum that stretches from one side of the room to another. One end of the continuum is internal; the other is external. Now ask everyone participating to move to a place on the continuum that reflects the way they would answer these questions:

• In your understanding of the reason for the church's existence, where along this continuum would you say that Christ intended his church to focus its attention: internal (primarily upon itself) or external (primarily outside itself)? (People vote with their feet by standing at the place along the continuum that reflects their answer.)
• Where along this continuum does our church invest its primary energy, finances, staffing, and facilities?
• Where do you think we should be in this regard?

As you might imagine, almost without exception, we find people gathering in the middle to the external end on the first question, and much more heavily toward the internal end of the continuum on the second question. Generally, they gather in the middle on the third question. It seems pervasive: there is a gap between our understanding of the nature of the church and the way we actually do church.

Nearly everyone agrees that the primary mission of the church is captured in texts such as the Great Commission and in images of salt, light, ambassadors, witnesses, and a host of other metaphors focused on impacting the world around us to help bring the reign of God to reality. The people of God are tasked with being a blessing to those around us.

To be sure, there are multiple commands to create a spiritual body that works in harmony; confesses Christ as Savior; and is marked by love, deep fellowship, a servant spirit, and profound humility.

In healthy congregations and parishes, the gap between where we invest the majority of our resources and what we sense to be our essential calling is under constant evaluation. In dysfunctional and self-absorbed communities of faith, the question is seldom asked and often belittled.

I believe this "mission gap" is at the heart of our crisis of attendance and support. When a congregation spends its time primarily tending to its own needs, when the care of members is the first priority for clergy, when members' expectations are primary, when the essential question we ask is "Do I like this?" ... then we have a fundamental problem of alignment. No stewardship campaign or outreach effort will be able to overcome this foundational misalignment.

As long as our first thought is self-care and self-fulfillment, we will be at odds with the spirit of Jesus Christ. Whatever success we have will be shallow, vapid, and transitory.

On the other hand, the churches that are inviting people to join them in living out the mission described, taught, and demonstrated by Jesus are finding an audience. Their attention is focused not only on "what I need from the church" but also upon "what our community needs from God and us." Seeking to balance these two polarities is at the heart of being the people of God in the 21st century.

It is amazing the transformation that comes when this balance is restored to a proper ratio. Infighting, selfishness, gossiping, backbiting, and judgmental attitudes have a way of melting in the face of passion for reaching and ministering to others. When a congregation gets properly focused on loving the city or community where it is located as Jesus loved the world, and especially Jerusalem, then an equilibrium is established that puts our internal concerns into their proper perspective.

Having our pew vacant, or hearing our preferred musical style in worship, or getting the attention and acclaim we think we deserve shrinks in comparison to the fulfillment we receive from feeding the hungry, giving a drink to the thirsty, clothing the naked, visiting the prisoners, welcoming the stranger, and caring for the sick.

This balance between internal and external focus is at the heart of what is right and what is wrong with most congregations today. We need to get this right, not just because of what it means for the coming year, but for what it means in our future.

For all our lack of clarity about what happens when we die, there are some things we can know without question. We do not need to wonder what will happen in the end. We have the authoritative story from the one who will be there. Jesus has told us in exquisite detail in Matthew 25:31-46 what awaits each of us.

We would do well to read these verses in church each week and to align our church's schedules, budgets, staffing model, and most especially our priorities accordingly.

Critical Questions to Ask Each Year

Bill Wilson

If there is one recurring theme to the conversations I have regularly with clergy, lay leaders, and denominational employees, it is viability. In a myriad of ways, people are asking viability questions about ministry, congregational life, finances, staff models, facilities, organizational structures, mission, and just about every aspect of religious life today.

At the outset of each new year, let me suggest some critical questions regarding congregational finances of the previous year that you need to ask and have answers to.

• How much of your budget receipts came from persons over age 70? age 75? age 80?
• How much of your budget receipts came from persons under age 35?
• What percentage of your budget receipts came from your top five donors?

Most established congregations will find the answers to these questions sobering. Reading that we are at the end of the era of congregational life being defined by rising budgets and attendance is one thing; actually coming to grips with that being true for you is another. Until we are honest about our own situation, however, we will never have the deep resolve to rethink congregational life that is necessary for us to be successful going forward.

Most congregations will find that their budget is heavily funded by a pocket of loyal givers who are primarily senior adults. It doesn't take a social science degree to understand the danger here. Soon, many congregations will face enormous financial challenges as their primary supporters move off the scene. Many congregations are only one or two funerals away from a real crisis. What is a concerned congregation to make of this reality?

• *Learn the difference between loyalty giving and passion giving.* Ask any fundraiser for a hospital, university, or nonprofit, and they will confirm this truth: The era of people giving out of a sense of loyalty, duty, and love for an institution is waning. As the Builder generation passes off the scene, they take with them a deep commitment to institutions and giving out of a sense of duty or obligation. In their place come the Boomers and their offspring, who give primarily out of their sense of passion and desire to make a difference in the world. Most congregations still design their giving campaigns for the group that defined them in the past, rather than their future.

We must learn to talk about stewardship in terms broader than obligation and duty. Thankfully, Jesus was the one who linked giving to meaning and purpose in life. Now, we must learn to speak his language on this subject.

- *Learn to live and talk about creating a congregational culture of generosity in the midst of a societal culture that promotes self-absorption.* While Jesus taught a life of internal abundance, 21ˢᵗ-century American cultural leaders preach a message of fear and scarcity. Many congregational leaders allow their thoughts on the economy to dwarf their faith. Far too many finance committees walk by sight, rather than by faith. We face significant headwind on this. Everything around us says "grab hold of as much as you can and don't worry about those around you." How can we create an oasis of people who actually believe "it is more blessed to give than to receive" and "to find your life, you must lose your life"?

  Healthy congregations will find themselves teaching an increasingly alien message about possessions and money that will evoke reactions and pushback from those overly invested in American consumer culture.

- *Broaden your understanding of stewardship to match that of Jesus'.* Reading the Gospels leaves one with the distinct impression that Jesus rejected the notion of obligatory giving and instead taught that all of life is a gift to be managed as though it were on loan from our creator. Jesus taught about living in gratitude for the privilege of being his son or daughter for a season here on earth. The ways we handle our money, possessions, influence, career, and education are all part of living out a unique mission as a steward of a treasure we have been given.

  When was the last time you taught your high school juniors and seniors that their choice of vocation and/or college is essentially a question of stewardship? Despite the fact that we are talking about donations and dollars, the truth is that the primary issue is not money. Financial metrics provide specific evidence that something foundational is amiss. While these are helpful for sounding the alarm that what we are doing is not viable or sustainable longterm, they are more symptomatic than the actual problem.

Over time, we must ask harder questions regarding why we are here and what we are doing.

Endings and Beginnings
David Hull

I write these words in the midst of a most unusual week. I spent the first part of the week in the home of my deceased parents. Their house is for sale. Most of the furniture has been divided up among family members, but there is still "stuff" to go through.

In the stark quiet of an empty house there are papers and files to review for keeping or tossing, books to give away to the library, clothes to take to the Salvation Army, and trash to be taken to the recycling center. My body aches from carrying too many boxes down from my dad's third-floor study. The biggest challenge, however, was not physical.

The hardest part was knowing what to save and what to discard. Everything I touched had been important to my parents, but that does not mean it will find a home in my house or in my sister's house. Discarding something that was once important to people you love is hard to do, but it is necessary to move forward.

I left the work at my parents' house and traveled to my daughter's home, where I am now babysitting my two-year-old grandson. What a contrast in experiences—all during the course of a few days!

Everything is new for Liam: each day brings new friends at daycare and church, new words to learn, new books to read, new experiences to cherish. The sheer silence of an empty house is replaced by Pop joining Liam at Cherub Choir on Wednesday night. No longer are there old clothes to throw away, but new clothes from grandparents to try on in an attempt to fit his ever-growing body. Signs, sights, and sounds of life are everywhere.

Endings and beginnings: both are important for healthy churches. The same experiences that I am going through this week in my personal life are the rhythm of healthy churches. Think for a moment about appropriate endings. Events, programs, ministries, buildings, mission endeavors, (and the list could go on to include things such as prejudices, attitudes, and fears) that were important to people we loved sometimes need to be ended. They do not need to have a home in the church of the future. These are often hard decisions to make. What needs to stay around? What needs to be discarded?

Perhaps the following questions will help you wrestle with finding the answers:

- Does this ministry help us accomplish our mission and vision for the future? If not, why are we keeping it?
- Will this facility be a barrier to our ministry vitality and growth? If so, is it time for an ending?
- Is this attitude or mindset within the congregation reflective of the mind of Christ? If not, is it time for it to be taken out for recycling?

Healthy churches are able to experience appropriate endings. Through effective leadership, clarity of mission and vision, vibrant congregational conversations, and collaborative processes, churches can move to have appropriate endings for things that were once very important to members of the congregation. That is how families move forward. Everything from the past does not find a home in the house of the next generation. Healthy churches know how to recycle!

Healthy churches also know about how to begin something new. If there is a need for appropriate endings, there is also a desire for energizing beginnings.

What new thing are you allowing God to do in your church? What "new song" is the tune of your ministry? Are you loving the world God loves with the wide-open arms of a bright-eyed two-year-old?

Perhaps these questions will help you think through energizing beginnings:

- Where do we see God already working in our corner of the world that we can join in and be a part of this mission—even if we have never done it this way before?
- What are the strengths and gifts of people within our congregation that have not yet been invested in ministry? How can we equip and empower these folks to speak the new words and sing the new songs of sharing God's love?
- What is the human need around us that cries out for an expression of hope?

We read in Isaiah 43:18-19, "Do not remember the former things, or consider the things of old. I am about to do a new thing; now it springs forth, do you not perceive it? I will make a way in the wilderness and rivers in the desert" (NRSV). Healthy churches know about appropriate endings—"do not remember the former things." They also know about energizing beginnings—"I am about to do a new thing."

I look around the room at the home of my daughter's family. In front of me is a chest that was in my sister's bedroom as a child. Not all of the old has come to an end. Some of the old remains and is handed down from generation to generation. On top of the chest is a new little pair of boots to be worn by one who experiences new things every day. That is how families move forward from generation to generation. The same is true for healthy churches.

Changing Seats

Bill Owen

I had my choice between the window seat and the aisle seat. Sitting by the window offers a great view, but it makes me feel cramped, if not trapped. There are benefits to the aisle seat. You have greater freedom to stand or move when you like. You can stretch at least one leg into the aisle.

I chose the aisle. I chose comfort. It is the decision many churches face.

Eric Swanson and Rick Rusaw explore such thinking in *The Externally Focused Quest—Becoming the Best Church FOR the Community*. It's a good read on getting the church into the community. Swanson and Rusaw believe that "incarnational churches" go to the people instead of waiting for the people to come to the church. These churches are focused on helping all believers live out their calling, especially among people who do not yet follow Christ.

Such churches are window-seat churches. They are externally focused. They have an eye for others, not just themselves.

Such vision garners buy-in from its members. They see success not by the number of worshipers on Sunday but by the impact and time spent in the community offering love and hope to a world desperately searching. They strive to be Christ beyond the walls. They pray for and care about what God's doing in the world as they find creative ways to partner in it.

I haven't walked into a church yet to hear members willing to say it is a waste of time being incarnational (taking church to the people). What I do hear people saying is that it is primarily the role of the pastor to care for the people inside, to meet their needs.

No doubt, churches still need to be places where people are comforted, cared for, and inspired. But it doesn't have to be either/or.

Statisticians all agree: The 21st-century American church is at a crossroads. We have a decision to make: Will we choose the window seat or the aisle seat?

At the Center for Healthy Churches we find that the spiritual, emotional, and organizational health of churches often comes when our attention is focused beyond ourselves. In pure market terms the church today has to be more socially aware and responsible. The church must be more interested in making an impact in the community as opposed to being almost exclusively focused on increasing returns for insiders. This need leads me to wonder:

• What might the church be if a new leadership model would emerge where the pastor becomes a coach, facilitator, even community organizer and not simply a person responsible for the church's well-being?

- What might the church be if we would choose possible discomfort and start dreaming about what God is doing in the world and then join hm there?
- What might the church be if our metrics would focus more on impact outside the walls as opposed to simply "nickels and noses" within?
- What might the church be if our communication strategies (social media, web presence, etc.) would focus on those outside our normal patterns and relationships?

Healthy congregations in the 21st century gather around ministry and not the minister, Kingdom issues in place of comfort, and matters of justice instead of just us.

At the CHC, we encourage pastors, leadership teams, and congregations to choose the window seat!

A Pivotal Question

Bill Wilson

Tom Ehrich, one of my favorite thinkers about church in the 21ˢᵗ century, recently told me he is down to one pivotal question for the congregations he works with: "Is your primary orientation inward or outward?" He contends that, until we get this right, our internally focused planning and programming will obscure the most important task we have been given.

I think Ehrich is right. Many of us would agree with his words but fail to fully appreciate the implications of such a shift in our orientation To ask this question is to embark on a fundamental and often uncomfortable shift for many congregations. We have been trained to provide services for our constituents (read: members) and to work hard at meeting their expectations. Clergy and lay leaders spend untold amounts of energy seeking to provide just the right kind of food, environment, worship format, program, facility, etc. for those who attend our church. We have spawned what my colleague Nelson Grenade terms "the concierge minister." Such ministers are expected to provide whatever the congregation wants, even if it conflicts with their core convictions about the church.

Inwardly focused, self-absorbed congregations produce highly anxious leaders who live in fear of offending a constituent and with a nagging sense of building a church that Jesus would not attend.

While we may talk about "outreach" to the community, often what we actually mean is some form of "in-drag." The only way we know to help people is to pull them into our facilities and then try to fix whatever ails them. We have a gnawing sense that our efforts are producing less and less return on our investment, but we really are not sure what to do in lieu of what we have always done. Such is the dilemma of many a loyal and faithful congregation as we live into the 21ˢᵗ century.

Reorienting ourselves toward an outward focus is more than simply lip service to a generic missions program or tossing a few crumbs to the less fortunate around us. It is to take seriously both the great commandments and the great commission, and to seek to integrate them into everything we do and say.

To be outwardly oriented is to recognize that God is at work both within and around the church and to seek out that activity and name it. One pastor I know simply invited his congregation to start noticing and naming "where I saw God at work today." The energy has been contagious as the congregation awakened to the possibilities of working with the Spirit in ways that have been too often overlooked.

Part of our reorientation will be the recognition that our scorecards and metrics will need to change. Our traditional scorecard items of "nickels and noses" are not adequate for a future that is outward focused. Balancing our obsession with attendance and finances with a hunger to measure our impact on our larger community is a seismic shift for many churches. It may help to recognize that this is at the heart of the way Jesus taught us to live out our faith.

Dave Ferguson, the lead pastor of Community Church in Chicago, suggests we need a new set of metrics to adequately reflect our outward orientation: "Adequate metrics for your church will reflect your understanding of the mission of Jesus."

If the mission of Jesus takes seriously not only those inside the church but also those outside, then we might consider expanding our scorecard and metrics to include our impact on the following:

- the local crime rate
- the high school dropout and graduation rates, test scores, and college admission percentages and acceptance
- the divorce rate and marriages restored
- the number of orphans and widows ministered to and prisoners reached, the amount of poverty averted and adequate housing provided, the number of hungry people fed, etc.
- clear discipleship thresholds identified and measured
- life-changing stories told and encouraged
- the hours spent off church property by staff in ministry

To shift our orientation from self-preservation and self-service to an outward orientation built upon a deep love for our city/community is to make the same transformative journey the disciples made as they walked alongside Jesus.

Initially, the disciples were fixated upon what Jesus could do for them (see Mark 9–10, for example). Gradually, on the far side of the Resurrection and as the Spirit opened their eyes and hearts, the disciples became obsessed with what Jesus could do for everyone. More than an evangelism campaign, their primary focus and concern became sharing this good news with their external community. Self-preservation gave way to sacrificial love for others.

We may discover that the pivotal question for every healthy faith community remains what it has always been: Is your focus internal or external?

10 Things Churches Can Learn from the Masters

Barry Howard

The first time I walked onto the grounds of the Augusta National Golf Club in 2002, I was overcome by the lush beauty. I have been privileged to attend the Masters tournament several times through the years. On each visit I have been inspired when I step foot on this immaculately manicured acreage—which is a rare combination of botanical gardens, nature preserve, and golf course.

When watching one Masters tournament on TV, I recalled my previous visits to the property. I began to reflect on 10 things the church could learn from the Masters:

1. *Hospitality is welcoming and winsome.* From the parking attendants, to the ticket takers, to the groundskeepers, Augusta National evokes a friendly vibe as staff members greet patrons with "Welcome to the Masters!" and a hearty smile. A hospitable sense of welcome is a trademark of healthy congregations.

2. *Not everything has to be high tech.* Technology is important. I utilize a smartphone, a laptop computer, and a tablet. And I served churches through the years that embraced technology, striving to have the most recent computers, the most up-to-date audio technology, the most cutting-edge video screens, and the most elaborate lighting. I am not anti-technology, but at the Masters it is nice to see thousands of patrons staring at a low-tech, manual scoreboard manned by volunteers, which happens to be one of the most iconic scoreboards in the world of golf. Churches should remember that technology is one tool in the toolbox, and if we become codependent on technology, it can become a liability rather than an asset in ministry.

3. *Appreciate silence and celebration.* The aura of Augusta National alternates between the roar of the crowd and a holy hush. I am always amazed that thousands of golf enthusiasts can cheer with loud enthusiasm, and yet a few moments later they can stand still in focused silence as a golfer is about to putt. Healthy churches appreciate and make space for both silent meditation and jubilant celebration.

4. *Simplicity and excellence often work in tandem.* The kitchen staff at Augusta National has mastered the art of making egg salad and pimento cheese sandwiches—nothing fancy, just simple sandwiches. Excellence in the local church doesn't require glitz and glamour, but often emerges in doing simple things well.

5. *Spectators cheer for the golfers, not against them.* In other sports, and even at other tournaments, fans may boo or jeer at the opposing team or their least favorite golfer, but not at the Masters. Church is a place to "encourage one another" without prejudice.

6. *Golf has a discipleship program called "drive, chip, and putt."* This catechism is designed to teach basic skills and disciplines to boys and girls ages 7–15. Healthy churches emphasize and exemplify the basic tenets of the faith, giving opportunities for the next generation to practice "on the course."

7. *Bad things happen to good golfers.* Even at the Masters, good putts lip out and the false front causes the ball to release and trickle into Rae's Creek. Wind direction changes, and weather is unpredictable. Yet the best golfers are required to be disciplined enough to put the last shot behind them and focus on the next shot. Likewise, healthy churches help others to put the past behind them, and the future before them, and to "press toward the mark of the high calling of God in Christ Jesus."

8. *New terms, new rules, and new norms take some getting used to.* While watching the Masters on TV in recent years, did it sound a little different hearing the announcers referring to "patrons" instead of "fans," and "penalty areas" instead of "hazards"? Or are you still adjusting to seeing players putt with the pin "in" the hole? Were you surprised when no penalty was assessed for knocking the ball off the tee during a practice swing? In church we like to say that our message is timeless but our methodology is always changing. Churches must exercise patience as our "patrons" adjust to our evolving nomenclature and a rapidly changing culture.

9. *Treasure and maximize diversity.* At Augusta National, no two holes are identical. At many golf courses, the trademark characteristic might be big greens or postage stamp greens, lots of undulation or no undulation, elevated greens or elevated tee boxes. At Augusta National, however, the rich diversity of landscape, elevation, and undulation is a part of the appeal. Churches often struggle when navigating diversity, but healthy congregations perceive diversity as a strength: they find ways to leverage their diversity for missional purposes.

10. *Everyone loves a good redemption story.* In 2019 a previous champion who had fallen to the wayside due to injuries and poor personal decisions won the Masters. Through hard work he rebuilt his swing and his game, and is in the process of rebuilding his reputation. Among many other things, church is a place of spiritual redemption, a place where the prodigal is welcomed home, a place where grace covers a multitude of sins, a place where we celebrate recovery, and a place where all stand on level ground before the cross.

Augusta National Golf Club is not a religious place, but in its leaders' quest for excellence in facilities and engagement with their patrons, there are a few things we as the church can learn from them.

Communicate, Communicate, Communicate
Joel Snider

Pastors and other ministers want to know the best practices of a healthy church. Here's one: healthy churches communicate well, recognizing that it is almost impossible to communicate too much.

This practice sounds simple, doesn't it? But if it's so simple, why don't more congregations do it well? One reason is that they fail to see communication is more than making announcements or designing a Facebook page. In fact, communication is more than any one task. It is a core *process* with many, related components. The full process includes:

• *Quality of decisions:* A good communication process begins before there is anything to announce. This fact is particularly true when communication includes information about a change or something new. Church initiatives and changes almost always derive from a decision. Quality decisions include as many people as possible in the development stage. They are collaborative. The more individuals who are included in the development of the decision, the more people who are involved in the creation of the information itself.

Whether it is a new ministry, a change in an existing schedule, or a policy revision, invite people to work with church leaders. By doing so, you also enlist a wider group of informed advocates who can speak for the decision and answer questions from people you might never encounter. Participant buy-in is some of the most effective communication possible.

• *Quantity of messages:* Communication specialists estimate that it takes telling a message 16 times for the information to spread throughout an organization. The number may seem like overkill, but it rarely is. The larger your church, the more you should consider 16 times as a bare minimum.

Today, people get their news from a variety of sources: Twitter, TV, websites, etc. In the same way, church members get their information about congregational life in many ways. Therefore, effective church communication is *multi-channel*: Facebook page, twitter, newsletter, group texts, website, and targeting small group leaders who can help disseminate information. Simply making 16 announcements on Sunday morning will not get the message to everyone. By increasing the number of communication channels, you improve the likelihood of reaching more people.

A corollary of this principle is the need for appropriate lead time to get information spread throughout a congregation. It's difficult to communicate important matters 16 times in a week. If you have information vital to a decision, a new ministry, or a schedule change, it's better to delay a target date in order to communicate thoroughly than to abbreviate communication in order to meet a deadline. Start early enough to give your message time to permeate the church family.

• *Clear and accurate information:* Accurate facts and clear information are basic components of healthy communication. The more channels you use to disseminate information, the harder it is to keep facts accurate across them all. One person may be responsible for posting an event to Facebook, while another develops the newsletter. A third sends out an email blast. We increase the chance for factual mistakes every time we add a person to the list of those responsible for getting the word out.

The process of checking and rechecking times and locations is as mundane as it is important. Facts must be accurate. Changing the time of a meeting or event may not seem like a significant issue to you, but it may be to individuals who are embarrassed that they arrived late because they received inaccurate communication.

• *Consistent practices:* The next component of healthy communication is the alignment of what we do and what we say. If you don't see this effort as communication, consider an incident involving my mother-in-law years ago. She attended a church meeting where the members voted to spend money on resurfacing the parking lot. When she left the meeting, she realized the parking lot had already been resurfaced. You may think this is not a communication problem, but the message she "heard" was that the congregation's decision didn't matter.

Unequally applied policies, procedures that are ignored, and information provided to a few—all carry damaging, unspoken messages that undermine relationships and trust.

All of these components are parts of the same process. They are interrelated and require constant coordination. Staff meetings and calendar checks bore most ministers. I can't imagine any person who felt the call to ministry could have anticipated spending hours each week in such dull and ordinary tasks. There is a way, however, to view attention to these components of the communication process as a higher calling. Try seeing them as a part of congregational care. Every time you practice effective communication, you are safeguarding the congregation from self-inflicted injuries and potential conflict.

If these tasks seem too simple to be vital, read in Part 2 how ignoring pieces of the communication process leads to avoidable problems in a congregation. You will also see how paying attention to a healthy communication process is easier than repairing the problems of failing to do so.

PART 4
Trusted Leadership

A healthy church has trusted leadership—both clergy and lay. A congregation that deeply trusts its leaders can face any adaptive challenge, respond with enthusiasm to any new call, and work faithfully through any conflict that may arise. Encouraging words and actions and clear communication by leaders embolden the congregation to step out in faith.

Trusted Leadership Begins Here

Bill Owen

Today's church faces great uncertainty and risk. To be alive and well calls for trusted leadership. Imagine two lists: One contains the qualities a pastor should have. Another includes the attributes most pastors would say they wouldn't choose to lead the church today. What might we include when it comes to "must haves?"

• dynamic communicator
• people person
• task-oriented
• effective fundraiser
• inspiring team leader
• vision-caster
• humble servant

And we could go on. I'll leave it to you to think about those qualities we'd prefer to set aside. Could it be that one term could find itself not just in, but even atop both lists? If so, it might be "vulnerability."

In her book, *Daring Greatly: How the Courage to Be Vulnerable Transforms the Way We Live, Love, Parent, and Lead*, Brené Brown takes us to Teddy Roosevelt in 1910:

> It is not the critic who counts; not the man who points out how the strong man stumbles, or where the doer of deeds could have done them better. The credit belongs to the man who is actually in the arena, whose face is marred by dust and sweat and blood; who strives valiantly; who errs; who comes short again and again, because there is no effort without error and shortcoming; but who does actually strive to do the deeds; who knows great enthusiasms, the great devotions; who spends himself in a worthy cause; who at the best knows in the end the triumph of high achievement, and who at the worst, if he fails, at least fails while daring greatly.

In the introduction Brown riffs on Roosevelt's words, which she says perfectly capture why we find being vulnerable such a hard thing to do:

> When we spend our lives waiting until we're perfect or bulletproof before we walk into the arena, we ultimately sacrifice relationships and opportunities that may not be recoverable, we squander our precious time, and we turn our backs on our gifts, those unique contributions that only we can make. *Perfect* and *bulletproof* are seductive, but they don't exist in the human experience.

163

Maybe you recognize yourself here. As a minister, too often I expended energy covering up inadequacies, hiding limitations, presenting a false façade. I realize that effort was built on an assumption that I had to be the smartest one in the room.

When a leader shuns such vulnerability, he or she tries to do everything alone. Executive leadership coach Lolly Daskal writes:

> We all know the mythology of the lone wolf leader—the one who has all the answers, who never compromises, who doesn't trust anyone else. In the real world, though, the best leaders know when to ask for help and make use of wise counsel. They know they can't accomplish everything on their own and work instead to find the support system that will help them become the best leader they can be.

I'm convinced that trusted leadership begins here. Leading with vulnerability takes tremendous courage. Here's what it may look like:

1. *Trusted leadership asks questions rather than simply giving answers.* Educators and psychologists agree that people who ask good questions are much more likely to be intelligent and innovative than those who always have answers. Always having "the answer" is often nothing more than a cover for low self-esteem, a fear of vulnerability, and a need to dominate a conversation. Remember Jesus as a little boy sitting among the teachers, "listening" and "asking questions." As Jesus did, so must we.

2. *Trusted leadership builds strong, engaged teams.* Leaders who present themselves as always having "the answers" close themselves off to others. None of us, in recognizing our vulnerability, should pretend we are able to "go it alone." When we ask others, "Can you help me with this? What are your thoughts on this issue? Are you willing to work on this together with me?" we are expressing our vulnerabilities in a courageous and positive way that opens the door to curiosity and engagement. Trusted leadership builds strong, innovative teams by listening and asking more questions.

3. *Trusted leadership fosters a culture of healthy and constructive feedback.* It takes great courage to invite discerning feedback. However, pastors (including ministry staff) do not always appreciate criticism—however gentle, appropriate, and constructive it may be. In fact, I often observe that anyone who offers feedback is labeled a troublemaker and then marginalized. Trusted leaders don't insulate themselves with only "yes people," counting on them to tell them what they want to hear.

The Bible is filled with examples of people of little or no particular status giving honest feedback to leaders. Think of Nathan and David, the Old Testament prophets and political leaders of Judah, and Paul and Peter at Antioch.

One way to build such a high-trust culture is to have a group come alongside the pastor and staff on a regular basis. One solution might be to invite discerning members to form an advisory group (whether formal or informal) that would meet regularly to give feedback about what is being overemphasized and what is being neglected in terms of the church's ethos or culture.

Whatever the approach, every pastor would do well to consider who speaks truth and to decide if they are willing to listen with humility and to ask questions that broaden perspective and engage others.

It could be that not only your effectiveness as a leader depends upon such vulnerability, but also the church's future.

A Guide to Building High-trust Leadership

Bill Wilson

Some of the best days I have known in ministry have revolved around high-functioning staff friendships and relationships. Seeing plans come together, an organization take off, or a worship experience exceed expectations is meaningful beyond words.

Some of the hardest days in my life have revolved around low-trust staff members and relationships that soured or became conflicted or were broken. Seeing the worst part of a person who is also a fellow staff member is haunting. I suspect that every minister I know can affirm those two statements.

Having a church staff that functions in a healthy way is not easy. Nearly all the conflict calls we receive at the Center for Healthy Churches deal in some way with staff members. The variations on the theme of staff conflict take many forms. Sometimes the conflict is between staff members, and other times between staff and laity. Some congregations are abrasive toward their staff, and some staff members are abrasive toward their congregation. Whatever their form, staff issues nearly always figure in the mix of a conflict call.

In my conversations with many clergy, the primary source of concern and frustration with ministry is something related to staff. Many pastors worry about their staff culture and fear that it is undermining the ministry of the church. It never fails: when clergy get together and talk about the hardest parts of their ministry, their staff situation is at or near the top of the list.

There is no magic cure to this perennial issue, of course. While there are best practices and habits that can create a healthier culture, there is no magic pill or Bible verse or staff model that will solve all our issues. Staff members are flawed, sinful, incomplete human beings. That fact means we will always find ourselves in some sort of stressful situation when they are involved. Perhaps it helps us understand the pervasiveness of our issues when we realize that Jesus faced many of the same dynamics with his disciples.

The best help I have found is the ability to reframe the primary issue into one of trust. Building a high-trust culture is at the heart of a healthy church and its staff. Low-trust cultures cripple churches or organizations and doom them to perpetual high anxiety and conflict.

I've lived in both, and the joy of a high-trust staff culture is exhilarating. The ability to follow your calling without fear is invigorating. I hope you have had the joy of that experience.

Low-trust cultures breed insecurity, bitterness, and frustration. Nothing is taken at face value, and motives are constantly questioned or assigned. Sadly, for many clergy, this is the norm for their experience in churches. It is often cited as the single most influential factor in someone's decision to leave vocational ministry.

Building trust is more than reading books or echoing proper rhetoric. Being able to act in a trustworthy manner is at the heart of those staffs that work together collaboratively and humbly. In this arena, as in most, we act our way toward a healthy future first. Save all the talk; show your convictions by how you live.

I like this list that Stephen M.R. Covey, in *The SPEED of Trust: The One Thing That Changes Everything*, has put together of behaviors that can positively impact a leadership team if practiced diligently:

- Talk straight.
- Demonstrate respect.
- Create transparency.
- Right wrongs.
- Show loyalty.
- Deliver results.
- Get better.
- Confront reality.
- Clarify expectations.
- Practice accountability.
- Listen first.
- Keep commitments.
- Extend trust.

Each of these behaviors is a critical contributing factor to building high-trust cultures. Each must be practiced in moderation, for too much or too little is toxic. I hope your staff and congregational leaders have an ongoing conversation around the issue of trust. If not, please start one. Doing so will inevitably increase your ability to work together and enhance your church's impact and influence.

If you can trust the leadership of your church or organization, amazing things can happen. If not, then you will find yourself frustrated and discouraged. Once you name and frame the issue, there are ways to build trust and recover the joy Christ intends his people to know. Might it be so for your leaders, your staff, and your congregation.

What Does Real Leadership Look Like?

Bill Wilson

One year I had the privilege of teaching a week-long Doctor of Ministry seminar in a seminary to some very bright and thoughtful students. In that seminar we focused on leadership that is adaptive, visionary, innovative, and entrepreneurial. We read some fine books on the subject, and each student came to class having interviewed a leader in their life circle who embodied such traits. We also added a field trip to visit additional leaders, while also conducting live and online interviews. It was a refreshing and invigorating week of learning for me.

As a way of summarizing, each student created a substantial reflection paper on the topic and summarized his or her insights into the topic and how those might translate to the student's unique ministry context. The students' wisdom was profound, and I found myself learning from them and their reflections.

Some of the most helpful thoughts had to do with what makes a leader truly effective and Christlike in the current leadership climate that ministers and other leaders find themselves. In summary, here are some of our thoughts:

- Effective leadership is much less about knowledge and *much more about relationships.* We agreed that there is an abundance of people in leadership who know many facts, have read many books, and can describe accurately many theories but who fail miserably as leaders. One of the things that most often distinguishes effective leaders is their ability to be fully present with others and to care unselfishly and deeply for others.

- *Humility, or a serving spirit,* is foundational to the task of ministry. From the corporate world we heard a similar refrain about how effective leaders are not primarily interested in self-promotion. We noted that the people who do the finest and most Christlike work as leaders are humble and self-effacing. We cited many instances of deflecting praise or sharing credit. Pride, in all its manifestations, is at the heart of most of our leadership flaws.

- Effective leaders are always *curious and learning.* Paired with humility, curiosity creates an appetite for learning from others and seeing others in our field as sources of knowledge rather than competitors. We noted how our best leaders tend to be nondefensive and see those who disagree with them as an asset and not a liability. One person noted: "I learn much more from my loyal opposition than I have ever learned from those who always agree with me. They keep me honest, and as aggravating as they might be, I need them."

- The finest leaders *assume the best about others.* Many examples emerged from both ends of this spectrum. Some leaders see hidden agendas everywhere and assign motives to nearly everyone. They demonize their opposition and create rivalries and win-lose scenarios. Meanwhile, our best leaders practice an abundance mentality that expects excellence from others and presumes the best from those in their church or organization. They create a culture of high-trust goodwill rather than a culture of doubt and suspicion.

- Ministry leaders who make a difference *start internally and work toward the external.* They are disciples who practice their faith when no one is watching. They order their private and personal lives in such a way that the gap between word and deed is constantly shrinking. Their integrity starts with their family, their friendships, their habits, and their spiritual disciplines. False leaders start with external appearances and give token attention to internal transformation.

- Leadership that *honors the ways of Jesus* is increasingly difficult. Humility and service are definitely not in vogue in most ministry settings today. We are taking our cues from culture and being conformed to an image that violates our core calling to be transformative servants.

- *Spiritual and emotional intelligence (SQ and EQ)* need to be our primary metrics for measuring and assessing Christian leaders. This means cultivating the vertical (spiritual) and horizontal (relational) dimensions of ourselves and allowing the intellectual and technical skills to follow in a supportive fashion. Much of our hiring, training, and education reward the opposite.

- Effective leadership in the church and all its organizations and institutions is only possible with great *humility, confession, prayer, and healthy fear.* Healthy dependence upon God is too often confused with weakness or a lack of strength. Instead, when we are weak, we are strong in the power of the One who calls us.

I came away from the seminar grateful to be a student learning from these students. I am grateful for their humility and their openness to God's leadership in their lives and vocations. May their tribe increase, and soon, for the church today desperately needs them.

The Essential Skill for a 21ˢᵗ-century Pastor

Bill Wilson

Increasingly I focus my time and attention on discerning what is the primary leadership skill needed among pastors for this season of the Protestant church in America. While it is dangerous to paint with too broad a brush, it appears to me that pastors of established churches (as opposed to church plants) that are not mega-churches face a similar scenario: Their churches are almost inevitably in decline. This is especially true if they compare their growth/decline to the growth/decline of the community around them. Thus, the essential skill set needed as a leader can be described as that of a turnaround leader.

Unfortunately, training as a turnaround specialist is a relatively unexplored concept in theological training, and very few ministers enter the ministry with those talents cultivated and honed. Most of us have had to learn on the job, as the season of church growth has given way to widespread decline.

There is, however, a growing body of work available related to turnaround skills in the corporate arena, and we can learn a great deal from them as we navigate these uncharted waters. Translating ideas from one world to another is always risky, but there is merit to understanding how others have stopped the decline of an organization and brought fresh vitality, energy, and direction to people who thought their future was bleak.

Scan the Internet for articles about the psychology of turnaround leadership, and be prepared for a lengthy reading session. After perusing dozens of them, what emerges for me are some core principles that seem to have relevance for ministers in churches facing decline and longing for turnaround leadership. For example,

* *Turnaround pastors provide vision and passion.* Declining congregations often have lost sight of their primary reason(s) for being and are dejected, dispirited, and depressed. A turnaround pastor sees something in them and in their setting and their DNA that, if properly nurtured, can become the fire that generates energy and passion for the future. Jesus saw something in his disciples and others he encountered that others simply could not see. He looked beyond their failure (Peter) and their liabilities (tax collectors) and invited them to imagine a future that was more than they could fathom or imagine. The ability to see what others cannot see is a key trait of a turnaround leader.

* *Turnaround pastors bring ways of creating dialogue, respect, and collaboration.* When congregations are in a season of decline, the congregational culture begins to descend into a season marked by secrecy, scapegoating, isolation, turf-protection, and passivity. Staff members and key leaders desperately need a catalytic leader who can make the covert overt and bring to life a culture where conversation and dialogue are normative. Fostering respect and a willingness to genuinely collaborate is one of the most essential

tasks a turnaround leader must cultivate. Finding scriptural support for speaking truth to one another and building a team that values diversity is actually fairly easy. It was the way Jesus assembled his discipleship team, and the way the early church was able to leverage the skills of a disparate band of followers into the greatest missionary force the world has ever seen.

• *Turnaround pastors are not afraid to engage and manage conflict.* Normalizing conflict as an inevitable and necessary part of being a high-functioning team (both lay and clergy) is a key ingredient in any turnaround. Inviting honesty that is couched in respect and a shared commitment to live in community requires a leader who can manage his or her own emotions and remain calm in the midst of the anxiety of others. The most effective turnaround pastors I know have learned to lean into conflict and see it as a friend when it is used to move a congregation closer to the dream God has for them. See how Jesus reacted in John 6 when his followers grew disenchanted with his trajectory and began to question him.

• *Turnaround pastors exude and live out of a spirit of confidence.* This confidence is rooted in their conviction that God is going to provide for and guide the church that humbles itself and submits to divine guidance. This confidence is not in the human skills of the pastor, but in the Spirit that inspires and sustains the people of God on our best days.

Turnaround ministry is now the norm for the vast majority of American clergy. It is rooted in our belief that God has more in store for the church than we can see or imagine. It requires a diligent retraining for most of us, and a willingness to speak the truth to a congregation in as loving a way as possible. When our efforts and the guidance of the Holy Spirit are joined together to bring the reign of God to bear upon our city or community, amazing things can happen.

What Future Leaders Do Differently

Bob Dale

We live and lead in a dark, chaotic world. Leaders see disruptive forces everywhere. Church leaders feel overwhelmed by the instability of their ministry fields. The U.S. military describes a "VUCA" (volatile, uncertain, complex, and ambiguous) environment, challenging their global planning and leadership efforts. In our shifting contexts, let's explore what future leaders do differently and how these traits can apply to church leaders.

• *Future leaders look long and then back-cast.*
 Faith-full leaders always look beyond their present moment to discern what God is doing just over the horizon. Amid instability, future leaders expand their time horizons, look further forward, peer carefully through "a glass darkly," and ask "longer" questions: What does God have next for us? What does God have for us after whatever is next?

In more stable eras, leaders found where they were and then forecasted from here to there. This step-by-step sequence of progress used fixed maps. During implementation, these maps had no way to adjust when their targets moved. I can't count the number of half-completed and finally abandoned strategic plan notebooks I've seen in pastors' offices.

Future leaders plan in GPS style. We target goals, move, and recalibrate as we learn. I met Edward Lindaman, key leader of the Apollo lunar mission and noted Presbyterian layman, after the Apollo program was concluded. When asked how the Apollo project leaders planned, Lindaman answered, "First, we found the moon." We all laughed at the obvious nature of that beginning. "Then, we back-casted from the moon to where we were." They identified stations between the earth and the moon, and then moved ahead by trial and success. The universe became the Apollo team's laboratory. They discovered new pathways and recalculated constantly. Foresight is fueled by insight and hindsight.

Finding the moon and then back-casting calls for constant learning when you're dealing with two moving targets. Do you suppose that's part of what Jesus meant when he called us disciples, lifelong learners who are always rookies in our world? Are you ready to take longer looks at God's actions in the world and then to back-cast in order to move in his directions?

• *Future leaders cultivate "edge" change.*
 Cultures and social systems are most dynamic and changeable on their edges. Think about the lively changes we see where seas meet shores, where neighborhoods connect (or collide), and when families interact at funerals. Margins are permeable, "yeasty" places. Edges invite creativity and new directions.

In fast-moving contexts, congregational leaders steward edges in flexible ways. Edge leaders are bi-focal. We stand on edges and look back at the centers of our faith communities with more objectivity. Then, from the edges, we turn and look over horizons to see what's ahead. Finally, we put those two "from the balcony" perspectives together for a clearer-eyed view of where we are now and where we're going next.

Edges are high-potential ministry arenas with lots of possibility. But, edges aren't easy settings for leaders. On emerging edges, there's a lot that leaders don't know. We feel outdated and outgunned. We travel light and shed outmoded practices quickly. We need partners who are strong where we aren't. We find safe places "to be" while we discern, at God's pace, what "to do." We create practice spaces to try new approaches on small scales and then, with fresh experiences, we try again. So, we ask, listen, pray, and learn as we move ahead. We live on the edge in a literal sense.

• *Future leaders tell "face" stories.*

The year 2008 was considered a "watershed" by futurists. On the brink of a dangerous depression, we elected America's first minority race president. But, most dramatically, a new worldwide connectivity gelled. For the first time, digital connectivity became possible for everyone. This technological breakthrough challenged future leaders to wed stories with electronics. Print, prose, and pictures now merge with pixels.

Think about the "3Ms" of future communication: message, mastery, and media.

With the future in mind, leaders sharpen and "story-ize" their message. Future leaders put faces on goals and needs to make their message more personal, more concrete, and more immediate. They know that stories are 22 times more apt to be remembered than simple facts. Then, future leaders master all the media at their disposal. Finally, future leaders match their available communication media options to their audiences. Leaders help their audiences hear comfortably and respond confidently.

From a practical viewpoint, since media is a major generational divide, future leaders will develop multigenerational staff teams. Then, every communication medium will be native to someone on the team.

In summary, to become a discerning and effective future leader, think longer horizons, promising edges, and eager faces. Ready? Go!

Pastor, Please Stop

Bill Owen

Becoming an effective, emotionally intelligent pastor requires more than delivering a good sermon, making timely hospital visits, and scheduling committee meetings. Outstanding pastors lead from their heart and their head. Their passions and enthusiasm set a charge into their organizations. But this is not easy.

In my early years of ministry I was so clever. I thought I could change the world. But as the years added up and I moved into the dog days of tenure, I faced many challenges: declining attendance, a shrinking volunteer pool, scarcity of leadership, and insufficient funding. Self-doubt, fear, and uncertainty nipped at my heels, chasing me like a hungry hound. Some days I wanted to throw up my hands in desperation.

This scenario happens to most all pastors. And when it does, I would advise them to STOP doing these five things:

1. *STOP focusing on your weaknesses.* It can keep you feeling inadequate and unsure of yourself. Left unchallenged, your "inner critic" will stifle self-esteem and hamper your effectiveness as a pastor leader. This voice must be countered. Choose a self-assessment tool such as the Clifton Strengthfinder to identify your positive qualities. Balance your negative thoughts with positive ones. Keep a list of your accomplishments throughout the year, and when you're feeling unsure of yourself, remember what you have already achieved. Focus on your strengths.

2. *STOP trying to be perfect.* You don't need to know everything when you start something new (or ever, really). You may be telling yourself, "If I don't know everything, then I know nothing. If it's not absolutely perfect, it's completely worthless. If I'm not at the top of my game, then I'm totally incompetent." Stop it. "I don't know, but I'll get back to you" is a perfectly appropriate response. You don't have to know the answer to every question. There is no more powerful attribute than the ability to be genuinely honest about your weaknesses or mistakes. Humility and graciousness are immensely attractive and inspiring in a leader. Nothing inspires trust in another human like vulnerability. Set your new standard as "growing" rather than perfect. Perfection is a mirage, so stop holding yourself hostage. Tell yourself, "I'm not failing; I'm growing!"

3. *STOP being your own worst enemy.* Don't waste time and energy chewing on mistakes. When professional athletes lose the big game, they review it, learn what they can do better, and get ready for the next one. Achievements and accolades are great, but keep in mind that your true value comes from within. Stay focused on the value that you bring to the table. Stop comparing yourself to other pastors or churches. Celebrate your strengths.

4. *STOP procrastinating.* Take action. Move forward. Quit thinking about what you know you have to do: Just do it. Often you feel stress because you freeze in panic. Putting things on hold only increases your feelings of incompetence. Deal with issues head on. Check items off your to-do list. Taking the first steps will allow you to truly own what you are capable of doing well.

5. *STOP going it alone.* It's okay to ask for help. Call someone in from the outside to speak into your context. At the Center for Healthy Churches we come alongside congregations and pastors to do just that. Surround yourself with people who recognize your talents and can remind you of them when you forget. Start or join a group of peers among whom you may share your passions, dreams, and challenges. Typically, there is no one harder on you than yourself, so you need friends and family to give you confidence, especially when you don't feel like you deserve it.

In my early years I was clever, so I wanted to change the world. Today I am wise(r), so I am changing myself.

Curbing an Epidemic

Bill Wilson

There is a consistent theme in the conversations I have with clergy and laity alike about what frustrates or challenges them most. Without a doubt, it is staff. Every pastor's gathering in which we ask for issues that need attention inevitably leads to a conversation about some aspect of staff. Nearly every lay person who calls ends up needing help with a staff situation.

This epidemic of conflict and frustration holds true regardless of denominational affiliation, theological orientation, worship style, size, location, etc. I recently conversed with a leadership team from a very large church (staff in the dozens), and their primary concern was staff communication/conflict. Later that week the pastor of a small church pulled me aside at a meeting to voice concern about an issue with his only other staff member—who was part time—and his wife!

Dozens of books, workshops, coaching, degree programs, and the like are devoted to this specific arena of congregational life. Why, then, is staffing the part of congregational life that seems to be chronically ill?

As with any complex issue, there are no simple answers. Flawed human beings attempting to do divine work in an increasingly secular culture with limited resources is a start.

Congregational models that seem imported from another era without adapting to a changing landscape don't help. Leadership styles copied from corporate culture rather than built upon spiritual values don't help. Too often our staff cultures mirror the disharmony and dysfunction of our culture rather than transform it with a vibrant alternative. So, where do we start with a healthy alternative for congregational staff?

At the Center for Healthy Churches we base our conversations in this realm on our conviction that healthy congregations/staffs/Christians engage in at least four consistent practices. We call them the "four C's":

1. They constantly *clarify* identity and mission.
2, They manage *conflict* in a proactive and redemptive fashion.
3. They *communicate* clearly, regularly, and honestly.
4. They build authentic *community* intentionally.

When staff members practice these four habits, they produce higher levels of satisfaction, effectiveness, and genuine leadership. When they fail to pay attention to any of the four, dysfunction is the result.

By the way, the first of the four C's is the most indispensable. It is the most internal and difficult to observe and quantify and the easiest to skip. We are tempted to assume it is self-evident, but it is also the one most frequently missing. Without it, you invite confusion and frustration into your own life, the life of your staff, and the life of your congregation.

Clarity of mission and vision for a staff member starts with a sense of personal and individual divine call. Your primary motive for ministry matters. If working at a church is simply a job, a way to make money, a way to work out your unmet needs, a way to impress your grandmother, or anything other than your response to God's personal and profound call upon your life, then you will find ministry to be a source of constant frustration.

Even then, the life of a divinely called minister is by definition a challenging journey to bring hope and life into the hard and difficult places of life. Along with bringing deep joy and satisfaction, it will cause you to doubt your sanity, your calling, and your faith. Without clarity around one's personal call, any minister is a candidate for a host of missteps. The same is true for a staff team.

Being clear about why you are on the journey, where your congregation is headed, and what the objective of your congregation actually is will prove indispensable. When the mission/vision is fuzzy or unfocused, staff discord is imminent. When the mission/vision is lacking, others will supply it, and it will usually be self-serving rather than Kingdom-serving. When the mission/vision is incongruent with a church's DNA or the biblical witness, then conflict will erupt.

Before a staff needs to worry about programs or strategies or creative ideas for being relevant, they need to get clear about the deeper question of clarity of purpose. Healthy staffs spend concentrated and regular time clarifying not only the broad mission of the church, but also the specific call of their church in their time and place of service. While it is easy to trot out the Great Commandments and Great Commission, what we are talking about is a deeper understanding and articulation of what those mean in your zip code.

Healthy staffs quickly learn that such conversations must include the congregation if they are to be sustainable and truly shared. Once substantial clarity is reached in the larger community, then the staff members assume their roles and goals based upon this shared vision of the future.

Let's start with this antidote for the epidemic of staff conflict: Clarify your mission and vision.

7 Ways to Invest in Your Staff Culture

Phill Martin

"Culture eats strategy for breakfast." I am not sure where I first heard this phrase, but I have certainly come to appreciate its validity when it comes to congregations. Most sources attribute the quote to the late business management guru Peter Drucker, who had a significant influence on business leadership and also greatly impacted non-profit management.

Why is this quote important to congregations? Most congregational experts agree that churches must have a clear and current vision. This vision should be based on the unique context of the community and the strength of the individual church. Vision must drive strategy. It is no longer enough to follow the prescribed denominational model or emulate the ministry of a well-known successful congregation or pastoral leader. Mirroring another strategy most likely will not work in a different context.

So, when a congregation invests time and money in the process to create a great new or refreshed vision, with a clear strategy to implement the vision, it is critical that the cultures of both staff and lay leadership not sabotage the strategy. The investment to build and keep a strong positive culture can be major, and the rewards measured in the success of the well-executed strategy are worth the investment.

Although a typical congregation invests 44–55 percent of its operating budget for staff expense, the additional cost in time and money to build and maintain a positive culture is worth the investment. Consider these seven ways to invest:

1. *Invest in understanding the strength of the individual team member and collective strength of the team.* CliftonStrengths is a great tool to name the unique gifts of each member and then see how combined the team strengths make for a strong culture. Spiritual gift assessments are also helpful in understanding team members' gifts, and both help staff have common language to understand each other better.

2. *Invest in honest feedback.* Using 360-degree tools and surveys can be a great way to measure feedback that will help direct and build culture. These tools help team members understand perceptions and identify blind spots. This knowledge is helpful in creating healthy individual development strategy.

3. *Invest in developing team members.* Each member of your team needs to be a lifelong learner stretching to improve skills and understanding. Emotional health balanced with spiritual well-being and physical wellness help a team member to bring positive support to the whole.

4. *Invest in community.* Social events, playing together, and investing in the lives of each team member can build and sustain a culture. When you pray for and care about the human side of teammates, the desire for the team to succeed grows.

5. *Invest in trust.* Help the team understand what builds trust and what tears down trust. Teams who have ongoing conversations about trust, and put in place ways to recover trust when it is broken, have a greater chance of success.

6. *Invest in team-building activities.* In addition to the work of building a community, find ways to build the collective competency of the team. Consider being a team that reads together. Use books to build a common language and expand ideas. Consider off-site events to allow focus and a change of pace. Enlist an outside facilitator to train and motivate. Reach out to other church leaders to provide new insight and lead spiritual growth for the team.

7. *Invest in establishing a staff covenant, and then review and renew it often.* A shared vision of what our mutual commitment to each other is helps to hold the space for trust, but covenant commitments require accountability. So be sure to know this investment could lead to the necessity for difficult conversations.

These seven investments are not a guarantee of the success of the strategy, but they will go a long way toward being sure that your culture is a resource to implementation rather than a cookie monster eating away at the strategy. Start with an honest conversation about culture. If you need an outside voice or assessment, the Center for Healthy Churches team is available to walk with you.

Holding Your Staff Accountable

Bill Wilson

Whenever I have an opportunity, I suggest that the starting point for bringing health and effectiveness to a church's ministerial staff is the critical work of clarifying mission, vision, and purpose in the congregation. That clarity then becomes the "north star" for every decision, every investment of resources, every staff position, every event that a congregation chooses to engage in. What comes next? May I suggest that accountability is essential for a healthy and functioning staff?

We find that many times congregational staff members operate in a bizarre congregational world devoid of healthy accountability. Without a thoughtful, rational system in place, evaluation and accountability disintegrate into personal opinion and judgments made without benefit of facts. Expectations are fuzzy. Ministers find themselves pushed and pulled by individual tastes and priorities. Congregational bullies show up and exercise inappropriate influence. Motives begin to be assigned. Facts take a distant backseat to innuendo and gossip.

Other times, congregations are victimized by clergy who seem to operate without rules or fail to practice rudimentary work habits. Clergy too often operate in silos, content to pitter-patter around their ministry corner without concern for the church as a whole. Clergy who are not held accountable make mistakes that no one calls them on, and thus fail to learn valuable lessons. Boundary violations are inevitable, as most church members are reticent to "call foul" on a man or woman of God. There must be a better way!

- *Accountability for clergy teams begins with healthy peer pressure.* Patrick Lencioni in *The Advantage* goes so far as to say that "peer-to-peer accountability is the primary and most effective source of accountability on the leadership team of a healthy organization." Rather than looking to the pastor or personnel committee as the primary source of top-down accountability, healthy ministerial teams hold each other accountable to common goals without fearing backlash or defensiveness. Such a culture is essential if a staff is going to truly function as a team, rather than independent contractors.

- *Peer-to-peer accountability requires high trust and a leader who is willing to confront difficult situations and hold people accountable.* Lencioni notes that no one will engage in peer-to-peer accountability if they sense that the team leader "balks when it is time to call someone on their behavior or performance." Such a truth raises an interesting irony. "The more comfortable a leader is in holding people on a team accountable, the less likely she/he is to be asked to do so."

 # good - safety (+/-)

180

I once came as pastor to a congregational staff that had never been given permission to disagree or hold one another accountable. Predictably, staff meetings were dreadful. Body language and attitudes said, "I'd rather be anywhere but here."

Our times together were perfunctory and subdued, with little genuine engagement and almost no give and take. Frustrated, I went to a trusted colleague and begged him to openly disagree with me about a proposal, just so we could show that we could have a vehement conversation and emerge with a better product.

At our next staff meeting, after I rolled out my latest marvelous idea, he simply responded, "I have a problem with this." You could have heard a pin drop, as the group braced for the inevitable sharp response. Instead, we engaged in honest and heated debate that produced several excellent upgrades to the original idea. Finally, we walked out laughing together and went to lunch. From that point forward, staff meetings and the staff culture gradually shifted toward more honest feedback and accountability. Staff meetings and retreats became times we anticipated as our opportunity to build deep fellowship and connect to our mission and vision.

At the heart of accountability is a deep motive that cares enough about someone to say the uncomfortable word. Lencioni says we only hold accountable the people we love: "To hold someone accountable is to care about them enough to risk having them blame you for pointing out the deficiencies." While we may think the kind and gracious thing is to let unwanted behavior slide, failure to hold someone accountable is ultimately an act of selfishness.

Far too often, clergy are ambushed by a dismissal that comes with no warning and no sense of having ever been confronted about their performance. There is nothing kind or loving about that.

• *Ministerial accountability includes distinguishing between metrics and behavior.* It is easy to note rises and falls in attendance or participation. It is more complex and profoundly more important to address concerns about behavior. The reason? "Behavior issues almost always precede or cause downturns in performance or results."

Healthy ministerial teams develop good practices around holding one another accountable. They spend time affirming all the ways each of them as individuals can help make the team better. Such "deposits" into our emotional bank accounts with one another make the inevitable "withdrawals" tolerable and even appreciated.

If you wish to inject health into your staff relationships, practice appropriate accountability.

Staffing for Survival

Bill Wilson

What is the most important staff position at your church? As a former pastor, I must declare that we cannot function without a pastor. But then what would we do without a music/worship leader? We cannot live without leadership for children or youth, can we? What about Christian formation? Outreach? Pastoral care? Missions? Administration? Singles? Recreation?

While all these traditional positions are obviously important, let me suggest another role that every healthy congregation with a viable future must pay close attention to. Whether it is a solitary assignment to one person or a front-burner focus for every staff position, the role of missional strategist is indispensable.

Don't like that title? How about Coordinator of Mission/Vision Implementation? Maybe Congregation-World Intersection Specialist? Minister of Mission (no S at the end of this title!). I like Passion Coordinator, though I suspect that might invite some misunderstanding. One more: Call Commander!

While these titles may be confusing or cumbersome, the task I am addressing is emerging as an essential ingredient in the congregational mix of the 21st century.

The era of staffing a church based solely on the attractional model of congregational life is drawing to a close. The attractional model, which has defined us for nearly 50 years, suggests that the main arena of ministry are programs offered at the site of the church.

Build it large, staff it fully, offer high-quality programs and events, and stand back waiting for the crowds to show up—and for years they did. Churches became synonymous with programs and facilities. Large numbers of people showed up at church on a regular schedule to consume an overflowing banquet of opportunities the staff served up for them. Staff members were professionals who led clearly defined pockets of church life (usually age groups) from a position of authority and expert knowledge. Often prone to overfunction, clergy were expected to be part entertainer, part concierge, part scholar, and part R&D coordinator.

Laity often were made to feel inferior ("Stand back, please don't touch . . . leave that to the professionals!"), and were relegated to showing up faithfully and providing funding for professional clergy to work their magic. One unintentional but nearly inevitable result was a critical spirit among church members that evaluated the hired pros based on that week's performance. Reduced to consumer status, lay members began to comparison shop and frequently found their pastor or specialty minister lacking. Much as with football coaches, congregational win-loss records (usually attendance and offerings) became the standard for judging success or failure of the ministers and the church.

While we were consumed with "build it and they will come" church life, something dramatic happened. The world stopped coming. Oh, I know enough of them still come to enable us to hold out hope that our methods still work. And there is at least one "growing" church in your community that seems to defy the trends, but much of that growth is transfer growth that chases after programming for the sake of children, youth, personal music tastes, or charismatic preaching. The actual percentage of the United States population that attends church regularly is a minority of the population, increasingly smaller in young adults, and may well be far smaller than the 40 percent that surveys suggest.

The logical conclusion is that, if they are not interested in coming to us, we must go to them. This is not to suggest that being an attractional church is no longer viable. I believe the vast majority of our churches will be engaged in excellent attractional models of ministry for many years to come. The opportunity we must seize immediately is to add to our attractional life the element of a missional imperative. Such an addition is a needed balance to our tendency to stay home and expect the world to come to us.

• Someone on your church staff (in addition to your pastor) needs to wake up every morning thinking about how to engage your church with your community and world.
• Someone must be charged with linking the individual gifts, talents, and passions of your congregation with the needs of the community you live in.
• Some group of laity needs to have as their primary task the movement of the church into the community with the good news.

Between them, staff and laity will begin to take seriously what it means to pray that God's kingdom will come to your neighborhood, as it is in heaven. If you do not pay attention to this, your church will die.

This sounds dramatic, but I believe it is true. Slowly, but inevitably, if you fail to practice the Great Commission in your zip code, you will cease to exist. Let those who have ears listen . . . and staff accordingly!

4 Traps for Clergy and Their New Congregation

Bill Wilson

In a recent conversation, a minister asked me what I thought are the major traps that most often snare ministers when they move to a new congregation. Great question! Healthy churches and ministers pay attention to potential trouble spots and act in a proactive way to avoid getting derailed early in the new relationship. Several come to mind:

1. *The trap of expectations:* Coming into a congregation as the new minister is a wonderful season of new beginnings and possibilities. People await you with great expectations. Often those expectations are exaggerated and grandiose. You are seen as the one who will reverse decades of decline, inspire apathetic congregants, make everyone happy at all times, and never disappoint. Sometimes the grandiosity is in the mind of the minister. You think this church is everything your last church was not. The grass looks so green on this side of the fence! Your own foibles and bad habits are overlooked in your infatuation with your new opportunity.

   Unrealistic expectations, wherever they originate, are a set-up. They lead us away from God's design for us and his church and trap us in impossible situations. You will never succeed as the messiah, and the congregation will soon expose its cracks and fissures and remind you that this really isn't heaven on earth. Talking about this and anticipating the inevitable disappointments is an essential component of a healthy relationship between minister and congregation. The humility that comes when we acknowledge that we are all earthen vessels and deeply flawed is a great place to begin this relationship.

2. *The trap of agenda:* Your arrival invites the congregation to imagine new possibilities. This is a wonderful and divine part of the opportunity. However, it is helpful to remember that all of us have agendas. Some are overt; others are quite covert. Simply put, some congregants will see your coming as an opportunity to advance a cause or seek a role that has been thwarted previously. Your arrival is a new day that will bring frustrated persons out of the woodwork. Others will assume they will have the same intimacy or insider status that they had with the previous person in your position. Some will have been deeply disappointed by your predecessor and will greet you with frosty indifference.

   Your job is to be aware. Avoid the trap of believing everything you hear. From search committee members to the most detached congregants, personal agendas abound. Watch with a degree of prayerful detachment those around you. Get up on a mental balcony in every meeting and during every conversation and ask yourself what is really going on. Constantly ask yourself: Why this? Why now? Your coming evokes a wide range of personal responses that you will be wise to take notice of in those early encounters.

3. *The trap of talking:* Since clergy are seemingly paid to speak, the usual pattern is that we do—profusely, often, and repeatedly. Watch out for the trap of verbosity. The entry into a new congregation calls for a season of diagnostic rather than prescriptive conversations. If your medical doctor walked into the exam room and immediately began a monologue about his or her ideas for your health, without ever asking for input from you, I hope you would jump up and leave the room. I'd offer the same counsel to a congregation and its minister.

Your role in the early days of your ministry is to have your ears wide open, your eyes wide open, and your heart wide open. There will be a time to speak the truth you bring to the situation, but initially your talking should consist of words of invitation to others. Ask many, many questions, especially around the themes of heritage and hopes.

4. *The trap of silence:* While listening is needed in your early days of service in a new place, after 100 days on the job, you had better have something to say! There are those who counsel a full year of observation before making any move toward acts of active leadership. The pace of our culture dictates a new reality, however. Your learning curve has been shortened and you must understand the trap that your silence as a leader, should it go too long, will be misinterpreted as your lack of ability to lead. Your first 100 days offer you a never-to-be-repeated opportunity to define yourself and establish some trajectories for your ministry. Pay attention to this time with careful and prayerful thought. In our coaching of new pastors, we encourage breaking down your first 100 days into 10-day blocks of time and becoming exceptionally deliberate about the proactive use of those days. These are days to emphasize relationships over tasks, so plan your time accordingly.

After 100 days, emerge from your time of study and observation with clear and compelling observations. The people need to hear from you. The rest of your first year will be a time to begin an extended congregational conversation that will shape the church's agenda for the near future. Use those days to engage people around "what if" questions. Invite them to dream with you and God about possibilities. Tell them what matters to you and what you love about them. Share with them a generous vision of the future and invite them to join you in creating that vision and making it a reality. Speak up!

Beware the traps and enjoy the ride. It really is a marvelous opportunity to start anew.

Leadership in Turbulent Times

David Hull

At Christmas in 2018, I gave and received a great book. Let me introduce it to you if you have not already found it. *Leadership in Turbulent Times* is the latest book by historian and leadership expert Doris Kearns Goodwin. She builds on her earlier books about Abraham Lincoln, Theodore Roosevelt, Franklin D. Roosevelt, and Lyndon Johnson to present this current book.

Instead of camping out in this miserable crisis for the rest of his life, Goodwin tells how that, instead, each man used the turbulent times of personal and political crisis to make him a better person and leader. Her book describes the early years of each man when he showed great promise for leadership in his community. A second section of the book depicts the season of crisis that forged the leader into greatness. In the final section Godwin shows how each man demonstrated a leadership trait that shaped the country and that can become a model for our leadership today.

As I read about each president, I was fascinated by his personal story of triumph on the other side of turbulence. I also learned much from the leadership lessons that each one taught as he made a great impact on the nation he served. According to Goodwin,

- Abraham Lincoln demonstrated "transformational leadership" as he "entered the presidency at the gravest moment in American history. His temperament and absolute determination helped win the war, save the union, and end slavery."
- Theodore Roosevelt exhibited "crisis leadership" as he "guided his countrymen through a long battle designed to restore fairness to America's social and economic life in the wake of the Industrial Revolution."
- Franklin D. Roosevelt portrayed "turnaround leadership" as he "delivered a sustained, reanimating energy to a nation suffering from the Great Depression and losing faith in democracy."
- Lyndon Johnson showed "visionary leadership" as he "gained office in a moment of national tragedy. His legislative mastery galvanized a domestic agenda that achieved more for civil rights than any leader since Lincoln."

There is a lesson here for churches that are trying to be healthy. Sometimes the greatest strength in leadership comes on the other side of turbulence. It was certainly the case in the lives of these four presidents. I see many churches struggling in turbulent waters today. Attendance is declining, financial resources are dwindling, buildings are aging, the culture seems to be ignoring the church, and the polarization of our politics makes unity in the church more difficult each day. By all measures, these are turbulent and difficult days to be leading churches. But the question is, "Will we let this turbulence make us bitter or better?"

I was moved by Goodwin's book that "tells the story of how they all met with dramatic reversals that disrupted their lives and threatened to shatter forever their ambitions. Nonetheless, they all emerged better fitted to confront the contours and dilemmas of their times." I pray that will be said of the church on the other side of our turbulent days!

How do we live through the turbulence of the church today so that we will one day be better fitted to "confront the contours and dilemmas" of our times? My reading about the presidents took my mind to a character in the Bible who faced his own turbulence.

The Apostle Paul called it his "thorn in the flesh." He prayed again and again for this trouble to be removed—but it remained. Finally, he realized that the turbulence of the thorn was helping him to lean on the power of God in his own weakness. It was at the intersection of his own weakness and God's power that Paul found strength beyond what he had ever known: "For when I am weak, then I am strong" (2 Cor. 12:7-10).

What if in these turbulent days of ministry in the church, we approached our thorn in the following ways?

- Instead of focusing on tweaking outdated programs, we get serious about prayer that seeks God's guidance into new forms of ministry.
- Instead of expecting declining numbers of clergy to solve the challenges of the turbulence, we all take responsibility for the ministry of the church.
- Instead of bemoaning the fact that our church budget is not what it once was, we dream about the possibilities of a reimagined budget that has been shaped by prayer and greater ministry engagement of all church members.
- Instead of spending funds we do not have to maintain buildings we do not need, we dream about how to be the best stewards by redeploying the assets we do have.
- Instead of believing that our best years are behind us as a church, we live with expectant hope that God's work through us in the future will be greater than what we have ever known.

These are turbulent days for the church. But they also may just be the very best days of preparation for something new that God wants to do tomorrow. How will the story be written for your church?

Necessary Leaders

Joel Snider

I have known dozens of churches well. Some I served; some were served by colleagues. Others were neighboring congregations. A few of these churches handled difficulties well. They took the initiative to deal with problems in the earliest stages. They set constructive boundaries and did not allow avoidable conflict to escalate.

Many of the churches I've known, however, avoided issues, simply hoping they would resolve themselves without pain or discomfort. People in these churches prayed that everyone would just get along, or they sacrificed a minister instead of addressing the underlying dynamics. This second group of churches watched members disengage from participation, or leave for other congregations as they grew wary and weary of growing problems.

I have no statistics or hard data to back up my conviction, but I have observed one crucial difference between the two kinds of congregations. I see one clear factor that separates them from each other. Healthy churches all have the necessary leaders who will make hard decisions in the right spirit. They have the leaders who will act in the best interest of the congregation, even when facing criticism. The other churches do not.

If I were a young minister, considering a call or appointment to a new congregation, a critical, human factor in my discernment process would include determining if the church has necessary leaders among its membership. If I still served a congregation, I would find ways to develop as many of these leaders as possible.

What are the characteristics of necessary congregational leaders?

- *Necessary leaders understand their proper role in the church.* We all use the expression "my church," but necessary leaders recognize that this statement reflects participation, not ownership. In multiple letters, the Apostle Paul tells us that Christ is the head of the church. Therefore, necessary leaders always remember that Christ has entrusted the church to them as human stewards of its mission and relationships. As stewards, they seek God's will and reflect the spirit of Christ in how they lead. Unhealthy leaders assert control over the congregation and its decisions, assuming whatever they want must be God's will for the church.

- *Necessary leaders function according to biblical standards.* A wise mentor once told me there is no difference between doing the wrong thing and doing the right thing the wrong way. In the kingdom of God, leaders are governed by the standards of Christ, not simple pragmatism. Necessary leaders practice principles such as speaking the truth in love (Eph. 4:15), handling disputes forthrightly (Matt. 18:15ff), and operating openly (1 John 1:5ff).

- *Necessary leaders have high emotional intelligence (EQ.)* Daniel Goleman reminds us that the greatest factor influencing effectiveness in any field is emotional intelligence. Necessary leaders possess the two major components of EQ: self-awareness and empathy. Self-awareness is vital because we humans can easily confuse our motives with God's will. Leaders with strong self-awareness can monitor their own motives, emotions, and reactions. Knowing themselves accurately, people with high EQ, consequently, can manage their own actions. They act and respond according to their principles instead of reacting emotionally. They also demonstrate empathy by keeping the good of the congregation in mind. Empathy allows them to read correctly the emotional climate in a crisis and to anticipate and appreciate the reactions of others.

- *Others recognize the integrity of necessary leaders.* Members trust necessary leaders because they have demonstrated that they act fairly, make wise decisions, and keep their word in a variety of settings. Time after time I have witnessed church members say, "I didn't agree with that action, but I trust the people who made it." Trustworthiness is more important than position or title. It is earned over long periods of time and after repeated instances of wisdom, transparency, and charity.

- *Necessary leaders don't bully, and they refuse to be bullied.* Edwin Friedmann says that most organizations act on the emotional level of their most immature participants. These are the people who threaten, demand, nag, whine, and manipulate—in other words, bully—to get their way. By their very nature, the leaders necessary to offsetting these dynamics neither use these tactics nor give in to them when they are used against them.

- *Necessary leaders act.* In moments of crisis or confusion, necessary leaders speak up, step forth, or make hard decisions. Based on their sense of stewardship and operating out of their understanding of biblical principles, they take responsibility and act.

If you were trying to discern who the necessary leaders are in your congregation, consider these questions:

- Whose opinion do people seek routinely, and why? Are these persons trusted or merely opinionated?
- In a recent conflict and how it was addressed, which laypersons were involved and how did they function? Who was mature and principled?
- When something unpopular was accomplished or addressed, who did the congregation trust in the decision-making process?
- Who can be trusted not to act on self-interest alone?
- Who consistently acts on obvious, Christian principles?
- Who would you say has genuine spiritual maturity?

These questions could be asked in an interview with a committee designated by the church to secure a new minister. Or, they could be used to create a list of potential necessary leaders for further development.

I believe there is no more important task for a minister than to recognize and cultivate a culture of necessary leaders. Sooner or later, the health and direction of your congregation will depend on them.

Ministry in the Meantime and Mean Time

Guy Sayles

Ministry happens in the "meantime" and in the "mean time." The meantime is a season of sometimes bewildering change and troubling transitions. It's an interval between a past we know well and a future that isn't yet clear, and between a familiar way of doing things and an emerging way of doing them. One indication of this interval is a leadership gap that exists in many churches: An older generation of experienced leaders is passing from the scene, and younger generations have not yet developed the skills for, or shouldered the responsibilities of, constructive congregational leadership. We live and serve in the tension between what has been and what will be, and this meantime calls for discernment, perseverance, and courage.

Meantime also refers to the climate in which ministry happens these days: It's a "mean" time. The tone of public debate is coarsening, and verbal violence is increasing. It's common to reduce complex issues to bumper-sticker or tweet-sized slogans aimed at the single goal of winning an argument, and it's uncommon to engage in thoughtful listening and speaking with the purpose of mutual understanding. Concern for the common good is eroding. Political polarization and partisan wrangling are more intense than they have been since the late 1960s and early 1970s.

These factors adversely affect ministry. Conversations about a church's challenges and opportunities too frequently reflect the stridency of public debate. Add to the corrosive tone of public debate other factors that make this a mean time:

- Decades of *worship wars* have splintered some churches into factions organized around differences in musical taste, matters of style, and differing opinions about what attracts "young people." Many congregations are a coalition of "churches within a church." In some places, the coalition is strong and based on a sense of common mission; but, in others, it's fragile and reflects unresolved conflict. In churches where the coalition is fragile, ministry is difficult.

- Uncertainty over the value of *"institutional religion"* continues to grow. Responding to people's hunger for spirituality and recognizing their caution about institutions is a Catch-22 for ministry leaders. How do we place legitimate focus on the structures and processes that make it possible for a church to serve people's genuine needs without overfocusing on institutional imperatives?

- Related to uncertainty over the value of institutions is confusion about *the relationship between tradition and innovation.* There's a difference between healthy tradition and deadly traditionalism. In the familiar words of historian Jaraslov Pelikan, "Tradition is the living faith of those now dead, while traditionalism is the dead faith of those yet alive." Tradition is the foundation, not the whole structure. Without a secure foundation, the church is unstable; but without open windows to let in the refreshing winds of change, the church becomes a suffocating shell. How do we strike the right balance between "the old, old story" and new ways of telling it?

Here are a few suggestions for vital and effective ministry in the meantime and in the mean time:

- *Model civility.* In public statements (remember that social media, whether one's own outlets or the church's, are all public) about hot-button issues, focus on issues far more than on personalities and on matters of justice, peace, and compassion that clearly flow from commitment to the rule and reign of God more than from the agenda of a political party. Ground what you say in solid biblical and theological reasoning. Speak "the truth," as you see it, "in love," as Jesus has shown it.

- *Have conversations about difficult issues without the pressure of immediate decisions.* It's important to discuss hard things in settings that allow people to speak and listen with the simple but crucial goal of mutual understanding. If a decision impatiently waits in the wings, discussion quickly becomes debate and curiosity about another's views becomes a campaign for one's own.

- *Pursue structures and processes that are lean and nimble.* In many congregations, there's a widespread but largely unspoken awareness that "the institution" is more complex than it needs to be and that "tradition" has a louder voice than the Spirit. Some congregations are trying to take a journey to a destination for which they don't have the right equipment, and the equipment they have is heavy. Maybe it's time for a conversation (remember, not tied to an immediate decision) about how the church has organized its life together and to ask how effectively it serves God's dreams for the church and world.

- *Nurture yourself.* Tend to your physical and emotional health by practicing Sabbath in ways that fit your temperament and circumstances. Spend unhurried time with family and friends. Have fun. Pray. Trust that God's Spirit is creatively at work and will bring life out of the chaos of the meantime and mean time.

Wanted: Agile Leaders for Seismic Eras

Bob Dale

We live in a "blur world." Leaders are constantly challenged, disrupted, and disoriented by change. With so much turbulence, we're almost surprised by any signs of stability and continuity.

But the globe hasn't always seemed to spin so fast. Ten years ago, when my mother was moving toward death, I talked to her almost every evening. As I thought about those nightly calls, I often identified a "research question" to ask her (if she felt well enough). Most of my research questions were about family lore. I wanted to fill information gaps about how my family had moved across generations to the present.

One evening I asked how she and my dad had learned about the attack on Pearl Harbor. Her answer stunned me: Our part of the Ozark Mountains blocked most radio signals, so we rarely listened to news programs. Eight days after the bombing, my parents finally learned about the event during a grocery shopping trip.

Think of it. In our 24-hour news cycle, when technology and social media keep us globally connected every moment of every day, it's hard for us to imagine how the onset of a world war could have gone unnoticed.

Discovery moves at varying paces. Churches and cultures move with different levels of awareness and at different speeds; sometimes it's a marathon, and other times a sprint. Typically, churches move in slow motion, getting buffeted by cultural tsunamis. Generally, cultures morph much faster than congregations, especially at hinge points. The differences between those marathons and sprints sometimes disqualify leaders. Consider these shortening timelines for leaders:

- The Agricultural Age, spanning 10 centuries or so, formed the Old Testament and Early Church eras. Nomads settled on lands and cultivated crops. Cities grew. Churches were planted.
- In the mid-1700s the Industrial Age, a time when many denominations emerged, introduced us to power-driven machines and manufacturing. Churches acted like machines.
- During the late 20th century the Information Age arrived without warning. Suddenly, a knowledge-based world with its automation, technologies, and telecommunications overran churches.

Check your cultural clock. The Agricultural Age lasted for nearly a thousand years. The Industrial Age lasted for roughly 400 years. The Information Age may have a shelf life as brief as only 50 years. Cultural turning points are speeding up and becoming seismic. Traditional churches, more comfortable with marathons, have collided with our Information Age's sprint culture.

Churches, uncertain in their careening worlds, are desperate for agile leaders to reorient them and move them forward. What do agile leaders do that helps churches deal with environmental "blur"?

Max DePree was far ahead of other leadership theorists. A quarter-century ago, he foresaw a new improvisational image in *Leadership Jazz*. He realized that jazz band leaders were ideally suited for volunteer organizations during fluid eras when maximum agility is demanded.

Jazz, like leadership, is performance art. Think of the musical process and how it parallels contemporary leadership, especially for teams. Consider the parallels between jazz and leadership.

• At the beginning of a performance, jazz band leaders establish a musical base line. Then, they return to that same base line at the performance's end. But, the middle of the performance features improvisation, with each member of the band stepping to the front and playing variations on the basic theme. Everyone shares the spotlight. Everyone innovates.In chaotic times, churches are challenged to find their enduring theological foundations and to build on them creatively. In dizzying transitions, congregations must stay anchored even while under full sail. And, all of the leadership team's members have a chance to contribute their best gifts.

• Jazz band leaders stay connected to their group. Jazz is community music, played by combos. Without community connections, the group loses orientation and gets off-key. Congregation leaders connect and work from the inside outward. Shared calling and teamwork root the church's ministry.

• Jazz band leaders tell "C-shaped" stories. In literature, C-shaped stories have three elements: a beginning point or dilemma, a movement or saga-like journey, and a resolution that returns to the earlier threshold without tying up all of the loose ends. Open-ended stories grab our attention and take us on emotional pilgrimages. Agile leaders anchor our identities and move congregational narratives forward. Journeys of exploration and discovery engage our souls and selves. As Louis Armstrong testified, "You blows what you is."

Agile leaders know when to step to the front of the stage and make quick corrections. They regain balance after a stumble. They get traction again after a slip. They learn fast. They try, with new information, to meet new challenges in new ways. Then, they step front and center and live out their congregation's theological base line. May it be so for each of us.

An Old Treasure: The Rule of St. Benedict

Guy Sayles

"A wise scribe," Jesus said, "is like the master of a household who brings out of his treasure what is new and what is old" (Matt. 13:52). There's an old and valuable resource in the leadership treasury to which I regularly return, *The Rule of Saint Benedict* , written in the sixth century by Benedict of Nursia (c. 480–547) to guide the monastic communities that sprang up in response to his call for holy living and church renewal.

Many monastic communities in the Western world follow a version of Benedict's *Rule*. In 2015 I spent some time with the Carmelite monastics who live and work at the Nada Hermitage near Crestone, Colorado (www.spirituallife.org). While there, I immersed myself again in the ancient wisdom that Benedict's Rule has for contemporary leaders.

- *Leadership grounded in listening to God:* The *Rule* begins, "*Listen*, my child," and this summons to receptive listening for God's voice is a constant refrain. There are instructions about how to chant the Psalms, how to observe silence, and how to benefit from the reading of books. While some of the specifics might strike us as archaic, their intention still matters: to enhance our awareness that we are never on our own even when we are alone.

  Contrary to how we might feel in some of the most challenging circumstances we face in life and ministry, God is both with us. In the context of a prayerful pattern of expectant listening, we can count on God to guide us and to provide what we need to answer the call God has placed on our lives. Expectant listening is an indispensable gift and demand of leadership.

- *A rhythm of solitude and togetherness:* Benedict knew that a vital spiritual life and good leadership require solitary reflection, prayer, and rest and also times of shared worship, celebration, and work. His *Rule* structures the functioning of a monastic community in a way that gives all its members an opportunity to honor their need for both solitude and togetherness.

  We're aware that some leaders are introverts for whom solitude comes more naturally, while others are extroverts for whom the times with the community are more enjoyable. Benedict pushes us to realize that, whatever our default mode, we need to tend to both ends of this polarity. Introverts invest the renewal they gain from aloneness in their engagement with others, and extroverts use the energy they gain from community to tune their hearts and minds to the gifts that come from silence.

  Similarly, in his appropriation of family systems theory for religious leaders, Edwin Friedman says that clergy need to be self-differentiated from, but to stay connected to, the congregations they lead, all the while remaining a non-anxious presence.

Benedict's wisdom about solitude and togetherness helps us here. The task of self-differentiation—knowing our own nonnegotiable values and taking stands consistent with them—requires time away from the pressure and demands of community life, time for disciplined and strategic thinking. The challenge of staying connected—nurturing relationships even with people who stand in different places than we do—grows from a commitment to a quality of community life in which love for one another does not depend on agreement with each other.

- *Awareness of individual needs:* Benedict's *Rule* aims for a community of essential equality among its members, but Benedict knew that equality of status does not always mean sameness of treatment. Demands depend on the capacities and conditions of individual members. For that reason, the *Rule* instructs the Abbot or Prioress to have particular compassion for children and the elderly and to recognize their need to be treated less strictly with regard to the time of their meals and the amount of food they receive. Similarly, assignments of physical labor should consider the relative strength and health of the monastics; they should neither be "idle, nor so wearied with the strain of work that they are driven away."

  Leaders need to know the people they lead well enough to recognize their current abilities and their emerging potential. Without such knowledge, it's possible to frustrate them by expecting too little of them, or to dishearten them by giving them more responsibility than they can healthfully bear. Effective leaders seek a balance between challenging others to develop their latent gifts and not demanding so much of them that they risk burnout.

- *Always beginning:* Benedict said that he wrote his "little rule for a beginning." Thomas Merton, who lived in a community governed by the *Rule,* observed, "We will never be anything but beginners, all our lives." It's good news: the journey to effective leadership and, even more, into Christlikeness begins anew each day.

Prophetic Priests, Priestly Prophets

Guy Sayles

In my work as a pastor, I often felt an inescapable tension between the "priestly" and "prophetic" dimensions of my calling. To simplify a bit: Priests help us with our relationship with God, while prophets call us to reflect our relationship with God in our relationships with other people, with culture, and with the systems and structures of society.

The primary locations of a priest are the sanctuary, hospitals, nursing homes, prisons, gravesides, counseling offices, living rooms, front porches, and restaurants where conversations about life's challenges unfold over a shared meal. Priests listen more than they talk; and, when they do speak, they use the language of prayer and blessing.

The primary locations of a prophet are the streets, city hall, the county courthouse, community centers, media outlets, creative studios where art and music are made, and board rooms. Prophets show up anywhere decisions are made or opinions are shaped that affect the common good. Prophets spend a great deal of time in discernment and analysis; and, when they speak, they mainly question *what is* and describe *what could and should be.*

While the priest's work is primarily within the church and the prophet's focus is most often beyond it, we're living in times when these distinctions are breaking down. "Out there"—in public realms—a pastor will find many people, not necessarily connected with a church, who yearn for the listening, guiding, and healing ministry of a priest. They long to be heard, to have their spiritual needs taken seriously, and to have someone help them honor the surprises of the sacred that appear in their experience.

"In here"—in the church—a pastor will find more and more reasons to raise prophetic questions about the relationship of faith to culture and to the principalities and powers. I think that, in days ahead, church leaders will increasingly need to find wisdom, grace, and courage to address the ways in which the culture tempts the church to baptize and affirm an order of things that is at odds with God's kingdom of justice, mercy, and peace.

Carlyle Marney cautioned pastors not to be "hand-tamed by the gentry"—not to allow the security afforded to priests to silence the prophetic impulse. In my work as a pastor, I tried to heed that caution. It wasn't easy. By temperament and training, I was more comfortable with the priestly role. I knew how difficult it is to distinguish partisan political issues from overarching issues of truthfulness, character, and justice. I was reluctant to speak painful truth to people I loved, and I was aware that congregations don't welcome prophetic voices, especially from within.

Thankfully, though, I have an uneasy conscience. It wouldn't let me completely default on my prophetic responsibilities. At the very least, it caused me to worry about my failing to perceive, pray, and speak as one who desired for "God's kingdom to come and God's will to be done, on earth as it is in heaven."

- I worried that I was like the establishment authorities in Assisi during the time of St. Francis' renewal movement, staying smugly and disapprovingly inside the cathedral, while he danced with hope and joy with the poor and the struggling.
- I worried that I was like officials of the church in Germany and Rome who turned away from Martin Luther's invitation to reform and sought to silence his voice.
- I worried that I was like the moderate white ministers to whom Martin Luther King Jr. wrote from the Birmingham jail, ministers who agreed with his goals but fearfully stood on the sidelines, cautiously, gradually, but ineffectually nudging their churches away from prejudice and segregation.

Worries like these haunted me and haunt me still. Though they make me uncomfortable, I'm grateful for them. As I wrestle, as we all do, with what faithfulness means in the face of complex and controversial issues, I need such worries to keep me from settling for the status quo. They push me to use my voice to amplify the voice of Jesus who speaks in the cries of the oppressed, marginalized, and victimized.

Poet William Stafford said: "Your job is to find out what the world is trying to be." That's the job of a prophet: to find out what the world is trying to be—to discover and declare God's dreams for the world. Prophets trust, and invite others to trust, that God is bringing order out of chaos, peace out of conflict, and hope out of despair. They rest in, and invite others to rest in, the awareness that God is lifting up love amid the ruins of fear and raising up life from the shadows of death. They challenge themselves, and they challenge others, to join God in that saving work.

How Do Leaders Become Leaders?

Doug Haney

Recently my friend, Joe, and I were playing golf in Dallas. Inevitably when we play, our conversation turns to church. Joe is a trusted friend and former chaplain. As we talked about the ebb and flow of church life, we both spoke admiringly of our church's leaders. Joe described one of our leaders as non-anxious.

In family systems terms, "non-anxious presence" is used to describe a leader who is clear in one's calling and sense of purpose and calm in the face of criticism and conflict. Joe and I have been blessed with non-anxious leadership. (To be candid, being consistently non-anxious is a lofty goal. Even learning to be less anxious can be a worthy emotional and spiritual goal and will have a profound effect on church and family systems.)

But then I began to wonder, how is it possible to be non-anxious? Where does this quality come from? How do leaders become leaders? Since I've been a member of several church staffs and observed lots of leaders in action, let me offer some observations based on experience.

• *Being non-anxious is a multi-generational gift.* I don't exactly mean to say this is a matter of good genetics and a healthy early environment. Are some leaders just lucky enough to have been reared by others with the right stuff? I'm not sure it's that simple. I do think that when we reflect on our heritage, in every family tree we find people who are models of strength and tenacity. But we have to take the time to explore, to know the stories of our ancestors, to see that we are part of a great cloud of witnesses. Even with the imperfections of every human family, there are always stories of people whose lives glow with a trait or a quality that is life-giving.

All of my grandparents Haney and Pruitt were children or teenagers during the Great Depression. Their life stories of survival, endurance, and resilience are a rich legacy for me. Our pastor, George Mason, weaves into sermons stories of his father who was a ship pilot in New York. These stories show a deep awareness of his own family. Great leaders tap into an inheritance, a reserve of tenacity, clarity, and courage—especially when times are hard.

• *Being non-anxious comes from "doing the work."* I picked up the phrase, "doing the work," in counseling. It means being willing to take a hard look in the mirror and being strong enough to make changes in your life—being willing to bend.

My brother and dad are both Georgia Tech alumni. Many years ago, I attended a class at Tech with my brother. The class was on the strength of materials. The professor lectured on the use of metals in the construction of, for example, an airplane wing. The metal employed must allow the wing to bend without breaking. This is described in physics as elasticity. To be sure, every metal has its breaking point, but the capacity to flex is essential.

Non-anxious leaders are brave enough and self-aware enough to keep "doing the work." Through prayer, nurturing relationships, and even therapy when needed, leaders are willing to grow and develop and choose to become healthier and happier people. Even small changes can make a great difference. Bending without breaking does not mean abandoning principles or convictions. But it does mean speaking with clarity while staying connected. Great leaders "do the work," managing their own anxiety and not taking on the anxiety of others.

- *Being non-anxious is a gift of the Spirit.* How do we explain a courage and perseverance that is not our own? Remember the times when though the storm raged you experienced a strange calm, the gift of being centered, a faith that "all things shall be well." This is the gift of the Spirit who was present at Creation. This is the Spirit who hovers over the waters, the dark places of despair, the scary times of uncertainty. God is with you even when you are so overwhelmed it is difficult to imagine creative solutions or promising outcomes.

I will not gloss over the pain and hurt that leaders must endure. Denial is not helpful. Still, the word of the Lord comes to those in the valley of dry bones. And the breath of God fills us with life. Great leaders keep going, buoyed by the winds of the Spirit who is ever making all things new. Thanks be to God.

3 Virtues of a Healthy Staff Team

Jayne Davis

What is the best team you've ever been a part of? This is an important question to ask if you value team ministry and want your next hire to be a good fit.

Good teams work together toward a common goal. They understand what the mission is and will give all they can of their time, talents, and energy to help the team to succeed.

If, however, individual team members are too focused on their own agenda, only doing what they need to get by, or leaving a trail of interpersonal destruction behind them as they go about their work, the team will feel the negative impact. Trust will be difficult to build and momentum hard to sustain. The team will spend far too much time holding back or cleaning up messes and not enough time focused on the work God is calling them to do.

The mission of the church is too important for our staff teams not to be as healthy as they can be.

In his best-selling book, *The Ideal Team Player*, business author Patrick Lencioni identifies three virtues as being at the core of his own organization's team and critical to his work helping businesses and churches to become healthy. Ideal team players, Lencioni says, have three virtues in common: They are humble, hungry, and smart.

Think about these three words for a moment. Do they describe you? Your ministry team? Your church?

1. *Humble:* When ministry leaders are humble, they define success collectively, not individually. They are confident, but neither arrogant nor self-deprecating. They are not afraid to honestly acknowledge the skills and talents they bring to the team and are willing to share those gifts in any way that will help the team and advance the mission. They are quick to give credit to others on the team for their contributions. Humble leaders are able to be vulnerable and to build trust. They can hold others accountable and engage in honest conflict because it's not about them, but about the team. "Humility," Lencioni says, "is the single greatest and most indispensable attribute of being a team player."

2. *Hungry:* Ministry leaders who are hungry are self-motivated and diligent. They are constantly thinking about next steps and opportunities, always looking for new ways to contribute to the team. They are tireless in their desire for more—more to do, more to learn, more responsibility—and they will go above and beyond to accomplish the church's mission and to help the team succeed.

3. *Smart:* Being a smart ministry leader has less to do with degrees and IQ than it does with emotional intelligence. Smart leaders are wise in how they deal with people. They have good judgment and intuition. They understand the subtleties of group dynamics and how their words and actions impact others.

The power of these three simple words—humble, hungry, and smart—Lencioni says, is the required combination of all three of them.

- If you're humble and hungry but not smart, you're likely to hurt people along the way.
- If you're humble and smart, but not hungry, you'll frustrate your team members who are working hard.
- If you're hungry and smart, but not humble, you're the skillful politician, willing to work hard, but often for your own benefit.

Many folks on your team probably have a fair level of health in all three of these areas. But, if we're honest, we're probably not equally strong in all three. We all have a growing edge, a place where we're holding back or where we've got work to do.

Lencioni offers a self-assessment to help with self-evaluation relative to the three virtues of an ideal team player. For each virtue there are six statements. You are invited to use a rating scale to indicate how each statement applies to how you think your teammates may see you and your actions on the team. The statements themselves give helpful ideas on how you might practice these virtues more fully.

What would happen if everyone on your team was willing to be honest about the virtue that is the weakest of the three for them *and* be willing to work on it for the good of the team?

However you go about it, whether you care more for each other on your team or whether you focus on becoming humble, hungry, and smart, be intentional about developing a healthy staff team culture. Ministry is hard. Ministry teams shouldn't have to be.

Do You C.A.R.E. Enough?

Jayne Davis

Since 1944, Hallmark greeting cards have been advertised with the famous tagline, "When you care enough to send the very best." Whether encouraging soldiers overseas, cheering up the sick, celebrating the graduate, or expressing your love to the one you've chosen to spend your life with, Hallmark promises to help you to be the kind of friend or parent or spouse that you truly want to be... "when you care enough to send the very best."

What about the kind of church staff team member you truly want to be? I don't think I've seen a card for that in the Hallmark store. Until then, there are other ways you can be intentional to C.A.R.E. enough; to take the time and the energy to do the things that deepen relationships and build the kind of trust that is foundational to everything else you do as a team.

• *Celebrate:* How do you celebrate as a staff? In the Genesis creation account, God stopped at the end of each day, looked at what he had done and said, "It is good." How many times in ministry do you finish one undertaking or event only to jump right in to the next? We need the same rhythm in our work that God gave to creation. Celebrate along the way. Remind one another that ministry is not a destination, but a journey to be enjoyed together.

Whether it's the birthday of a staff team member, sharing the stories of the seventh-grade campout, or finding a volunteer to lead the kitchen crew, there's always something to celebrate.

Make it a habit to ask one another, "What are you celebrating today?" Pay attention to your team members. Notice things to celebrate in their ministry. Frame the picture. Tell the story. Find ways to look at your work together and say, "It is good."

• *Affirm:* How well do you affirm your fellow staff members? While celebration is about what we do, affirmation is about who we are. As Jesus was about to begin his earthly ministry, he heard the voice of his Father: "You are my beloved Son. With you I am well pleased." As he was about to head to Jerusalem, to face betrayal, suffering and death, Jesus heard the voice of his Father again, saying to those who would walk closest to him in those last days, "This is my Son. Listen to him."

We all need affirmation. It's why we count our "Likes" on Instagram and Facebook posts like they are silver dollars spilling out of a slot machine. Who on your staff team brings a calming presence? Offers insightful observations? Lightens heavy conversations with humor? Who pays attention to the details? Or remembers to include everyone?

Everyone brings a gift to the team that makes the team stronger. Too often we take these things for granted. We all need to hear that what we do matters. Regular and consistent affirmation helps us to lean into the work that is ahead of us. It's not to puff us up; it's to remind us who and whose we are and the divine gift we bring.

- *Respect:* How deeply do you respect your co-workers? Respect can take many forms. We can respect someone's position or their talents. We can respect the boundaries of one ministry area from another. All of these are good things.

One of the most challenging ways that we respect one another is by speaking the truth in love—with emphasis on the "in love" part—to C.A.R.E. enough to say hard things to one another. This involves risk and humility and a good bit of self-examination. Too often we sweep a lot under the rug, pretending there's not a big lump under the carpet, only to be resentful when we trip over it again.

A solid foundation of trust is built when we work through difficult situations and subjects because we want the best for one another. A good word from *Cinderella*: "Have courage and be kind."

- *Encourage:* I completed my first triathlon in 2016. Of the swimming, biking and running, running is my least favorite part of the race. And it comes at the end. By the time I started the 5K, I was already tired. The first mile took forever, and there was little shade from the heat. I just wanted to stop and walk the rest of the course. But along the way, kids from the high school handed out ice cold cups of water. Whether as a drink or as a shower over the top of my head, they were welcomed gifts. They kept me going until the end, along with my family who had spread themselves out over the last quarter mile to cheer me on.

There are days in ministry when we just don't want to run anymore. We're thirsty, and the finish line feels forever away. Sometimes you're the runner and sometimes you need to be the cheering squad.

How do you offer your colleagues a cup of cold water? How do you cheer them on when there's still a long way to go? How do you show up along the way to remind them that they don't run alone?

How will you C.A.R.E. enough to be the very best staff team you can be?

Too Busy Not to Stop

Jayne Davis

More than 20 years ago, Bill Hybels wrote a terrific book, *Too Busy NOT to Pray*. In it he challenged our passive willingness to allow busyness to muscle out time for prayer in our daily schedules. Most of us know intuitively what we fail to practice in real time—that it's precisely because of our full and fast-paced lives that being grounded in prayer is critical to keeping our focus, activities, and well-being centered in God.

I would argue that the same is true for staff team development. We are simply too busy NOT to stop and intentionally nurture our relationships as a team, certainly for our own sakes but even more importantly for the sake of our churches and the work that God wants to be doing in and through them.

In the summer of 2015 our church staff blocked out four weeks when our team was our priority focus. Four weeks! That seemed like a great idea back in March when our August calendars had a whole lot more white space in them. As it turned out, it was a great idea. We'd been through a lot of transition. We recently had brought two new staff ministers on board, and we had a sense that our congregation was on the verge of a new season of vital ministry and we needed to discover together what God might have in mind. So, we kept other meetings to a minimum and devoted 2-4 days each week to listening, learning, and laughing together.

Whether you are in transition or in a rut, whether congregational life has bogged down or is revving up, whether you are a long-tenured staff or just getting to know one another, there are three areas of staff team development that will breathe life into your relationships and your ministry if you are willing to focus your attention on them.

1. *Team Dynamics:* In his book, *The Advantage*, Patrick Lencioni states, "Teamwork is not a virtue. It's a choice—and a strategic one." Too often we live under the assumption that good relationships just happen. We get surprised in marriage when we don't always communicate perfectly, frustrated when we discover unspoken expectations, or defensive when we respond to conflict differently. The same is true of a staff team. Building trust, communicating clearly and consistently, and handling conflict in healthy ways are foundational to a strong team. And they happen by choice, not by luck.

Our staff spent two days with a facilitator, working through some of Lencioni's material on building a cohesive staff team—telling our individual stories, using personality profiles to talk about our unique strengths and weaknesses and what they bring to the team, taking time to unpack the ways we communicate and handle conflict and what we might do differently.

When we understand one another better, we assume positive intent. The big-picture folks can listen and not feel challenged by the questions of the detail folks. The "people persons" can appreciate the structure brought by the task people. The introverts can have some time to think before being asked to respond. And everyone can feel that the gift they uniquely bring to the team is noticed and valued.

2. *Catalytic Conversations:* In his book, *Transitioning,* Dan Southerland says, "You don't find vision when you search for vision. You find God's vision when you search for God." If you want to discover what new life God wants to breathe into your staff team and into your ministry, expand your circle of conversation partners and listen for what God might have to say to you through them.

As part of my church's staff "retreat," we traveled to a church our size in another city and spent a day with the staff members there, listening to stories of what God was doing in their midst. We visited a refugee ministry to catch a glimpse of what might be next in our own work with Karen families. We met with our district attorney and were challenged and inspired by the needs of our community and what thoughts he had on how our church might make a difference.

Catalytic conversations take us outside of ourselves. They're shared experiences of listening and discerning God's voice that can reshape our collective hopes and plans for ministry together.

3. *Room to Breathe:* If fun and food are not a major part of staff team development, then something critical has been lost! We went kayaking, took a boat tour, spent a leisurely morning at a coffee shop just brainstorming ideas about the things we'd heard. We met and ate at each other's homes, went out to dinner together and, oh yeah, ate some more. And we talked about how we needed to do that more often. As in most relationships, the really good conversations come more informally than formally, and that takes time and room just to be.

You don't have to take four weeks for staff team development. Maybe you can do something once a quarter together. Carving out that kind of time was challenging for us, even a bit stressful. Rapidly approaching fall events and a September stewardship campaign all clamored for attention, along with the daily activities of ministry.

But much like the clarity and peace that come when you make time to pray, even and especially when you believe you are too busy, taking time to focus on our inner and outer life as a staff team surfaced and deepened many gifts in our midst that have better equipped us for the days ahead. These gifts included:

- Discerning God's leading
- Leaning on each other's strengths
- Trusting one another's intentions
- Avoiding unhealthy silos
- Benefiting from healthy conflict
- Folding in new staff members
- Most especially, simply enjoying the journey together

Which one of these gifts do you most want and need to unwrap as a staff team? How will you be intentional about making this happen?

Boundaries 101

Bill Wilson

The headlines are relentless. I wince every time I hear of a minister violating sexual or moral boundaries. I listen sadly as clergy describe unrealistic demands placed upon them by their congregation. Over the years I have seen the great harm inflicted on congregants and clergy alike by boundary violations.

As preparation for training to be offered by the Center for Healthy Churches, in 2012 I attended my first-ever "boundaries workshop." Wow. Going into the workshop, there were some things I already knew:

- I knew that boundary violations have become a pressing issue in ministry settings.
- I knew that clergy over-functioning and laity under-functioning (and vice versa) are a lethal mix.
- I knew that a minister with a messiah complex can be deadly.
- I knew from personal experience how sick clergy can be.
- I knew about laity who think they own the minister and his/her family.
- I knew from experience what it feels like to be a victim of boundary violations.
- I knew this topic is one that most of us would rather not address.

But at the workshop I learned many things that I didn't know:

- I had not realized how pervasive this issue is for the 21st-century church.
- I had not realized how reluctant we (I) have been to confront the congregational systems we have built that have enabled and even encouraged fuzzy boundaries.
- I had grown insensitive to how vulnerable every minister is to a multitude of temptations.
- I had not stopped to take in how many men and women, boys and girls have had their lives harmed by boundary violators.
- I needed to be reminded that for all the good that clergy can do for the sake of the Kingdom, an unhealthy minister has the capacity to inflict pain and harm that will carry its poison far into the future.

Now I know, and I can't un-know what I know. As a result, I've tried to capture my thoughts as I mull over the implications of clear and healthy boundaries for clergy and congregations alike.

- Boundaries are our friends. Just as clear rules make a game more enjoyable for all participants, clear boundaries make congregational life richer and more Christlike for all.

- The personal and internal issues that every minister and every congregant deals with will have significant impacts on the way they live out their calling in the church.
- Every minister needs someone to hold him or her accountable. This person or persons should have a name and a regular appointment on the calendar of the minister.
- Every congregation should have a relationship with a licensed pastoral counselor to whom they refer congregants with personal issues.
- Every congregation needs to establish a professional code of conduct for their clergy.
- Clarity about a wide array of expectations between clergy and congregation is sadly lacking in most congregations. Such clarity is indispensable for healthy ministry.
- Personnel committees have two essential roles: advocacy and accountability. Their job is a sacred trust that requires great maturity, spiritual insight, and emotional intelligence. They should meet regularly. Setting salaries is a minor task in their job description.
- Every church needs clear guidelines for how to do the ministry it has been called to. These must be composed in broad-enough terms to remain flexible as our contexts continue to shift and change. And, there must be an understanding that when rules rule, the kingdom of God is stifled.
- Every minister and every volunteer who works with children and youth should undergo a thorough criminal background check and be required to attend an annual boundary awareness workshop/review.
- Every church needs clear policies regarding online and social media communications for clergy and laity.
- Sexual and moral violations are the most obvious, but boundary issues run much deeper and are more pervasive than we are prone to imagine.
- If you think you are above and beyond the need for clear boundaries, you probably have a problem.

Since having my consciousness raised regarding the urgency of this issue, I've come to a greater appreciation for how difficult it is to be effective in ministry while maintaining proper boundaries.

Some of us were raised with better clarity in this regard than others. No one, however, can afford to take this issue lightly or ignore his or her own vulnerabilities. We must pay close attention to boundaries if we are going to be taken seriously in our community.

Every congregation and their clergy should covenant with one another to make healthy boundaries a high priority. What that will look like will vary from place to place, but it must be addressed—and it must become a high priority. Anything less dishonors the One we serve.

Conflict: It's Complicated

Tracy Hartman

Conflict: Just the word gives many of us a sinking feeling. And it seems to be everywhere these days—in our homes, in our churches and other ministry settings, and in our national and global interactions.

I once had the privilege of spending a week in Israel with a delegation of deans and seminary presidents from the United States. Over the course of the week we met with more than a dozen different scholars, government and religious leaders, educators, and journalists to learn about all facets of life in that beautiful country.

One of the things I learned is that if you ask three people in Israel about the Israeli-Palestinian conflict, you'll get five opinions. (Does this sound familiar to us who live stateside?) As we dug deeply into the conflict in Israel that folks on both sides live with every day, we were all reminded of some universal principles related to conflict:

• *Conflict often is complicated.* Whether at home, at church, or in the public square, there is always more than one, or two, positions on every issue (in addition to the levels of conversation detailed below). We will only make progress on resolving conflict when we take time to listen deeply and carefully to all positions and all layers of a problem, before crafting our own response or counterargument.

We do well to ask questions, especially if we are new in a setting, such as: How long has this situation been going on? What are the presenting issues and the ones going on at a deeper level? Remember, only 10 percent of the iceberg is visible above the surface! When you think you understand it all, take a step back and look at the bigger picture once again.

• *We can't stay in our own silos.* I was surprised to learn that in Israel, most people are born and raised in very homogenous communities—even within different sects of Judaism. Young people often will not meet someone who thinks, feels, and believes differently until they enter the military or the university. By this time, generalizations and biases about those they consider "other" are deeply entrenched and hard to release. Some of the best peace work being done in Israel is led by folks who are integrating schools (for faculty and students) as early as the elementary level.

What about us? We are often as siloed in our social media, denominational, and political connections. How might our conflict resolution processes benefit from being in intentional communities together?

• *We need to keep looking deeper.* Several of our speakers reminded us that the conflict in Israel is about much more than boundaries and real estate; it is about the core identities of all involved. We do well to remember this, too. In *Difficult Conversations: How to*

Discuss What Matters Most, authors Douglas Stone, Bruce Patton, and Sheila Heen assert that difficult conversations have three levels or layers:

1. The "What Happened" Conversation: Here we often want to argue about who's right and who's wrong. Instead, we need to stop the blame game and truly hear each other's stories.
2. The "Feelings" Conversation: If we are not aware of our feelings, they can burst into difficult conversations in unhealthy and harmful ways. Drawing on emotional intelligence to identify and manage our emotions can help us bring feelings into difficult conversations in productive and healing ways.
3. The "Identity" Conversation: Determining what the identity issues are for us, and for those we are trying to resolve an issue with, will help us get beyond skirmishes over buildings, programming, and other important but often non-essential issues. Ask: What is really at stake for me here? For other partners in the conversation? Are there ways we can work together for a solution that will affirm the core identities of all involved?

- *We rarely get everything we want in resolving a conflict.* Working to affirm core identities, honor feelings, and work on the deeper issues does not negate the reality that compromise and concession are two key components in conflict resolution. Sometimes, we do need to draw a nonnegotiable line in the sand, but these instances are rarer than we often care to admit.

    There is almost always room to move toward one another, and when all parties agree to do this, progress becomes truly possible. If our rhetoric is inflammatory and unbending, however, we set ourselves up for failure.

Some of our teachers in Israel were more hopeful than others about a resolution to the conflict in their land, but all agreed on the need for ongoing, respectful, and intentional work together. Most agreed that the people in their neighborhoods and houses of worship were more willing to meet in the middle than their leaders. I'm betting that's true in our civic and religious conversations as well. Conflict is complicated, but those we serve might just be the ones to lead us forward.

Conflict as Blessing:
Please Don't Waste This Crisis

Bill Wilson

Ask any minister, "What is the worst part of your job?" and nearly all will tell you, "Conflict!" Ask any congregation member what they like least about their church experience, and most will answer the same. Conflict is everywhere people are, and it seems to be escalating. The incivility of our culture is having a toxic effect on ministry and congregations.

The FACT survey of 14,000 congregations found that, in the past five years, 75 percent of churches have experienced some level of conflict. At any given time, one-fifth of congregations are in active conflict. With our depressed economy and seismic job losses, many lives are deeply stressed. It comes as no surprise that churches are experiencing more conflict than ever. Regarding conflict as blessing seems foolish and naïve. Is it possible, however, to learn to manage our conflict constructively?

Church leaders are wise to address conflict early and proactively before it escalates to become divisive. The issue is not whether you will have conflict, but what you will do with it. Following biblical commands means handling conflict with openness, compassion, and as much transparency as possible. Speaking up early, rather than sweeping disagreement under the carpet, avoids a host of problems that over time can leave a congregation divided and deeply wounded.

Conflict within a congregation can begin as a simple difference of opinion over worship styles, carpet color, or youth activities; or it can be as shame-filled as division over clergy sexual misconduct or staff financial mismanagement. It always causes discomfort, and it can be downright painful. And yet, conflict within a congregation can be a catalyst for healthy growth.

In my experience, it is the rare adult who makes any significant life change without discomfort and pain. Throughout the Bible, God uses conflict to grow his people. Paul, Peter, Martha, Mary, David, and Jeremiah are examples of heroes who learned through the ache of failure and conflict. The letters to the early church are filled with instructions for managing conflict. We are not the first to walk this way.

Conflicts and crises make excellent teachers. They often lead to new and better ways of doing things. If a youth leader's misbehavior results in a safer policy for adult interaction with teens, the youth ministry is strengthened. If employee theft inspires a smart policy that minimizes risk, congregational trust is enhanced. When bitter argument gives way to thoughtful conversation, community is built.

At the Center for Healthy Churches, we believe there are several keys to navigating conflict.

• *Avoid triangulation.* During conflict, it is tempting for people to talk about each other to anyone who will listen. Instead, we are called to take Matthew 18 seriously and learn to talk to each other about the issue. Such conversations must come in from the parking lot to the fellowship hall. Leaders can facilitate opportunities for guided conversations in a manner that allows everyone to voice an opinion. Mature leaders can help others learn to discuss deep issues of differences, disagreements, and disappointments. When people feel belittled, ignored or disrespected, the outcome is very different from when they feel valued, included, and heard.

• *Anticipate conflict.* Healthy congregations have regular times to talk about life together. Opportunities specifically devoted to open discussion create a safe place for the congregation to ask hard questions and relieve anxiety. Meetings that include unstructured time for asking questions build trust. Congregational leaders who are willing to hear suggestions and critiques without undue defensiveness model maturity and deepen the fellowship.

• *Get help.* As with Paul and Timothy, in some cases, despite the best efforts of leadership and the congregation to remain open-minded and transparent, a polarity cannot be resolved. When conflict gets especially heated, a third-party intervention may be required to enable us to overcome our emotional anxiety and harmful habits.

• *Learn the art of graceful exits.* If a conflict escalates beyond reconciliation, our goal as Christians ought to be to bless one another and then separate. Often, in a worst-case intractable conflict, the two sides take their focus away from the issue and set out to destroy each other. This tears at the fabric of the church and decimates our witness for Christ. We can certainly do better.

While the church of Christ may be the scene of conflict, when we manage that conflict in a way that leads to a healthier congregation, we become a message of hope to the larger world. There may be no better way for the church to witness to a conflict-weary culture than to handle its own, internal differences with wisdom and grace.

Crisis and conflict awaken our passions and can motivate us to a better way. When conflict arrives, as it must, please do not waste the opportunity to seek to turn it into a blessing.

EPILOGUE

Leadership During Crisis

During the editing/production phase of this book, the United States and most of the world encountered a pandemic of epic proportions. As with all types of businesses and institutions, the rapid and deadly spread of the coronavirus sent church leadership reeling as they sought to keep their congregations safe. Pastors and other staff members were forced to make quick decisions and adaptations related to in-person gatherings and person-to-person ministry. During those early days of the pandemic, the Center for Healthy Churches published several blogs related to ministry in these changing and challenging times. The editors of this book thought it appropriate to add slightly modified versions of those blogs to this volume, offering guidance to ministers as they seek to lead in building healthy churches even during the current health crisis and perhaps during future crises.

COVID-19 and the Church

Bill Owen

There's no denying the stress in recent days surrounding the COVID-19 outbreak. The reaction has been fast and fluid. The Dow Jones dropped some 4,000 points in two days. The NCAA conference tournaments and March Madness were cancelled, along with NBA games and Major League Baseball and spring sports at all levels. Most recreational and entertainment venues—including Disney properties—closed, in addition to hotels, restaurants, businesses, etc. No wonder we feel a bit off-balance!

Emotions run high: anxiety, fear, worry, sadness. You may find yourself in a community where neighbors have tested positive for the virus. We've not known days quite like these. Churches and their leadership are not exempt. Church leaders are scrambling to find footing, to bring timely and proactive leadership when there really is no tried and true template.

Here are some simple reminders to help navigate this period:

- Move toward the issues we face, not away from them. It's healthier and more effective for everyone if leadership remains calm and confident as we address matters head on.
- Be honest, humble, and vulnerable as you move forward. Confess that together we will build this plane as we fly it. We'll need to be fluid and agile.
- Connect with trusted colleagues, peer groups, and sister churches to "discover" and "test" what is working for them. Surf the web to check for best practices.
- Communicate clearly and often through various channels with your church family— online media, social platforms, personal email, text messaging, phone calls.
- Engage and enlist others to join you, from ministry staff to lay leadership, as you connect with the church family and your partners in mission and ministry.
- Reaffirm your mission. Lean into your values as the body of Christ. As Simon Sinek would say, "Remember your WHY." Be the presence of Christ to one another and to your neighbors.

Here are a few "best practices" to consider:

- Livestream and/or broadcast Sunday worship on Facebook Live. Church members can join in "real time" and "chat" during the service to promote a sense of community. Engage laypersons, where possible, in the leadership and production of the experience.
- Utilize social media to convene and connect Sunday school and Bible study groups.
- Post ongoing and timely "updates" on your website. Include access to resources, including links to Sunday worship, a password-protected prayer list, and online giving.
- Encourage small groups to check on and care for one another via phone calls and texts.

- Determine the best manner to do pastoral care. Clearly communicate this plan to the congregation regarding pastoral care visits/contacts in homes and especially as it relates to hospital and healthcare facility policies.
- Keep church offices open, even if modified from regular schedules or staffing. If church offices must close, program telephone systems (if available) with clear and concise information related to church activities and events, along with immediate contact information to ministerial staff members in the event of an emergency.
- Pray for one another, your community, and our world. Remember those families directly affected by COVID-19 and the health professionals providing care, our government leaders, and the sick and most vulnerable.

At the Center for Healthy Churches we often refer to the uncertainty of "transition periods" in the church's life as a kind of "wilderness" journey. It's appropriate that the coronavirus pandemic began during the Lenten season. Lent is a time for spiritual discernment, prayer, and fasting. Remember it is God who is "our refuge and strength, an ever-present help in times of trouble" (Psalm 46).

- Face your fears with a bias of faith and hope.
- Engage your assumptions with facts and the good reason God has given you.
- Act on what we are learning from the medical and scientific professionals. Wash your hands; practice social distancing. Be a leader where God has placed you.
- Release your fears to God. Pray and take this seriously, but don't panic.

A Tale of Two Futures for Your Church

Bill Wilson

The coronavirus crisis has taken us off the rails that we thought were permanent and dependable. Congregations are facing a future that we have no precedent for or roadmap to navigate. There is a sense of disorientation, fear, and bewilderment among leaders and judicatories that are trying to manage a life they never imagined or prepared for. Each morning we awake wondering, "What can possibly happen today?" In fact, "managing life" is becoming an oxymoron as we increasingly feel out of control of what is happening to us.

There is also a sense that we are facing a crisis that, while portrayed as a medical or financial dilemma, may also be a crisis that requires a faith perspective to fully meet the challenge. Fear, loneliness, social isolation, food insecurity, job viability, along with heightened anxiety and dread, are now a daily reality for many people whose life previously was relatively stable.

Congregations face a future that is radically different from what they imagined at the dawn of 2020. Looking ahead, with a nod to Charles Dickens, one can make a good case that this is both "the worst of times" and "the best of times" for congregations.

As to the worst of times...

The great fear is that this dual crisis of health and finances will hit congregations hard in areas we are weakest.

Many established congregations are comprised of a majority of senior adults. This population is especially susceptible to the ravages of the virus. If the current trend lines hold, some of our most reliable and regular members are facing major medical challenges. Even if the illness spares them, it will impact their quality of life and may affect their willingness to fully engage in public activities for a very long time.

"Flattening the curve" is a strategy for stretching out the onset of the virus so that medical facilities can manage the surge in services needed. It also means that the outbreak of the virus will stretch out over many months. Therefore, it will probably be months before the "all clear" signal is given to return to regular routines such as church attendance. When we do, things will look very different.

Many churches in America run on very thin financial margins. Congregational reserves are modest at best, and fixed costs dominate most congregational budgets. Many established churches simply do not have the capacity to absorb a major loss of income over more than a few weeks. Our reserves have been dwindling as our churches have plateaued and declined over the last two decades, and many of us find ourselves with more facilities than needed for the numbers of attendees. The costs of running those facilities will continue unabated and may even escalate as deferred maintenance issues erupt and can no longer be deferred.

Many of our most devoted members live on investments and depend on resources that are threatened by the looming recession. The financial fear that a recession/depression brings may cause some of our most trustworthy financial supporters to pull back on their giving habits. And, we have legitimate concerns about the efficiency of online giving to make up the loss of financial support that physical attendance brings. Every pastor dreads the loss of a "snow Sunday" offering that never quite equals a normal Sunday's income.

The inevitable decline in receipts we all face means a sort of financial triage will be necessary for each church. We learned in 2008 that deep cutbacks in spending generally mean support for denominational and mission entities will rapidly decline, and layoffs and cutting of staff support or positions will soon follow.

Some observers of American church life have been predicting that the trend lines of the last 30 years pointed toward the closure of between a fourth and a third of existing congregations by 2035. Our current crisis may accelerate those trend lines to the point that we have less time to get our affairs in order than we had thought. Think months, not years.

The harsh reality is that the parallel financial crisis and health tsunami may wash away some of our churches that have "preexisting and underlying conditions" that make them particularly vulnerable to the future we are facing. Many others may be crippled to the point of questioning their viability. This is a nightmare scenario that is painful even to put into words. There is another way of imagining the future, however. Let's assume that we are entering a season of remarkable opportunity for the church.

As to the best of times…

The church, across the ages, has often been at its best in the face of its most challenging moments. From plagues to depressions to persecution to natural disasters to wars and pestilence, God's people have found their backbone and their calling in the midst of some of their darkest days. While the circumstances have often been overwhelming and devastating, it was often in our darkest moments that the lights of faith, hope, and love shone brightest.

Salvation history teaches us that God works in mysterious and counter-intuitive ways to bring the reign of God to bear upon our world. From Abram's call to abandon the known for the unknown, and on nearly every ensuing page of scripture, God is portrayed as leading his people into a future that appears fear-full, but is actually the place where we will see "more than we can imagine" unfold before our eyes. Jesus modeled for us and proved to us that life *will* conquer death, no matter how dark and foreboding the present circumstances seem.

Our culture and our world may well be more open and receptive to the good news of Jesus Christ than we have known in our lifetime. Our faith in politicians, science, financial markets, consumerism, nationalism, and many other things is being shaken to its core. For too long we have elevated these pretenders to a level of absolute loyalty that they do not deserve. These false idols are being revealed as just that, and there may well be a hunger to find something more substantive and enduring for people to believe in.

Combined with a surging hunger for meaning, the church has an opportunity to show the world what healthy people do in times of crisis. Rather than panic and devolve into self-absorption and self-protection, we run toward the needs in our culture rather than away from them. We refuse to demonize others but act out the story of the Good Samaritan on a daily basis. Local churches can lead the way to show their communities what "love your neighbor as yourself" actually looks like.

Every day brings increasingly urgent instructions to retreat physically *away* from others. While that is a physical necessity, a corresponding relational move *toward* others by Christ-followers is a massive opportunity for us to show the difference we make in a city or community. As churches and faith communities find ways to innovatively engage one another virtually and in ways new to us, we can extend that care to all of our community, not just our church members. Doing so will show our world that we are the ones who enter when many others exit their life.

I pray that the divisiveness too often present in congregations melts away as we lift our gaze and our attention to a common mission that unites us rather than those things that divide us. We simply do not have time or energy to battle one another.

One of my hoped-for scenarios is that when we emerge on the other side of this pandemic, we will experience a deep and profound appreciation for shared community, worship in the same room, small group interaction, and the role of faith in our life. We've taken for granted so many things that have now been ripped from us. Could it be that getting those back sparks a resurgence of interest in churches and ministry?

Innovation is going to be forced upon us, and for many churches that have resisted the need to innovate and experiment, that is a steep learning curve. What we might find is that forgoing corporate worship and small groups, while painful, thrusts us into a new world that we needed to enter anyway. The resulting openness to innovation, technology, and fresh ways of thinking about being church and not just doing church is the beginning of a rich season for many churches. Being relevant to the needs of others and cultivating the willingness to listen to new voices would be a welcome addition to many churches.

Surely, every church is going to experience a pruning season over the next few months. Finances and other metrics of success are going to decline. It may well be that pruning produces for churches what it does for fruit trees: fewer but higher quality fruit. Forced choices about what to lop off and what to keep will challenge us to reexamine why we exist and what our true calling is. That is a healthy exercise, even if it means real loss and pain.

So, which will it be? The "worst of times" or the "best of times" for your church? Actually, we know that it will be both, as Charles Dickens implied. There are hard and hard-to-imagine days ahead for every church and every one of us. However, that does not have to be the final word. We are a people who walk by faith, and not simply by sight. If we can look at what cannot be seen, if we can imagine possibilities where others see only unsolvable problems, if we can embody hope in the midst of despair, we just might find ourselves emerging from this crisis shaped to be more like the church Christ needs for the 21st century. Might it be so.

Applying Lessons from a Hurricane
Matt Cook

I still remember the moment I first saw the spaghetti models for Hurricane Florence heading right for us. I'm not a native North Carolinian, and most of the folks who'd grown up on the coast told me not worry too much until it was a lot closer. But every day that cone of uncertainty got more certain. And then Jim Cantore from the Weather Channel showed up—and we knew we were toast.

To be honest, at the onset of the Covid-19 pandemic it felt a little like déjà vu. We could see the virus coming. We hoped it wouldn't hit us, but as the days turned into weeks and word began to spread about cases in the United States beginning to grow, it was clear that a very different kind of hurricane was coming ashore. Most of us began to batten down the hatches, while hoping the damage wouldn't be too great.

I don't want to make myself out to be some high-level expert in crisis management here. That's a distinction no one really wants because it means you've got to live through enough major crises to get really good at managing them. But I do have a few hard-earned lessons to offer from pastoring a church through a hurricane and the recovery efforts.

• *Normalize the (ab)normal.* So much of what we're dealing with right now is uncertainty. In fact, the only thing we can count on is that life is not going to be the same anytime soon—maybe ever. Wrap your brain and heart around this fact as quickly as you can, and start lovingly, gently helping others do the same.

Worship, but worship differently. Practice discipleship and care for each other, but do these things differently. Give up the temptation to just sit and wait for things to calm down and go back to normal. Instead, start restructuring the way you and your church do ministry in light of the new normal. The good news is that doing so will almost certainly teach you and your congregation some really wonderful lessons along the way.

• *Communicate, communicate, communicate.* Normalcy and predictability typically go together. When things are normal, people know what to expect. Moments of crisis on the other hand are, by definition, moments of uncertainty. Everyone will be reacting to the crisis through the lens of their own personality and experience. But churches are social organizations. To be the church requires coordination of hearts, minds, and actions.

If your church is going to be the presence of Christ in the midst of a crisis, it will require a massive surge in the amount of communication you provide. In Wilmington, that meant communicating what was taking place on an almost daily basis. And the value wasn't purely logistical. It helped people stay connected, even when some of them had evacuated hundreds of miles away. When they returned home, however, they were already emotionally and mentally engaged.

Our current crisis will have much the same challenges and opportunities. While sheltering at home whether on a limited or regular basis, our routines and habits are completely disrupted. You can't change that for the people in your congregation, but you can creatively walk beside them and keep them connected by communicating more than normal.

• *And then, communicate some more.* The amount and nature of communication with your congregation will need to be preceded by a surge in communication among your staff team. Many church staff members complain good naturedly about the number and duration of staff meetings, but you're probably going to need to have a lot more of them in the coming weeks and months.

In a crisis everything is different. Existing patterns and programs go offline for a while. The tendency then is either for nothing to happen or for everyone to go off and do their own thing. But your strongest response to the crisis as a staff team is to figure out how to pull together in the same direction. Doing that when everything is different, however, requires significant communication. Check in far more often but for less time.

For almost a month after the hurricane hit Wilmington, we had a staff meeting every morning. The meetings didn't last long, but we all knew what was going on, what needed communicating to the congregation, and the impact we were having collectively because of that brief time we spent together.

• *Don't let the crisis blind you to the presence of God.* In the early days of the pandemic, I read about Winston Churchill's crisis management style during World War II. One of the things he was best at was telling the stories of how ordinary heroes were turning the tide of the war. They were living through one of the most difficult periods in British history, but those moments of collective celebration framed the difficulties in ways that minimized the hardship and amplified future hope. There's a powerful lesson here.

Crises are exhausting mentally and physically, but they can also generate some of the most powerful spiritual insights and blessings of your entire life. I wouldn't wish a hurricane on any church or community, but watching the power of God unleashed through the people of my congregation in the aftermath of the storm was one of the most amazing spiritual experiences of my life.

The nature of Covid-19 is very different because of social distancing, but I have no doubt that God is powerfully at work around you. Stopping consistently to recognize that and to lift it up for others to see and celebrate will be among the most important work you'll do as a minister in the coming months.

As the assistant director of the Center for Healthy Churches, I'm not on the front line of congregational ministry anymore, but I do get a front-row seat to see all the amazing things you're doing across the country. This is a challenging moment, but God tends to do transformational things in challenging moments. Our hope and prayer at the Center is that God is doing just that through your ministry and in your church. If there are ways that we can be of assistance to you in those efforts, please let us know.

Toward that end, we at the Center have decided to offer on a first come, first served basis free coaching to ministers in the coming months as you lead your church in responding to this crisis. For more information, e-mail us at contact@chchurches.org.

When Can We Breathe Again?

Phill Martin

As a church staff leader, are you in information and support options overload? These opportunities are coming to us quickly and with ever-changing details. New laws, technology, challenges, upset schedules, and unknown answers ... I know I'm in overload; perhaps you are also.

As church leaders, most of you are finding that remote church, working from home, and the goal of good pastoral ministry in a time of physical distancing requires more from your resources and energy than usual. So, what are you to do? Work harder and burn out? We all understand that this is not the solution, but it is harder than ever to accept limits and make your own needs important enough to act.

Across the country, during the past weeks and months we have been at different levels of action and restriction. Some of you are still going to the office, even if you are among a lot smaller group. Some of you are now home schoolteachers and childcare workers in addition to the added stress from job responsibilities. Some of you can still move around with a bit of normalcy, while others have to stay at home except for essential shopping and appointments.

I confess I am not a model of what you should do, but I'm watching what is happening, and want to suggest we take a moment to breathe. My Apple Watch is good at reminding me to breathe, and it shows me my level of movement. If you are like me, though, I ignore it more than I listen to its invitation to *breathe* and *move*.

In the early days of the pandemic, I hosted five open Zoom meetings with our association members, The Church Network. Those meetings varied in size, location, and church size but offered a time to talk to each other about what is happening on the ground. We discussed process, payroll, streaming, childcare, how to keep ministry moving, contributions, use of buildings for ministry, etc., etc. Sometimes we shared our best guess, sometimes we found real solutions, and sometimes we just identified good questions.

Not to compare these women and men to the most critical front-line doctors and nurses and food service workers, but the administrative part of church has become even more complicated and is pushing most everyone to the limit. In these sessions I let the conversation go for about 45 minutes, and then I suggested a shift. "You've been working on a great list of things that must have solutions, but my question to the group is: How are *you* doing?"

So, what are we to do? Following are a few possibilities:

- Breathe. I mean, really breathe. Check yourself and allow time to decompress, pray, meditate, and be still.
- Move. Spending 10-12 hours with email and Zoom meetings will wear on you.
- Check on your colleagues. If you are one of those who have a lot of new free time—and are tempted to tell us about how bored you are on social media—use that time to reach out to your teammates and their families or maybe a minister friend in another church or city.
- Ask some questions: What can I slow down? Is this a must for now? Do we have to do everything we used to do—plus some?
- Eat well, sleep enough, move, and remember to name what you are grateful for each day.

I agree with the many people, especially church staff ministers, who are predicting things will be different on the other side of this pandemic. It will escalate changes that were already in motion. It may create a significant pivot in how we do church. The good news is that we don't have to understand it all now or do it all this week.

So, B-R-E-A-T-H-E deeply.

Navigating Our Emotions
in Times Like These

Barry Howard

If it feels like your emotions are "all over the map" during these days of "physical distancing," you are not alone. In addition to altering our schedules and delaying many of our plans, the closures and life interruptions and limited person-to-person contact have likely disrupted our sense of emotional balance.

Stress can be a good thing. For example, the stress of preparing for the final exam motivates us to study diligently. Or, the stress of getting ready for a speaking engagement or a presentation at work inspires us to rehearse thoroughly. The introduction of multiple significant stressors simultaneously, however, can put us in a state of distress. Distress often upsets our emotional equilibrium.

Emotions are complex. I find it helpful to think of my emotional flow as a traffic pattern. When we are following a normal routine, our emotions follow familiar roads. For instance, when we arrive at an intersection, there is a traffic light or stop sign that prompts us on when to stop and when to go. The intersection entails certain risks, but we feel safe and confident because we are familiar with the pattern and we have a fairly high degree of certainty that others will follow the prescribed prompts.

When multiple stressors are suddenly and unexpectedly introduced into our life, however, our normative emotional traffic patterns are disrupted and often rerouted. Imagine that you are approaching a major intersection at the juxtaposition of a couple of four-lane roads only to discover that there has been a power outage and the traffic signals are not working.

Every vehicle approaching that intersection is trying to determine who should stop, who should go, and who is next. And because the normal standard (the traffic light) has been removed, chaos ensues until common courtesy is extended and cars proceed to navigate the intersection; the drivers share the same goal (to get through the intersection), but they do not have a mutually agreed-upon method for navigating the new dynamics. Describing a similar dilemma, Terry Pratchett cautioned, "This isn't life in the fast lane, it's life in the oncoming traffic."

In recent weeks and months, in an effort to minimize the impact of the coronavirus, the preventative measures we have been taking have also created new and significant sources of stress for us. Depending on our individual circumstances, we have dealt with stressors such as working from home, providing childcare at home, losing our job or dealing with reduced income, caring for a sick friend or relative, adjusting to economic realities, or losing in-person contact with our primary social group or community of support.

Based on their level of emotional intelligence (EQ), some individuals can manage one or two significant stressors without throwing their emotional balance into a tailspin. But for most of us, the sudden and simultaneous addition of more than a couple of stressors creates a traffic jam in our emotional traffic flow.

What is the best way for us to navigate the "rush hour traffic" of our new emotional realities?

- *Slow down.* Whenever we are navigating unfamiliar territory, we need to travel at a slower pace.
- *Anticipate emotional fluctuations.* Momentary surges in anxiety, frustration, anger, and melancholy are normal.
- *Exercise patience.* Be patient with yourself as the new normal actually becomes more normal.
- *Own your emotions.* Discuss your emotional fluctuations with a trusted friend, accountability partner, or counselor. Verbalizing your emotions may prove to be therapeutic.
- *Become grounded in your faith.* Let your spirituality serve as an anchor. Emotions are fickle, even when they are held in balance.
- *Fly by the instrument panel.* Like a veteran pilot landing a plane in the fog, make decisions based on what you "know," not how you "feel" at any given moment.

In this season of temporary shutdowns, heightened anxiety, and elevated concern, be assured that we are all novices, not experts, at dealing with the ramifications of a pandemic. And based on age, health, genetics, and many other factors, every individual has a unique emotional composition.

As we navigate the emotional turbulence within, let us be patient with ourselves. And let us be patient with others who are struggling with emotions that are "all over the map."

Now What?

Bill Wilson

In the early days of the coronavirus pandemic, my retired pastor friend Mike Smith and I speculated about what is on the horizon for congregations and parishes as we transition from the crisis of the moment to the long-term implications of the pandemic.

Here are 10 of our random and partially developed thoughts/questions, plus one pressing question we all need to ponder. Feel free to add yours to these as we all seek to navigate the choppy seas that are before us.

1. There will be no "light switch" moment when some horn sounds and life suddenly returns to normal for churches and parishes. Instead, we will gradually and painfully emerge from this pandemic and its impacts over the course of months and even years. Until there is a reliable vaccination for the virus (estimated to be 12-24 months), we should assume that many people will be wary of public gatherings of any type. It will probably be well into 2021 before large-scale physical worship attendance becomes the norm.

2. The adaptive change lessons we have learned are our new reality. Specifically, innovative methods for gathering the scattered church, engaging the de-churched, and meeting the un-churched and our neighbors are going to be our primary focus for the rest of this year and probably longer. We're going to need some new metrics, by the way.

3. We have learned so much so quickly! We discovered that we can connect with a wider range of church members than we thought possible, provided we are willing to go to them on a regular basis and in multiple formats via the Internet. If we've learned this much in a few short weeks, what will we know months and years from now? Our resilience and imagination are encouraging.

4. We've learned that we can quickly develop online content at low cost and in sufficient quality. Already, the notion that online worship must be a replica of sanctuary worship is fading. It is remarkable to watch the adaptation that is taking place as people explore the possibilities and creativity of virtual worship.

5. We've learned that we have people who are willing to connect with socially isolated members by phone, email, Facebook, Zoom, and other means. We can have meaningful ongoing contact even if we cannot be physically present with one another. The next generation of this contact will be fascinating to watch as we find new ways to create deep connections with one another.

6. We should assume a surge of mental illnesses, increased addictions, depression, loneliness, marital conflict, parenting frustrations, chronic anxiety, unresolved grief, etc. How are we preparing to offer help to those who are going to suffer most as the disruption continues?

7. When we do get back to whatever passes for normal, we will have a whole culture even more addicted to the Internet than previously. How will this impact the way we engage our church and/or fellow believers? We should not expect our folks to walk away from what has become indispensable to them.

8. Prior to the virus, most church staff members invested nearly all of their time in those who showed up for church on a regular basis. In the future church, will staff revert to such a pattern, or will they reconfigure their time to include preparing and using the Internet to stay in touch with the moderately and slightly connected members of the church and even the largely disconnected? If staff decides to reconfigure their use of time, what might that look like and how will it be received by relevant oversight groups?

9. Will congregations and ministers be willing to try to cultivate a congregation outside the core congregation, one that exists primarily via individual interactions with online content and communications rather than physical presence at designated times?

10. Will ministers and congregations be willing to build on their experience with Zoom and other providers to structure, promote, and resource online small groups? If so, what might be the impact of such an effort on former methodologies and on a church's reach and impact?

Finally, churches are being challenged to have the same conversations as retailers, universities, and hospitals: Is our building a necessity for delivering our services/ministry?

We will probably learn to answer this question as a polarity exercise. That is, the answer will simultaneously be "yes" and "no." Like retailers, universities and hospitals, we will find ways to be the church both in a physical location and in a virtual and scattered manner. We knew this diversification was needed, but the pandemic has fast-forwarded us into our future at warp speed. Going forward, we will not be able to un-learn what we have learned about being the church. Our new normal will see us regarding our physical location as one of many expressions of our church. In doing so, we will quite possibly become more of the gathered and scattered church Jesus had in mind for his followers.

Tomorrow

Mike Queen

Don't stop thinking about tomorrow.
Don't stop, it'll soon be here.
It'll be, better than before.
Yesterday's gone; yesterday's gone.

These lyrics from an old Fleetwood Mac song call us to let go of yesterday and look forward to tomorrow. While most of us are trying to do just that in the season of Covid-19, it is getting through our todays that proves to be the challenge. And what day is it for us who followed stay-at-home orders and continue to maintain physical distancing? As a friend of mine recently noted, "I think it is April, the 38th." The days do run together.

We have adjusted to online worship. We are becoming efficient at Zoom. We are learning to celebrate health care workers in hospitals and nursing homes. We are meeting new neighbors as we walk our neighborhoods. We are playing games, working jigsaw puzzles, cleaning out closets and attics, working in the yard. We're enjoying the sights, sounds, and smells of the season; and they are delightful.

But we have also seen the images of caskets in mass graves in New York. We all know someone who has died, but because of social distancing, we have not yet been able to pay our respects at a memorial service. Students of every age from elementary to college have been forced to adapt to distance learning, as are the devoted teachers who teach them. Graduations have been postponed or cancelled. Sports have disappeared. No proms, no gathering for worship, no haircuts, no coffee shop conversations, and no certainty as to when tomorrow will be normal.

A Methodist minister friend in London, Leslie Griffiths, said recently, "What dystopic days we are living through. I can't wait to build a future with lessons learned from this mess."

I wonder what lessons we will learn in the church and in our personal lives? Or if we will learn anything at all?

Across the years I encountered several married couples whose relationship was in trouble. Often one of them would say something such as, "I just want it to be like it used to be." My response to that was always, "Not good enough. If your relationship is like it used to be, then you will end up here again. Your goal needs to be to make the relationship better than it has ever been." As the song says, "better than before."

This does not happen automatically. It takes hard work to make things better than they were. To complicate matters even further, none of us knows when or even how we will begin to approach normal once again. Many experts have rolled out plans for "reopening society" as we know it. No two plans are the same. Some have a short timeline, while others stretch well into 2021. So as good as it may be to contemplate tomorrow, how do we live today—right now?

While there are many people still working full time and overtime, for many of us, we have a lot of time on our hands. Even old movies and TV reruns get old. Organizing family photos can only take so long. For me it has come down to this new kind of routine:

- I pray more intentionally than perhaps I ever have. While I have always prayed for others, I now pray for both my wife and myself. We are in our 70s with some underlying health issues. The whole thing is scary for folks like us. But, as I noted in a recent sermon, "When faith and fear collide, faith has something to say to fear."

- Almost by accident, I have begun to reconnect with people I have not spoken to in years. I recently talked with two old elementary school friends. I talked to a man from a church where I served as a youth minister in the late 70s. We had not spoken to in 40 years. So, every day I call someone from my past—a former classmate or college buddy or business associate or church member. The phone has become my best friend.

- I try to write at least three notes or letters a week to people who have meant something special to me in my life. Sometimes they are handwritten, while others are via email or Messenger. The point is that it is good to express gratitude for those who have nurtured us along the way.

- Every day I read, write, and exercise. And when this is all over, my prayer is that I will hold on to all of these disciplines, because they are blessing my soul and I believe they will bless my tomorrows.

So, as we live through these "dystopic days," what might you or your congregation consider doing today so that your tomorrows might be "better than before"?

7 Lessons from the Covid-19 Pandemic

Barry Howard

Church looks and feels very different right now. For the past weeks and months, as a proactive expression of love for our people and our communities, most of our churches have been gathering online for worship, Bible study, and committee meetings rather than assembling in person.

Pastors are learning to preach to cameras. Staff members and volunteers are learning new technology skills. Churches have been quickly setting up or upgrading their online giving platforms. Small groups and individuals have been responding to ministry needs with creative ministry actions.

Certainly, churches have not been the only ones affected by the "shelter in place" orders. Restaurants scrambled to revise their delivery system to take out or curbside only. Banks limited access to their lobbies to "appointments only," channeling most transactions to the drive-thru window. However, churches stereotypically are perceived as the most resistant to change.

As I have collaborated with other pastors and church leaders, it seems we are all learning a few things about ourselves that may be helpful in shaping the next chapter of ministry. Here are seven lessons to consider:

1. *Online is the next best thing to being there.* While online services are not likely to replace in-person gatherings, we are realizing that livestream worship is a good option for those who, for one reason or the other, cannot attend services on campus. We are also discovering that for some of our members, the increase in online options is a blessing. After the current health guidelines are lifted, online options should be perceived not as a replacement, but as an enhancement to a church's ministries.

2. *Each of us has a priestly responsibility.* The priesthood of the believer is multifaceted. Our priestly privilege includes having direct access to God, being accountable to God, and having an assignment from God. We have the privilege of "priesting" one another as we encourage each other, care for neighbors, build up the body of Christ, and share the teachings of Jesus through our words and our actions.

3. *Every home is a satellite campus of the local church.* Although we have known this for ages, we have become more adept at organizing our life at home as an outpost of faith formation, a house of worship, a chapel for prayer, and a launch point for ministry action.

4. *A campus is a valuable resource of the church, but it's not a church.* A brick-and-mortar campus can be an important tool for a congregation, but it is just one of many tools in a congregation's toolbox. A campus should always be perceived as a resource for the nurturing of our faith, not a source of our faith.

5. *We need the human touch and social engagement of spiritual community.* During these days of social and physical distancing, we have experienced withdrawal pangs from missing the handshake at the door, the passing of the peace, the hug from our favorite elder saint, and blending our voices in song while in the same room with others from our family of faith. While we are grateful for online connections, we will emerge from this crisis with a greater appreciation for the privilege of in-person meetings.

6. *Our members are more resourceful and creative than we realized.* Many members have jumped into action to sew masks for healthcare workers and first responders. Others have been proxy shoppers, delivering groceries and pharmaceuticals to those most at risk. A few members have written songs or poems to encourage or entertain others and then posted, published, or performed their artistry on social media platforms. In the future, we can enlist their skills to advance the ministry and liturgy of the church.

7. *We can function in a healthy way with fewer meetings.* Some committees are continuing to meet by video or conference call. Some are sharing monthly or quarterly reports via email. And others have postponed monthly meetings at least temporarily. All in all, committees are meeting as necessary, but less frequently than before the crisis. I expect that some monthly committee meetings may easily transition to quarterly meetings as we emerge from this pandemic.

Every major world event, including war, terrorist attack, health pandemic or ground-breaking discovery, has altered or revised the normative patterns and protocols of life on this planet. It is yet to be seen what the new norms will look like after COVID-19.

For many reasons, both spiritual and economic, it is doubtful that churches will have the option of returning to a pre-virus status quo. Churches that build on the lessons learned during the pandemic, however, may have the best opportunity to thrive and not just survive.

Pandemic Preaching

David Hull

John Ruskin once wrote, "Preaching is thirty minutes in which to raise the dead." This well-worn quote is worth hearing again. While our preaching during this pandemic may be shorter than 30 minutes due to online attention spans, the cultural moment that is tinged with death does call for the very best preaching from the church.

Fortunately, the full witness of the Bible gives the preacher themes from cover to cover that can speak the Word of God into this age of anxiety and confusion. Whether one is using the Revised Common Lectionary to navigate preaching during these days or developing a personal plan for preaching, perhaps the following biblical themes could be woven into the fabric of proclamation during this pandemic.

- *Creation:* The Creation account describes the great abundance of God. In the midst of this earthly paradise, God said, "You may freely eat of every tree of the garden . . ." (Gen. 2:16, NRSV). What a gift of generosity! But God also said, "but of the tree of the knowledge of good and evil, you shall not eat, for in the day that you eat of it you shall die." (v. 17). No sooner had God spoken of the abundance of the garden, God then spoke of a life within certain limits. We later learn that the sin of Adam and Eve was because they focused too much on what they could not have instead of rejoicing in the abundance given to them. Perhaps during this season we are once again being reminded about the limits imposed on us by nature. We can't have everything. We sometimes forget that. But we can still have access to the rich abundance of God's gifts for us. Good preaching can point our focus to all the other trees in the garden of God's creation that still provide fruit for us even in our time of limitation.

- *Exodus:* The grand story of the Exodus is an account of a people trying to escape bondage and finding their way to the land of promise. In the middle they experienced a long season of wilderness. In the days of wandering and wilderness, God was present, manna was given, fire continued to direct, water was provided for the thirsty, and a covenant was established for the community. As we wander in the wilderness between the bondage caused by a terrible virus and the promised land of a vaccine, God still provides. Good preaching can help us understand that the manna, fire, water, and covenant will still give us "strength for today and bright hope for tomorrow."

- *Exile:* Exile is when you are forced to live where you do not want to be. The Hebrews knew about this in the days of Babylonian captivity. We are clearly in an exile moment right now. It is one of the best ways to describe life—we are all in exile, longing for the pleasures of home. It is time to hear from the prophets again. Isaiah teaches us to understand the "little while" of this season as we are encouraged to "Come, my people, enter

234

your chambers, and shut your doors behind you; hide yourselves for a little while until the wrath is past" (Isa. 26:20 NRSV). Jeremiah tells us that this period of time may be long, and we are to make the most of these days as we "build houses and live in them, plant gardens and eat what they produce . . . and seek the welfare of the city where I have sent you into exile, and pray to the Lord on its behalf, for in its welfare you will find your welfare" (Jer. 29:1-14 NRSV). What does that look like for us today as we live in exile? This is rich material for the preacher. Prophetic passages abound that teach us how to live in exile. Good preaching will lift up these passages and bring them alive for us in our exile.

- *Kingdom of God:* Jesus talked about the kingdom of God more than any other subject. That should tell us something about its priority in our own preaching. These pandemic days have reminded us about the powerful community of the Kingdom. When life is normal, we often focus on our own individual church. We worship in one place and care for one community of faith. These days I sometimes worship with several different churches. My emphasis has become less about the one church where I serve and more about the community of churches that has now become accessed in a greater way online. Good preaching will call us to a greater awareness of God's reign in the world and will invite us beyond the walls of our church to participate in God's work in the world.

- *Goodness of God:* "And we know that in all things God works for the good of those who love him, who have been called according to his purpose" (Rom. 8:28, NIV). This pandemic may stretch our understanding of "all things" to the limit, but the promise is still true. What sightings of God working for good can we highlight today? What biblical stories of God working for good can help us to see more clearly today? Good preaching will help us to see the good that God continues to do in these difficult days.

- *Resurrection Hope:* It felt like we "missed" Easter this year. True, preaching to a camera in an empty room did not feel like the wonderful celebration of a large crowd at Easter. But we only missed Easter if we allow ourselves to ignore the wonder of the resurrection. Our preaching should proclaim the powerful message of resurrection not just on Easter Sunday, but on every Sunday as we walk through the "valley of the shadow of death." As we read in 1 Peter 1:3, "Blessed be the God and Father of our Lord Jesus Christ! By his great mercy he has given us a new birth into a living hope through the resurrection of Jesus Christ from the dead" (NRSV). Good preaching will return to this theme of resurrection every week so that all who hear may be stirred with hope.

We have "thirty minutes in which to raise the dead." Preach well, my sisters and brothers, during these difficult days when people are hungering for a good Word from God.

Lessons from the Ancient Church
for the Present Crisis

Matt Cook

In the second and third centuries two different pandemics swept the ancient Roman world. Many Roman cities were densely populated, which made them perfect breeding grounds for communicable diseases. (By some estimates, ancient Rome was three times more densely populated per square mile than modern-day New York City.) And of course, the Roman world lacked what modern medicine has taught us about microbiology and epidemiology. The most reliable estimates suggest that somewhere between a quarter and a third of the Roman Empire perished in the second-century epidemic alone.

When the pandemics hit, the wealthy and powerful were able to survive far more easily. They had the resources to sequester themselves at home or even better to relocate to the country where they were not surrounded on all sides by the sick and dying. They didn't know exactly what was causing people to die, but they knew that staying behind likely meant death and getting away likely meant living. So, they left.

One obscure religious cult, however, seemed to defy the odds. There were all kinds of bizarre rumors about this particular cult: strange initiation rites, political subversion, cannibalism—just to name a few. But when the pandemics hit, they not only stayed in the cities, but also survived in larger numbers than the surrounding population. The members of this obscure religious cult had a name for themselves: "Christians."

The leaders of the early church saw what took place in their midst in miraculous terms, and if you believe that miracles are possible—and I do—then you can't completely discount that idea. It's just as likely, however, that what those early Christians did without realizing it was make small contributions to the health and well-being of those around them. Dionysius, the Bishop of Alexandria, said that many Christians "took charge of the sick, attending to their every need, and ministering to them in the name of Christ."

Such care started a virtuous cycle. Simple kindnesses such as a cold cloth on a feverish forehead or food provided to people too weak to feed themselves meant those people survived in greater numbers. And the combination of Christians surviving in larger numbers drew more people into the circle of care who also survived in larger numbers. Many then became followers of Jesus both as a result of the kindness they could explain and their survival that, lacking a medical explanation, seemed miraculous.

I've been wondering lately what a virtuous cycle for the 21st -century church might look like in the midst of this pandemic. Statistically, as with plagues historically, the pandemic is hitting the vulnerable among us the hardest. The pandemic is hitting the poor harder—the homeless and the working poor who don't have the luxury of staying home and doing their work from the comfort of their living room on a laptop (as I do).

It's hitting senior citizens harder: nursing homes are in the very highest risk categories. And it's hitting minorities harder, particularly Black and Latino populations.

I am currently serving as the transition pastor for a congregation, and we are having the same conversations as your church about when we might return to worship—something we all want, and something we all need. And yet I think the most important thing we can do to worship God isn't to gather in a building—as much as I want to—but to proclaim by our words and actions that Jesus is Lord. The early church did that not by asking other people to risk their lives so they could continue to worship, but by risking their own lives to care for the sick, many of whom were among the most vulnerable populations of that day and time.

What would it look like for us to risk what matters to us to bring life to those at risk? First Baptist Church in Lee's Summit, Missouri, is located about 20 miles outside Kansas City. Like a lot of churches, its leaders started having conversations about the challenges the pandemic was creating for them. But they also recognized that the most important thing for them to do in this moment wasn't to hunker down into preservation mode but to proclaim by their actions that Jesus is Lord.

So, on March 22 (their second Sunday of online only worship), they decided to give away half of all the offerings they received that week to their neighbors who were being impacted by the coronavirus. They gave half to a local nonprofit that helps the poorest of the poor in their community and the other half to employees of shops, restaurants, and bars in their community that were experiencing lost wages. (Imagine you're a bartender and the owner comes in and hands you a check and tells you it's from the Baptist church down the street. I bet that'll get your attention.)

I am not going to criticize you if your church decides to start gathering again sooner rather than later. I do, however, wonder if a socially distanced congregation that can't hug or linger after worship is over is really the most powerful symbol that the church is being the church. I'm not hearing people complain about not spending more time in the building. I am hearing everyone, Christians and non-Christians alike, talk about the loss of connection. People need to be seen and heard and loved, and as terrible as this pandemic is, the witness of history is that the church truly being the church is exactly what the world needs in a moment like this.

Adaptive Change During a Crisis— Kairos Time!

Deborah London Wright

Like many people at the start of this pandemic lockdown, I went all Marie Kondo on my home. In the process I came across handwritten notes from a talk Ron Heifetz (Godfather of Adaptive Change) gave several years ago. An audience member posed a question to Heifetz after his speech that went something like this: I get how to approach adaptive change when you have the luxury of climbing on the balcony and studying the patterns. But what if you're faced with a crisis? How might adaptive change inform the best response?

As I entered week 10 of SIP (Sheltering in Place), those notes came to mind: Stages of response matter. Our default switch as eager problem-solvers is to rush in and fix. It's a natural reflex, and one we frequently fall into the trap that Heifetz describes as slapping technical fixes on adaptive challenges. Based on his sense of staged response, I discerned four distinct serial stages our churches must go through during the pandemic.

1. *Triage, or assessing the immediate damage and danger:* For the church in the middle of Lent this became, "How to get everybody through Easter!" or, as we joke, suddenly every pastor we know became a televangelist! Suddenly after years of patiently coaxing often reluctant church teams into using Zoom as a tool for distance coaching, there's one thing I know for sure: I'll never have to teach a congregation how to use Zoom again! They all became masters overnight. (Adaptive note: Necessity is the mother of innovation!)

2. *Fragility, or locating the cracks:* I live in earthquake country. When a quake hits, immediately after the initial triage, officials start looking for cracks in bridges, overpasses, buildings, power grids, systems, etc. In the church our job is checking for the financial, mental, physical, and spiritual "cracks." This includes helping our churches, preschools, food ministries, etc. apply for SBA/PPP loans and denomination-based funds and services. Our pastors are checking in on their flocks to see how they're coping. Attention is especially needed for non-WiFi and shut-in folks. Some ministers/leaders are offering Zoom coffee hours, prayer groups, Bible studies, deacon phone trees, grocery shopping, meal deliveries, etc. We also need to check in on our ministers, most of whom are exhausted, overfunctioning, and feeling isolated. For most, virtual worship is at least twice as taxing as "regular" worship. Clergy Zoom gatherings can offer a safe space, if we are sensitive to the very real issue of Zoom fatigue!

3. *New normal, or facing our nemesis at this time:* As churches enter the third stage of adaptation, it's all about re-entry and gathering again for in-person worship and other functions. How will we do things differently? There may be no such thing as "regular" again. When a church burns down, the power to go back to what was "normal" is dominant—to rebuild the sanctuary exactly as it was, even though there were flaws in that design. Finding the "new normal" phase will have technical and adaptive issues. Technically, we will need to determine how to do worship together safely. Many things require consideration: the offering plate, communion, baptism, passing the peace, printed bulletins, seating, sanitizing, singing, coffee hour, online giving, etc. The main point is that some old "normal" needs to fall away—bless it and bury it! Acknowledge with our folks that we may miss it. This is decidedly not about restoration. The temple may be in rubble, but let's not necessarily rebuild it as it was!

4. *Sorting, or observing deep discernment:* Think of Phyllis Tickle's notion of the "rummage sale" that Christianity holds every 500 years. What is essential and what is fleeting? This stage is all about asking the WHO, the WHAT, and the WHY—but not the HOW. Not yet! The HOW gets us stuck in technical fixes for adaptive problems. This is a time to experiment and fail. Try new things. See what adaptations from our SIP time we may keep, for example, continuing with certain committee meetings on Zoom or having noontime Zoom lunches with prayer, Bible study, or just fellowship. This can be a time of pulling out some real lay talent that has been lying dormant.

Just as I will never again have to teach a congregant how to use Zoom, I will never again have to encourage a congregation to imagine WHO and WHAT they are without a church building! That used to be a tough exercise, but no more. Hopefully we can deeply discern the WHO, WHAT, and WHY of church with experiential imagination now, and we will be the stronger for it.

As Churchill said, "Never let a good crisis go to waste!" Experiment, celebrate successes and failures, and discern the voice of the Holy Spirit. This is Kairos Time!

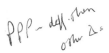

Contributors

William "Bill" Wilson founded the Center for Healthy Churches in January of 2014, following his service as president of the Center for Congregational Health at Wake Forest Baptist Health since 2009. Previously he was pastor of the First Baptist Church of Dalton, Georgia, where he served since 2003. He brings more than 33 years of local church ministry experience to the CHC, having served as the pastor of two churches in Virginia (Farmville Baptist Church and First Baptist Church of Waynesboro) and on a church staff in South Carolina. Bill has led each of the churches he has served into a time of significant growth and expansion of ministry. His work with churches and ministers is marked by a positive and unyielding belief that Christ-centered ministry is fulfilling and relevant. His deepest desire is to encourage churches and clergy to discover a vital and vibrant future. He believes that, as difficult as it is to be the church today, there has never been a day when the church is more needed.

Matt Cook is the assistant director of the Center for Healthy Churches. According to Bill Wilson, "Matt's joining CHC is both an answered prayer and testimony to the remarkable growth and potential of our group. At age 47, he represents the future for our efforts to engender sustainable health in congregations and clergy across the nation." Earlier, Matt served local congregations for more than 25 years, with nearly 20 years as senior pastor in churches in Texas, Arkansas, and North Carolina. He is a gifted and thoughtful leader who knows how to listen and how to sort out the issues a congregation needs to address as it prepares for the next season of vital ministry. In his work, Matt combines research and scholarly insight with an emphasis on strategic focus and missional awareness. He has training and experience in strategic planning, staff reorganization, and leadership development, in addition to assisting congregations in pastoral transitions. Matt is also a noted speaker and preacher in churches, at conferences, and on college campuses.

Robert (Bob) Dale is an Oklahoma Baptist University graduate and former assistant executive director of the Virginia Baptist Mission Board. He is a noted author, consultant, and coach who for nearly 50 years has been a thought-leader in the world of congregations as they engage the question of health and vibrancy. Following a distinguished career as a pastor, seminary professor and denominational leader, Bob now turns his focus toward coaching. In this role he is helping to guide a generation of clergy and laity toward a healthier understanding of leadership and maturity. He is also a coach for the Center for Healthy Churches. He and Bill Wilson are the authors of *Weaving Strong Leaders: How Leaders Grow Down, Grow Up, and Grow Together* (Nurturing Faith, 2016).

 **Jayne Davis** has served as the minister of spiritual formation at the First Baptist Church of Wilmington, North Carolina, since 2001. Prior to going into ministry, she was the executive director of a non-profit organization and worked as a strategic planning consultant for early childhood initiatives. Jayne is a certified coach, working with individuals and churches and with the Center for Healthy Churches and the Cooperative Baptist Fellowship of North Carolina. She is also the co-author of *Hopeful Imagination: Traditional Churches Finding God's Way in a Changing World* (Nurturing Faith, 2014).

 **Doug Haney** has served as minister of music at Wilshire Baptist Church in Dallas, Texas, since 2004. He previously served at Providence Baptist Church in Charlotte, North Carolina, and at churches in Mississippi, Alabama, and Georgia. At Wilshire he directs the choral program and supervises the churchwide music ministry, with major responsibilities for worship. Wilshire's sanctuary and youth choirs are renowned for their quality and innovative approach to traditional worship.

 **Tracy Hartman** most recently served at Baptist Theological Seminary at Richmond as a professor of preaching and practical theology, and previously as director of the seminary's supervised ministry and Doctor of Ministry programs. She is the author of *Letting the Other Speak: Proclaiming the Stories of Biblical Women*, the co-author of *New Proclamation Commentary*, and a contributor to the *Feasting on the Word* and *Feasting on the Gospels* commentary series. A popular preacher, she is active in Baptist life and has served as a staff member and interim pastor at several Virginia churches.

 **Barry Howard** is now pastor of the Wieuca Road Baptist Church in Atlanta, Georgia, after serving as senior pastor of the First Baptist Church of Pensacola, Florida, from 2005–2017. With more than 40 years of experience in the local church, he has worked with the Center for Healthy Churches in training future pastors and is passionate about congregational health.

 **David Hull,** an active leader in community and denominational life for 35 years, joined the Center for Healthy Churches team in 2014. He recently retired after serving as associate pastor of Second-Ponce de Leon Baptist Church in Atlanta, Georgia, and before that as pastor of the First Baptist churches of Huntsville, Alabama, and Knoxville, Tennessee, and also at churches in South Carolina, North Carolina, and Kentucky.

Jim Kitchens, a native of Mississippi, has served Presbyterian churches in California and Tennessee for almost 35 years. He loves helping congregations prayerfully discern how the Spirit calls them to adapt to changing cultural contexts. Jim is the author of *The Postmodern Parish: New Ministry for a New Era.*

Phill Martin is the CEO of The Church Network (TCN), an interdenominational professional association of churches and individuals that exists to connect, develop, and strengthen church leaders in administration. His passion is to engage and connect individuals and organizations to help them reach their maximum potential. Phil enjoys coaching, teaching, mentoring, and connecting people with information and resources. He is also a coach with the Center for Healthy Churches.

Larry McSwain is a long-time educator at McAfee School of Theology, Shorter College, and the Southern Baptist Theological Seminary. He specializes in congregational research and in training others in strategy-planning processes and conflict ministry. While Larry is now in retirement, he continues to be a vital resource to the Center for Healthy Churches.

Bill Owen is a congregational consultant and coach for the Center for Healthy Churches after a 32-year pastorate at Mt. Carmel Baptist Church in Cross Plains, Tennessee. An experienced leadership coach, he also has worked as a cognitive coach among educators, particularly secondary school teachers, with a focus on innovation and personalized learning. He brings these skills and experiences to his work with and love for congregations and ministry staff development. He works extensively with the Strategic Transition Education Program (STEP), designed specifically for churches and their leaders during interim periods in a church's life.

Mike Queen has served churches in North Carolina for the last 40 years. He retired after 25 years as pastor at the First Baptist Church of Wilmington, but continues to serve in various interim positions. Mike, along with his colleague Jayne Davis, founded a ministry of encouragement called Hopeful Imagination to work with traditional churches dedicated to finding God's way in a changing world. They are the authors of *Hopeful Imagination: Traditional Churches Finding God's Way in a Changing World* (Nurturing Faith, 2014).

Guy Sayles serves as a congregational consultant and coach after a 13-year pastorate at the First Baptist Church of Asheville, North Carolina, and four years of teaching at Mars Hill University in North Carolina. He is part of the adjunct faculty of the Gardner-Webb University Divinity School. Along with his other interests of teaching, preaching and writing, Guy works with the Center for Healthy Churches to foster congregational health and depth.

Steve Scoggin is a minister, professor, licensed professional counselor, certified Franklin Covey facilitator, and Associate Certified Coach (ACC). He is president of CareNet., Inc., a wholly owned subsidiary of Wake Forest Baptist Medical Center in North Carolina. Along with his responsibilities of providing leadership to a statewide outpatient counseling network of 32 clinics, he also is adjunct assistant professor in psychiatry and behavioral medicine at WFBMC. He specializes in executive coaching and consulting, having worked with executives and organizations in the private, public, and non-profit sectors.

Craig Sherouse retired in February 2019 after 11 years as senior pastor of the Second Baptist Church of Richmond, Virginia. His 47 years in local church ministry—43 of those as senior pastor—included his native Florida, in addition to Kentucky, Georgia, and Virginia. Craig has training and experience in strategic planning/visioning, coaching, team building, and pastoral transition. He is a coach and consultant for the Center for Healthy Churches.

Joel Snider retired in 2016 after a 21-year pastorate at the First Baptist Church of Rome, Georgia, and a total of 40 years in active ministry. Joel has an active coaching practice with a wide variety of clients, including ministers, small business owners, and financial planners. In his work with the Center for Healthy Churches, Joel focuses on creating a faith development ministry with young families and churches, in addition to consulting for minister search committees and congregational health. He also serves as a coach for the CHC.

Deborah London Wright is a minister in the Presbyterian Church (U.S.A.) and a principal with PneuMatrix, an adaptive change consulting group based in northern California. She has returned to working directly with presbyteries and congregations after 25 years as a corporate chaplain, bringing adaptive change rooted in spiritual formation.

CPSIA information can be obtained
at www.ICGtesting.com
Printed in the USA
FSHW020705010820
72079FS